OHIO
ON THE
MOVE

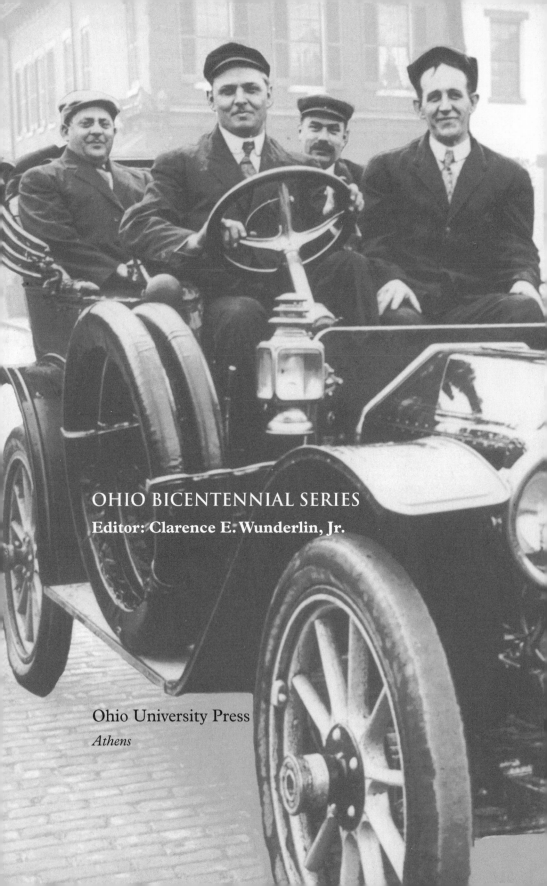

OHIO BICENTENNIAL SERIES

Editor: Clarence E. Wunderlin, Jr.

Ohio University Press

Athens

OHIO
ON THE
MOVE

Transportation in the Buckeye State

H. ROGER GRANT

Ohio University Press, Athens, Ohio 45701
© 2000 by H. Roger Grant
Editor's Preface © 2000 by Clarence E. Wunderlin, Jr.
Printed in the United States of America

Ohio University Press books are printed on acid-free paper ♾ ™

06 05 04 03 02 01 00   5 4 3 2 1

The publication of this book was made possible in part
by the generous support of the Ohio Bicentennial Commission.

Library of Congress Cataloging-in-Publication Data
Grant, H. Roger, 1943–
    Ohio on the move : transportation in the Buckeye State / H. Roger Grant :
editor's preface by Clarence E. Wunderlin, Jr.
        p.   cm. — (Ohio bicentennial series)
    Includes bibliographical references and index.
    ISBN 0-8214-1283-3 (cloth : alk. paper). — ISBN 0-8214-1284-1
(pbk. : alk. paper)
    1. Transportation—Ohio—History. I. Title. II. Series.
HE213.03G73 1999
388'.09771—dc21   99-29728

In memory of my mother,
Marcella Dinsmore Grant Dearinger
(1903–1996)

CONTENTS

ILLUSTRATIONS

Chapter 4

Chapter 5

Chapter 6

Chapter 7

EDITOR'S PREFACE TO THE
OHIO BICENTENNIAL SERIES

THE OHIO COUNTRY—and the state that Congress carved out of it—has occupied a central place in the development of the transatlantic world since the mid-seventeenth century. Its significance was easily recognizable to the explorers, traders, and missionaries of the Western European maritime powers who traveled there from the early seventeenth to the late eighteenth centuries. During this second phase of the imperial conquest in the New World, the Ohio Country stood out because of its strategic location, the wealth of its natural resources, and the diversity and skills of its Native American peoples. Beginning his *State Centennial History of Ohio* with a brief discussion of Anglo-French competition for strategic advantage in the New World, Rowland H. Rerick offered this assessment of the the Ohio Country's importance:

> It followed naturally that this land, now mainly included in the State of Ohio, became a battle ground and the cause of war in other regions, from the beginning of European rivalry in North America. It was the most important region of the continent; the key to all the country west of the Alleghanies; commanding the commercial outlet toward Europe of a vast and fertile country, destined to be the richest in the world. (17)

Initially a key fur-producing area, the Ohio Country became a command post of commerce by the beginning of the eighteenth century. After 1700, numerous Native American tribes from the Great Lakes region joined refugees, increasingly organized in multi-tribe villages, in moving into this region, which had been largely depopulated by constant warfare after the mid-seventeenth century. With the rising demand for deerskins in the mid-1700s, the Ohio Country became a center of commercial hunting on the North American continent. Many Native Americans converted from trapping to hunting in order to enjoy the fruits of the buckskin trade, thus adding the skills of a modern commercial hunter. They harvested white-tailed deer by the thousands each year in the forested valleys, meadow edges, and blackwater swamps of the Ohio Country. The deerskin trade of the second half of the eighteenth century established several Ohio villages as mercantile outposts and helped transform Pittsburgh and Carlisle, Pennsylvania, into major centers of Trans-Appalachian commerce.

The importance of the land and its Native American population was recognized in the thirty-year struggle for dominance and independence waged by French and British soldiers, their Native American allies, and Anglo-American colonists. The contest for control of that "key to all the country west of the Alleghanies" led to a global war for empire after 1753. The struggle was resumed in the American Revolution, with almost constant backcountry warfare in and around the Ohio River Valley. Throughout the period, Ohio Country Indians were key political and military actors, influencing the imperial contest.

The state of Ohio and its people assumed prominence in the nineteenth century. After 1800, a third phase of Western imperialism commenced with the industrialization of the European powers and the thinly populated Atlantic coast of North America. In the introduction to this book, historian H. Roger Grant observes that Ohio's continued prominence is "understandable" in the era of industrialization. He reminds readers that Ohio again occupied a key location, possessed crucial natural resources, and received a diverse and skilled European population that produced great wealth through industry.

The first two factors, location and resources, cannot be overemphasized in explaining Ohio's socioeconomic development. Ohio was the crossroads of the Midwest, with important canals and trunk line railroads traversing the state. Its position at the edge of the great Midwestern prairie land allowed agriculture to flourish. In addition, abundant supplies of the raw materials necessary for basic industry could be found in or near Ohio. Indeed, the Midwestern manufactures, based around mining, basic iron and steel, and the fabrication of metal products, developed rapidly in the late-nineteenth century because of the extensive exploitation of the region's plentiful natural resources.

The diversity and skills of the European peoples who settled Ohio made possible this industrial "success story." Settlers from New England, the Middle Atlantic states, and Virginia transformed the Ohio Country and propelled it toward statehood during the last decade of the eighteenth century. The strength and skills of the first immigrants from Germany and the British Isles proved essential to building the state's canals and railroads, as well as the factories of early Cincinnati. European immigration at the turn of the last century gave Ohio the large, diverse, and efficient workforce it needed for a rapid expansion of mass production industry.

The state's diverse population also provided a base for the nation's two major political parties after 1854. Ohio became an important center of American political life, influencing partisan struggles and providing talented leadership for service at the highest levels.

Although the importance of Ohio's location and resource base has diminished somewhat in the postindustrial age, the diversity and productivity of its population have assumed an even more crucial importance. The state of Ohio, after almost two hundred years, maintains its prominence in political and economic affairs.

The approach of the state's bicentennial, with the attendant publicity and commitment of resources, affords scholars a unique opportunity to reevaluate Ohio's history. To that end, the state has created the Ohio Bicentennial Commission. Supported by state funding, the commission has already underwritten academically based scholarship on a wide variety of historical topics. Numerous local and county projects have also been initiated around the state with the goal of advancing the study of local history.

In an effort to promote a more systematic assessment of the state's history, Ohio University Press has embarked on the publication of a series of monographs and special projects. When he first envisioned the Ohio Bicentennial Series, David Sanders, director of the press, had in mind the generation of a body of scholarship that would commemorate Ohio's statehood by offering specialists, students, and knowledgeable generalists a comprehensive picture of its development. The first special project, a volume of documents, will make the textual record of the state's past more accessible for the student in the classroom and the general reader outside the academic setting. Other special projects include an illustrated history of the state and a biographical dictionary of Ohio governors.

The series will also include monographs that will provide fresh assessments of important aspects of Ohio history. One group of works already in progress will focus on key societal groups, charting the "progress" of these specific categories of Ohioans over time. Books on Ohio women and on utopian communal experiments exemplify this type of study. A second group of monographs will take a topical approach, examining a field of history as Roger Grant does in this book on transportation.

For all these works, I have asked specialists in the relevant fields or subfields of history or related disciplines to provide readers with a fresh synthesis of the old and the new. Authors of these works will synthesize "old knowledge" already existing in a multitude of sources and, whenever possible, present the findings of their most recent research, adding a pinch of "new knowledge." The first contribution to our series, *Ohio on the Move* by H. Roger Grant, is a perfect mix of interpretation and discovery.

The "progress" Ohioans made in transporting themselves and their various cargoes is the subject of this new book. The author has assessed the primary modes of transportation in seven chapters. Thus, each chapter establishes a discreet category of analysis within which Professor Grant evaluates the influence of technological and organizational change over time. But the full measurement of Ohio's modernization can only be determined by looking across the separate categories, across the sweep of Grant's book, as it moves from pathways and roads to interurbans and aviation.

Ohio on the Move is a model of synthetic scholarship. Grant's blend of old and new can be seen in chapters on canals and railroads, in which he weaves each narrative from a mountain of published scholarship. His talents can also be seen in his treatment of bus lines, trucking companies, and commercial aviation ventures, where the author was forced to supplement a meager amount of existing scholarship with original research. In these sections, Grant introduces readers to such pioneering firms as Green Line Bus Company and Great Lakes Stages, Inc., that offered intercity bus service between the two wars, recounts the accomplishments of innovative trucking firms during the interwar years, and tells the fascinating story of early commercial aviation in the region through brief portraits of firms like Lake Central, a major local service carrier, and TAG Airlines, a little-known "niche" company.

Few historians have an extensive knowledge of the economic, technological, and business history of a state; none has the grasp of Ohio transportation history possessed by H. Roger Grant. I am especially pleased that Professor Grant agreed to launch the Ohio Bicentennial Series of Ohio University Press with this outstanding volume.

CLARENCE E. WUNDERLIN, JR.

Associate Professor of History
Kent State University

PREFACE

FEW AMERICAN states can claim a richer or more important transportation heritage than Ohio. Every major form of public conveyance has held a strong presence in the state. From the canal age to the interurban era, the Buckeye State has been a national leader.

It is easy to see why. The Northwest Territory, out of which Congress carved Ohio, possessed an inviting climate and vast natural resources, including massive stands of hardwoods, fertile soil, and an array of minerals. The territory's strategic position between the Northeast and Middle Atlantic States and the trans-Mississippi West also guaranteed its importance. When modern Cleveland boosters proclaim their city to be "the best location in the nation," they are hardly promoting a falsehood. Natural resources and location drew settlers, and over time Ohioans created great wealth. Residents quickly sensed that progress depended heavily on good transport, and they strove mightily to make improvements. Always receptive to better forms, residents embraced replacements, whether successful or not. As a result everything in vogue was tried and the best became commonplace.

This work is not a definitive account of transportation in Ohio. Such a study would be immense; indeed, the state's railroad past alone is vast and complicated. Instead, I have attempted to highlight major events and trends while providing essential details that explain the long-term importance of transport and the state's premier role in a changing picture.

Although this study is primarily a synthesis of pertinent scholarly monographs and articles, I have employed a variety of sources. This was necessary because the secondary literature is mixed in both quantity and quality, with much available on canals and railroads and virtually nothing on commercial aviation, intercity bus lines, and trucking companies. Where appropriate I have included some primary research, including materials from my earlier book and journal article projects.

Several individuals have helped improve this book. George Knepper, a former colleague at The University of Akron and the foremost living authority on Ohio's past, graciously read a draft of the manuscript. Robert P. Barnett, Jack Gieck, Cornelius Hauck, John Humiston, George Krambles, John V. Miller Jr., David and Sally Riede, and Charles Stats added information, insights, and illustrations. The skilled and dedicated specialists in the interlibrary loan division of the R. M. Cooper Library at Clemson University also made a significant contribution. Finally, Samuel Girton, an artist in Athens, Ohio, creatively produced maps of Ohio's network of canals and electric interurbans.

This book is the result of the organizational talents of Clarence Wunderlin, a member of the Department of History at Kent State University and the general editor of this Ohio bicentennial series. The debt to my wife, Martha Farrington Grant, is also considerable. This is the nineteenth book she has helped craft.

OHIO
ON THE
MOVE

1

ROADS AND HIGHWAYS

C ONTEMPORARY Ohioans likely define *transportation* as automobiles and trucks moving along paved highways. Although vehicles and roadways are a product of twentieth-century technologies, the use of a defined land route, trail or road, has an ancient past. When the earliest Euro-Americans moved beyond navigable waterways, they commonly traveled trails made by Native Americans or wild animals. For example, the Portage Path, which connected the Cuyahoga and Tuscarawas Rivers, likely dated from the Adena period (ca. 1000 B.C.– A.D. 600) or even earlier. These trails usually traversed a dense wilderness of hardwoods and some conifers and sensibly followed ridges, crossed streams where waters were shallow, and avoided marshes and swamps.[1]

Once the Northwest Territory, created in 1787, began to attract settlers, better access became essential. As a result new or improved trails soon connected with land and water routes from Connecticut, Pennsylvania, and Virginia, the principal homes of thousands of adventurous immigrants. By the time Ohio entered the union in 1803 several key avenues penetrated the eastern and southern sections of the state, making it possible to walk, ride on horseback, or travel by cart or wagon to this land of promise.[2]

Take the case of Connecticut residents who located in the Western Reserve of northeastern Ohio. Although these settlers could trek across the state of New York to Buffalo and sail from there for harbors along the southern shores of Lake Erie, a more direct overland access was deemed vital, particularly by the Connecticut Land Company, chief purveyor of Western Reserve real estate. Fortunately, by the mid-1790s, a road was emerging between Buffalo through the Holland Land District of southwestern New York and the Pennsylvania–Western Reserve border. Promoters logically sought to link the strategic settlement of Cleveland, situated on the east bank of the Cuyahoga River near its mouth, with this eastern connection. In 1796 survey work began between the Pennsylvania line and Cleveland, and early the next year leaders of the company decided upon a route and the details of the project. The latter involved the following: "[T]he small stuff [trees] to be cut out 25 feet wide and the timber to be girdled 33 feet wide and sufficient bridges to be thrown over streams as are not fordable." The road took shape quickly and opened by the end of 1798. For decades it served the area, although local governments made alterations and improvements.[3]

While the Girdled Road gained local recognition, another contemporary artery, Zane's Trace, became much better known and was the only road of any length during Ohio's formative years. The driving force behind it was Col. Ebenezer Zane (1747–1812), an uprooted Virginian. "No better man than Ebenezer Zane could have been found to cut a road through Ohio," concluded historian Clement Martzolff in 1904. "His influence in the new settlement, his wealth and his general knowledge of the country made him the logical man to assume the responsibility." Early on, this farmer, entrepreneur, and land speculator showed his desire for better land transport, blazing a trail during the Revolutionary War era between Pittsburgh and Wheeling, Virginia (after 1863 West Virginia). Then in 1796 Zane won landmark federal backing for his more than two-hundred-mile "bridle path" between St. Clairsville, in Belmont County, near Wheeling, and Maysville, Kentucky, opposite Adams County. This route would be shorter and less expensive for mail service than the Ohio River between Wheeling and Maysville, and it would be usable when ice blocked the channel. As an incentive Congress gave Zane "the tracts of land, not exceeding one mile square each, at Muskingum, Hock-hocking and Scioto where the proposed road shall cross those rivers, for the purpose of establishing ferries thereon." These three places held value beyond locations for river ferries; they had considerable potential as town sites, a promoter's paradise.[4]

As with the Girdled Road, Zane's Trace rapidly materialized; it opened during the summer of 1797. Soon pedestrians and animals, usually pack-horses with burdens of several hundred pounds, appeared on the path. Almost immediately Zane's Trace became popular. The path provided a practical way for individuals possessing land warrants in the Virginia Military District to reach their new homes in southern and southwestern Ohio. These hardy settlers from the Old Dominion and from other parts of the southern backcountry traveled the crude forest pathway known as the Wilderness Road through the Cumberland Gap into Kentucky, passing Maysville, before they crossed the Ohio River and reached Zane's Trace.[5]

Since Zane's Trace had taken on such great importance, Ohio lawmakers in 1804 approved an upgrade, creating what became the Ohio State Road. This improved artery generally passed through the same communities as the trace, although it veered from that route when surveyors found a better one. Still, specifications permitted contractors to leave stumps a foot high in the twenty-foot-wide road; public funding was skimpy, the state investing at a rate of only fifteen dollars per mile. Being heavily aligned to the Democratic-Republican Party, Ohio politicians overwhelmingly embraced the Jeffersonian commitment to the notion of that government is best which spends and governs least.[6]

By the early decades of the nineteenth century, Ohio possessed hundreds of miles of primitive roadways. Usually they were designed to connect with bodies of water, the principal trade avenues. By 1816 in Cincinnati, for example, six locally sponsored roads extended into the hinterlands, giving farmers direct access to the city, where their agricultural goods could be marketed, processed, and shipped by river to New Orleans. These radial routes from the Queen City included the North Bend Road to the west, the Hamilton and Lawrenceburg Roads to the northwest, the Dayton Road to the north, the Lebanon Road to the northeast, and the Columbia Road to the east.[7]

Military trails also improved travel, especially in northwestern Ohio. The War of 1812 became more than America's second war for independence; the conflict altered the state's transportation map. Significantly,

3

Harrison's Road ran through Piqua, St. Mary's, and Defiance and Hull's Road connected Dayton, Urbana, and Findlay.[8]

A contemporary interest in turnpikes likewise developed, with the first one being incorporated in 1809 for a project in Trumbull County. Although residents saw these publicly chartered for-profit firms solving their road needs, most endeavors lacked the capital and leadership to succeed, often failing before completion or soon thereafter.[9]

Because roads in frontier Ohio were notoriously bad, overland journeys became memorable experiences. Travelers often considered distance to be an enemy and, like sin, something they must continually fight. They repeatedly complained, especially during the spring mud season. When in 1811 Charity Rodman Rotch (1766–1824) and her husband journeyed across large expanses of the state before they settled in Kendal (later Massillon), she frequently commented in her diary on road conditions, and they were usually poor: "[R]each'd Shartlers Inn on the 27th [of May] a very comfortable Log house, and kind people perhaps 12 miles from Lancaster, in the morning rode two miles to Tarlton, & stopt at Lybrands Inn on—of getting a pr. of horses, the *mud* now being too deep for ours, to convey us comfortably." Somewhat later Marianne Parker Dascomb (?–1879) wrote to friends in Dunbarton, New Hampshire, about her trip in the spring of 1834 to Oberlin. "[A]t five o'clock we took stage for Elyria, which is ten miles from Oberlin—road very bad from ruts and mud. We were in constant danger of overturning." And she added, "Once when we came to a ditch in the road the gentlemen got out and took down a fence, so that we could turn aside into the adjoining field and ride around the obstacle."[10]

Ohioans, nevertheless, hardly considered the sorry state of their roads, which often made trips torturous, a crisis of epic proportions. If settlers had reasonably close access to waterways, the shortcomings were not so severe. Even if they did not, transportation of bulky or heavy goods usually could be managed during the winter months. With frozen soil, muddy conditions disappeared. If snow covered the roadways, large sleds pulled by teams of horses, mules, or oxen could travel with relative ease. At this time of the year farmers enjoyed greater freedom from their work and could concentrate on hauling chores.[11]

A community that desired to build good roads found a paucity of local funds; capital in rural Ohio was scarce. Governmental units, usually townships, dealt with this situation by allowing taxpayers to "work off" their modest yearly road assessments. However, these annual events, which became neighborhood parties frequently fueled by jugs of corn liquor, often accomplished little of practical value. The laborers of good intent usually lacked the skills, equipment, or availability at the best time of the year to fashion acceptable roads.[12]

Although state coffers hardly overflowed, some funding for roads was available. Significantly, on February 23, 1823, Congress granted Ohio 60,000 acres of public lands to construct the forty-six mile Maumee Road (later U.S. Highway 20) from Maumee southeastward to the Western Reserve, and eight years later awarded an additional 31,596 acres for the Columbus and Sandusky Turnpike. Most of all, the Ohio Enabling Act of 1802, which permitted statehood, contained a positive provision for land transport. The state's founders took advantage of the federal government's willingness to grant 5 percent of the net proceeds from public land sales in the state for roads. It was agreed that three-fifths of the 5-percent fund would go for laying out roads within the state and two-fifths for ones to and through it.[13]

The project that received Ohio's greatest financial backing from the Enabling Act was the National Road, the Grand Portage, from the Atlantic seaboard to the trans–Allegheny West. What emerged by 1817 was a modern road extending from Cumberland, Maryland, and connecting to Baltimore and Washington, D.C., to Wheeling and the Ohio River, and by ferry to the Ohio State Road. But this first federally funded avenue did not stall at river's edge; it would be pushed toward a terminus on the Mississippi River or farther west.

Although debate over the constitutionality of internal improvements delayed extension of the National Road, President James Monroe in 1824 signed a bill authorizing construction beyond the Ohio River. Soon funding for the link to Zanesville, paralleling the Ohio State Road, was granted, and engineers from the War Department sought to make a lasting thirty-foot-wide roadway, employing for the first time the McAdam Plan. Specifically, the surface was not to be covered by untreated gravel, but rather by a three-inch layer of broken stone, "which shall unite by its own angles so as to form a solid hard surface." In 1830 construction workers, many of whom were neighboring farmers, completed the Zanesville portion, and, complying to a federal mandate for creating a straight line across the state, three years later extended the road to Columbus and in 1834 to Indianapolis, Indiana. Ultimately, by 1840 the National Road, or pike, technically terminated in Vandalia, the former capital of Illinois; it failed to reach Jefferson City, Missouri, or even the Mississippi River at St. Louis because the iron horse was rapidly shattering the isolation of the region. In fact, the segment from Indianapolis to Vandalia was never completely graded, and in some sections not even cleared of stumps. Yet, the National Road was strong evidence of America's commitment to both expansion and cohesion, for by tying together the East and West it fostered a national economy.[14]

Although the federal government paid for much of the construction of the more than 600-mile National Road, by the 1830s the maintenance burden fell on the states. When Washington surrendered the road, the several states responded by erecting tollhouses for collection of user fees. In Ohio these collection booths stood about ten miles apart along the 225-mile span, becoming in 1836 the responsibility of the Board of Public Works, more renowned for its control of the canal system. From 1831 to 1877, the Buckeye State took in nearly $1.25 million in revenues, but this income was insufficient for upkeep, even though the road was built to high contemporary standards, featuring good engineering, state-of-the-art surfacing, and impressive bridges.[15]

Members of the traveling public did not worry about the economic health of the National Road; they wanted an all-weather roadway. Even though it became the best avenue across the state, Ohioans still fussed. Many objected to tolls, even though they received exemptions for attending church or funeral services, voting, or military duty. Maintenance shortcomings repeatedly prompted negative responses, and wagoners especially resented drovers, whose cattle, hogs, sheep, or turkeys slowed or blocked their passage.[16]

Still, travelers were usually pleased with the National Road in Ohio. In 1840 an English commentator, James Silk Buckingham, for one, praised the pike. "In the course of our journey from Wheeling to Zanesville, we found the road admirable all the way, as good indeed as the road from London to Bath." And he added, "[I]t was no ordinary luxury to travel on this smooth and equable National Road, where we were drawn at an uniform rate of about seven miles an hour. . . . and I

6

must say, a better road than the one on which we were now traveling could not be found in England."[17]

The ease of travel on the National Road prompted a creative, albeit largely forgotten, response, a prototype of the famed Pony Express of 1860–61. Although stagecoaches carried U.S. mail, in 1836 Amos Kendall, postmaster general in the Andrew Jackson administration, endorsed an unusual experiment. The government hired boys fifteen to seventeen years of age to race their horses along the fifty-six miles between Columbus and Zanesville. These plucky young riders, who changed their mounts every six miles, dramatically reduced the time of such a trip, covering the distance in five rather than the usual nine hours for stagecoaches. By 1838, however, cost considerations led to the discontinuance of this expedited mail service.[18]

Although no precise figures exist on how many individuals traveled the National Road in Ohio, toll receipts reflect general usage. During the forty-six years that the state maintained collection gates, maximum revenues occurred between 1837 and 1853, with 1839 being the peak year. Traffic then fell, especially between 1854 and 1861, likely explained by initial rail competition. The Civil War era, however, saw increased income that remained somewhat constant until the mid-1870s.[19]

The brisk traffic on the National Road can easily be explained. A strategically located, quality roadway always attracted travelers. Not only did this pike serve some of the most important communities in Ohio, including the capital, but it quickly became the direct route to the West. Moreover, scores of lesser roads radiated from this "Main Street of America," connecting to virtually every corner of the state. "The leading line of communication through Ohio is the great National Road, which is of importance itself as the trunk of a tree is to its branches," asserted the *Wheeling Times and Advertiser* in the late 1830s. "The traveler who seeks any portion of the state, almost, takes his start from the National Road as a central line from which divergence is easy and direct. Examine the leading stage routes and you will find the National Road the focus of all of them." According to *Mitchell's Traveler's Guide through the United States,* published in 1837, fourteen of the state's thirty-two established stage routes connected to the pike.[20]

The people who swelled the volume along the National Road were the "movers." These individuals and families, who had likely left their stony or generally infertile farms in the East to seek the richer soils of the Midwest, sought to realize the American dream on the frontier. Commentators commonly found the road "crowded with emigrants of every description;" their Conestoga wagons were ubiquitous. Drovers, stagecoach drivers, and wagoners were also frequent users. Local residents, too, if they lacked suitable, toll-free alternative roads, took the pike and contributed to its substantial traffic.[21]

As with contemporary canals and soon with railroads, a distinct corridor emerged along the National Road and other important intercity roads. The most distinguishing feature was the tavern or inn, usually located in an established village or town. The needs for these facilities were real; many travelers wanted food and lodging for themselves and perhaps for their animals. Travelers also sought to learn about road conditions and other information. Although camping, which usually necessitated bringing along a packhorse to carry provisions, made long-distance journeys possible, for some it was hardly a pleasant option. Since the National Road in Ohio largely followed a new course, structures designed to serve the public sprang up at convenient intervals; other older routes may have seen the evolution of bona fide taverns from rough-hewn log cabins or other pioneer buildings.[22]

Whatever the origins of these public houses, they catered to two general groups. The more obvious were the itinerants, many of whom were repeat patrons. For example, "drummers" with their wares and oddments passed on a frequent or regular basis and stagecoach drivers expected to spend the night with their passengers at preselected places. There were also local customers from the town and immediate countryside who likely came to enjoy food and drink, to gossip, or perhaps to transact business. And for everyone, according to one observer in the late 1830s, "[Y]ou obtain all the news, all the scandal, all the politics and all the fun." Although the several functions of the tavern and its successor institutions—hotels, tourist homes, and motels—never totally disappeared, after the Civil War the railroad depots often took over as centers for disseminating information.[23]

Potential patrons of a tavern or inn might encounter difficulties in reaching their destination, especially during wet conditions, unless they had access to a thoroughfare of the quality of the National Road. Through the nineteenth century and the first decades of the twentieth century, Ohioans struggled with their roads. Nevertheless, some progress occurred.

A notable improvement began in the early 1840s. William Renick, widely known in the Scioto Valley for his cattle breeding, animal marketing, and civic activities, successfully demonstrated that there was an effective yet affordable way to enhance travel. He recommended that expensive grading, ditching, and stone crushing be avoided; instead, he suggested placing on existing roads four to six inches of clean, unscreened gravel and repeating the process several times, packing and smoothing with each application. This approach cost about one thousand dollars or less per mile rather than the ten to fifteen thousand dollars per mile for an improved macadamized road. In a demonstration on the financially strapped Circleville-Chillicothe Turnpike, results were impressive: "[T]he road became sooner packed, was less rough, and constructed at a cost of not exceeding $1,200 per mile, bridges included." Although the Renick way did not create a fine macadamized roadway, it "would give all advantages of the same and with a little attention to repairs would be kept so." Turnpike operators and county commissioners took advantage of Renick's betterment: gravel was usually cheap and plentiful, workers, even the unskilled, could readily make the improvements, and the process far surpassed anything of comparable cost. Enthusiasm for graveling led to this popular ditty:

> The roads are impassible,
> Hardly jackassable;
> I think those that travel 'em
> Should turn out and gravel 'em.[24]

By the Civil War era, road betterments, often the result of repeated graveling, may not have satisfied Ohioans, but they applauded any progress. These improvements prompted a longtime resident of Medina County to pen a glowing, multistanza poem, which in part said:

> And we question if they can fully believe,
> The things which their senses so fully perceive.
> Let them look at highways now leading about,
> In contrast with the roads on which they came out.

Winding out then in a single direction;
Running around now to ev'ry mile section;
Guided then by spots on the trees blazed awide;
Guided now by fences along either side.

Then full of turns, roots and holes, everywhere:
Now, straight, well bridged, cast up and graded with care:
Now, the carriage with wheels glides smoothly away;
Then, 'twas lifting, tipping and plunging all day.

The few roads were then muddy, rough and crooked.
Used seldom by teams, but frequently footed,
Our swales and our swamps with cross-logs were laid.
With chinking between covered with dirt by a spade.[25]

While Ohioans poured tons of gravel over their primary arteries, they expressed only modest interest in plank roads. In the mid-1830s this fad swept sections of Canada and the East, and a decade or so later sections of the Midwest, particularly in the swampy Chicago area. Proponents of plank roads thought they had a better way to facilitate land travel, especially through marshy locales. They proposed placement of wide, heavy, hardwood planks across wood stringers, fastened by iron spikes or wooden pegs, to create a solid surface over the wettest and hence muddiest stretches. This was a refined version of the corduroy road, with its split-log construction, which for short distances was common in Ohio. Wherever stands of trees grew, plank-road builders could erect small sawmills to convert native timber into planks and then place them over existing public roads, thus saving the expense of grading, draining, and perhaps bridging. Fortunately, public and private road operators in Ohio built only limited sections of planked routes, in part because the Renick scheme limited the need for this innovation. The continual expense of upkeep of plank roads was the greatest shortcoming: if not repaired, surfaces, weakened by use and decay, menaced travelers. As an Oberlin resident succinctly described a local experiment: "Like all plank roads it was a comfort at the outset, and a nuisance at the end."[26]

Later in the century Ohioans would consider "iron roads," an obscure variation of the plank-road movement. During the hard times of the mid-1890s a workers' group unsuccessfully promoted a way to achieve better roads and, significantly, to hire the unemployed. One broadside outlined the concept:

Why would not plates of iron 6 or 8 inches wide be laid on solid dirt roads, filled in with gravel to prevent slush and mud and for the horses to travel upon? These iron plates might be stayed every 10 or 12 feet to keep them in place. This plan would employ idle labor and would be the source of a great deal of comfort besides saving the public a great deal more than it costs in a few years' use. . . . Buggies, wagons and the immensely popular bicycles could roll smoothly to their destinations.[27]

As this argument revealed, during the latter part of the nineteenth century a bicycling craze swept Ohio and the nation. Although the National League of American Wheelmen made its debut in 1880, a decade later the popularity of the cheaper and more versatile "safety" bicycle, with its pneumatic tires, triggered ever greater interest in this means of personal transport. Many Ohioans, in fact, expected the bicycle to eliminate the need for horses. Cycling became a favorite pastime of thousands who peddled on evenings, Sundays, and holidays, allegedly reducing the business of theaters, sales of pianos, and church attendance. Also, in the state's largest communities bicycle messengers peddled to pick up and deliver time-sensitive documents.[28]

This enthusiasm for bicycles not only led to a positive impact on the Ohio economy, most notably expansion of the infant rubber industry, but also resulted in modest improvements in roads, namely brick pavements. By the early years of the twentieth century scores of miles of brick "pavers" served cyclists and other travelers within corporate limits and also between some communities, the first major project having been portions of the Wooster Pike in Cuyahoga County. The state was in a good position to create this type of all-weather road; although relatively expensive, bricks were readily available. Yet the legacy of this craze was more than new roadways: it brought to the public's attention the miserable condition of the more than seventy-five thousand miles of country roads. Although an exaggeration, the observation that "the roads of this state resemble the condition described in the first chapter of Genesis—'without form and void'" had some merit.[29]

The widespread appearance of the automobile encouraged the public to lift Ohio out of the mud. While the earliest cars were owned by mechanics and tinkerers who might also be their builders, shortly after 1900, the state's wealthiest citizens, including bankers, businessmen, and physicians, started to buy these expensive vehicles from an increasing

Ruts and rocks made the main street of the Summit County village of Peninsula less than perfect, even in the best of weather. A horse and wagon move downhill toward the iron bridge spanning the Cuyahoga River. *(Author's Collection)*

number of local and out-of-state manufacturers. They could endure mechanical breakdowns and taunts of bystanders shouting, "Get a horse!" These self-confident individuals wielded considerable political clout and did much to sustain efforts for better roads. Events in Cleveland are illustrative. In 1900 the Forest City claimed the nation's second automobile association, the Cleveland Automobile Club. Although launched by prominent citizens to promote motoring as a sport and to provide automotive service functions, the organization quickly became a lobbyist for better roads, within the city and throughout the state.[30]

As automobile ownership rapidly increased, especially after the introduction of motorized buggies—called buggy cars, or high-wheelers —and the affordable and more dependable Ford Model T in 1908, and as residents grasped the pleasure of "motoring," Ohio became wholly infected with "good-roads fever." A statewide good-roads association, officially the Ohio Good Roads Federation, supported by motorists' clubs, Grange chapters, and other groups, directed this struggle for road improvements. Backers sought to convey to local civic organizations,

A journey on a Baltimore & Ohio passenger train, pulled by a high-stepping Ten Wheeler (4-6-0), was faster, smoother, and more dependable than a horse and buggy on a public thoroughfare. About 1913 a maker of "real-photo" postcards caught this scene of rail and road in Fredericktown, Knox County. *(Cornelius W. Hauck Collection)*

churches, colleges, and—perhaps most importantly—to county commissioners and state legislators the manifold advantages of improving roads. Ohio quickly became a national leader: its size, wealth, soil, climate, and "progressive men" contributed to its prominent role. In 1904, the general assembly created one of America's earliest highway departments, but its budget of ten thousand dollars restricted its functions to educational activities. Seven years later, however, lawmakers backed the McGuire Act, which formed the modern department, and then in 1913 a small highway levy energized this state agency.[31]

Aggressive lobbying at the federal level also brought about some noteworthy betterments. In 1912 pressure from good-roads groups prompted Congress to appropriate $500,000 to assist states and counties in building experimental intercity roads. This measure contained two principal stipulations: first, each state or county that participated must contribute two dollars to every one dollar given by the federal government (the first use of matching grants for roads); second, Washington must supervise

Pioneer motorists in Ohio simply endured as they traveled through ruts and dust. In 1910 a driver and his three passengers, dressed in white "dusters," charge through the Ohio countryside in a Cincinnati-built Ohio 40-A model automobile. *(Cornelius W. Hauck Collection)*

construction. One pilot roadway involved the twenty-four-mile section of the former National Road, known locally as the West Pike, between Zanesville and Hebron. The project was funded with $120,000 from the federal government, $140,000 from Licking County, $100,000 from Muskingum County (raised through county revenue bonds), and $80,000 from the state. Ohio officials also agreed to pay for upgrading the road across the remainder of Licking County to the Franklin County line. Although business interests in Zanesville, backed by a large brick manufacturer, bitterly objected to the plan by the federal government to use cement, workers began in 1914 pouring the latter in sections sixteen feet wide and thirty to ninety feet long, creating a prototype of future intercity roads. At the time, there existed only a handful of concrete roads nationally. To celebrate completion of the experimental road on May 18, 1916, hundreds of area residents motored over "one of the smoothest pieces of roadway in Ohio" and looked optimistically to the

Early motorists had an easier time driving in those Ohio cities where brick pavements predominated. In 1910 the Cincinnati occupants of a locally manufactured Cino automobile could confidently wear their Sunday best for travel about the Queen City. *(Cornelius W. Hauck Collection)*

future. "The trip by automobile over the old National Road is indeed delightful and will be enjoyed by residents of both Muskingum and Licking counties to the fullest extent," editorialized the *Newark Advocate*. "One may now jump into a machine and drive to Zanesville as quickly as he could go from Newark to Granville [seven miles] with a horse and buggy."[32]

Before the federal government began its major commitment to public roads using the Federal Aid Act of 1916, which authorized expenditures of $75 million over a five-year period provided that states matched on a dollar-for-dollar basis, the Lincoln Highway Association (LHA), like the West Pike experiment, achieved modest success in improving Ohio's road network. Initially called the Coast-to-Coast Highway, the LHA functioned chiefly as a self-help and lobbying scheme to span the country from New York City to San Francisco with a well-marked, all-weather road. Launched in 1912 by good-roads enthusiasts and led by

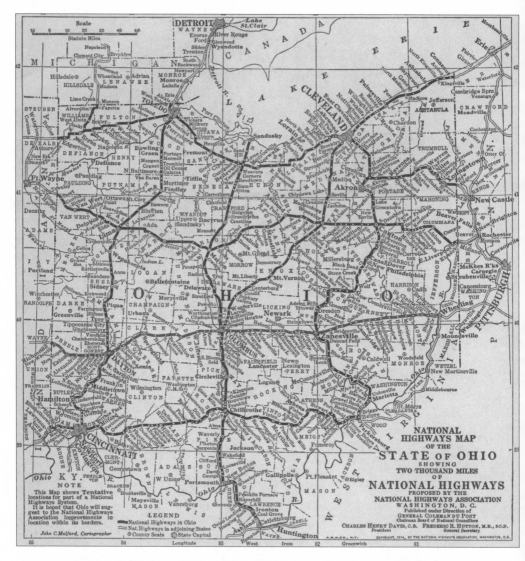

In 1914 the National Highways Association, a good-roads pressure group, proposed for the Buckeye State a network of two thousand miles of all-weather roads, including the "National Old Trails Road," the former National Road. *(Author's Collection)*

Prest-O-Lite Company [carbide auto lamps] executive Carl G. Fisher and then by the co-founder of the Goodyear Tire and Rubber Company Frank A. Seiberling, the organization laid out and identified with signage what in time became mostly U.S. Highway 30. The LHA paid with donated funds and materials for much of the upgrading of the route, especially with oiled dirt and gravel and with a limited amount of concrete paving (but none of the latter in Ohio). These contributions were hardly surprising since the list of LHA supporters read like a who's who of the automobile and cement industries, except for the conspicuous absence of Henry Ford.[33]

The Lincoln Highway sliced across the northern third of Ohio. At first it ran from East Liverpool through Lisbon, Canton, Mansfield, Marion, Kenton, and Lima to Fort Wayne, Indiana. Subsequently the LHA straightened the western portion, bypassing Marion, Kenton, and Lima. Local boosters in these three communities with an eye to trade and tourism resented this action, and in the early 1920s they successfully lobbied for improvements of the east-west artery through their localities, the Harding Highway, later U.S. 30 South.[34]

During the Roaring Twenties public funding from every level of government facilitated thousands of miles of better roads in Ohio. The role of Washington was especially pronounced. The Federal Highway Act of 1921 gave additional dollars to be matched on an equal basis with state funds, but unlike the precedent-setting 1916 law, it demanded support for "such projects as will expedite the completion of an adequate and connected system of highways, interstate in character." This legislation required that Ohio and other states identify no more than 7 percent of their total mileage as "primary" and that funds would be earmarked only for these roads. Soon the skeleton of a national network of highways emerged.[35]

By the early 1920s Ohioans correctly expected that better roads were to be part of their future. For example, the Lincoln Highway, soon to be U.S. 30, revealed a marked improvement from its initial self. Although hardly a "perfect" roadway, 69 miles of its 239-mile length were paved with brick and 6 miles featured concrete, mostly between the Pennsylvania line and Mansfield. The remaining sections sported long stretches of macadam, "maintained in excellent condition," and additional paving was planned. These generally good roads produced favorable comments.

17

"To travelers who had been puss-in-the-corner with highways all day, the broad, paved, clearly identified roads of Ohio were like awakening from a bad dream," observed a tourist who in 1926 crossed the state and the nation. "We found no better anywhere. They were smooth and wide and, chiefest of their blessings to wanderers, each road was numbered and at every turn or crossroad, the number stood affixed to a post too plainly for even the worst blunderer to miss. Ohio and Oregon, as far as our experience goes, have the best thoroughfares in the Union."[36]

During the 1920s and for decades to come, Ohioans, who sought better local roads, at times embraced a historic response: self-help. A resident of rural Jackson County recalled a popular do-it-yourself response to seasonal potholes and dust as vehicular traffic increased: "A load of crushed limestone mixed with used crank-case oil from a nearby garage . . . helps, but sure is messy." Urban inhabitants also employed waste oil. As late as the 1960s they poured it on rock roads to help prevent clouds of white dust from rolling into their homes.[37]

Not only did an ever-growing volume of automobiles appear on Ohio highways and byways, but motor trucks also became common. Local manufacturers, like G. A. Schacht Motor Truck Company in Cincinnati and White Motors in Cleveland, and out-of-state firms produced an increasing number of trucks prior to World War I. Some automobile owners even converted their vehicles into primitive "pickups." In 1913, for example, the Norwalk Produce Company acquired a four-year-old Overland touring car and removed the backseat, creating space for transporting egg crates to the local interurban freight station. Not surprisingly, trucks and modified cars mostly replaced horse-drawn wagons and carts for delivery services. But it was the European war that necessitated the use of trucks as ambulances and cargo haulers, resulting in rapid improvements in technology and operating performance. These advances, which included pneumatic tires and semitrailer units, were translated into more effective operations on the home front. In 1917 in Cincinnati, the Cleveland, Cincinnati, Chicago & St. Louis ("Big Four") Railroad (New York Central System) substituted trucks for boxcars, which were in short supply, to assemble less-than-carload (LCL) shipments from area plants. About the same time, regular express truck service began between Ohio and New England. With return to peacetime conditions, the number of newly organized or expanded trucking firms dramatically increased. A decline in vehicle prices and a rise in consumer credit coupled with substantially cheaper gasoline and tires as well as better roads largely explain this phenomenon. Still, mom-and-pop companies of financial instability and rapidly changing identity dominated the industry.[38]

Buses also joined trucks on Ohio roads. The earliest ones were touring cars, or sedans, in which usually the owner-operator picked up riders who paid cash fares. Often there existed no fixed route or formal schedule, although some "bus owners" who transported workers customarily began and ended their journeys at factories, hotels, public buildings, or stores. Word of mouth, newspaper advertisements, or printed broadsides announced the service, but regular commitment was not guaranteed.[39]

By the time of the world war this jitney, or taxi-cab style of bus service, was commonly evolving into more recognizable bus operations with fixed routes and printed timetables. In January 1918 the Green Line Bus Company distributed a schedule in which it listed five daily, except Sunday, trips between Cleveland and Strongsville and indicated that it maintained a waiting room at 4224 Pearl Road. Like steam and electric railroads, the firm added a variety of messages to its listing of arrival and departure times: "Children Under 12 Years Half Price; Special Trips for Parties; Full Fare for Dogs; $7.00 Worth of Tickets $5.00."[40]

Differing from the trucking industry, which remained highly atomized until after passage of the federal Motor Carrier Act of 1935, bus operations in Ohio followed the national trend toward consolidation. Although various small companies continued until automobiles severely cut into the short-haul market after World War II, bus patrons could use firms that offered more than trips to nearby communities. In the late 1920s, for example, Cleveland-based Great Lakes Stages operated a fleet of modern center-aisle buses between Cleveland, Buffalo, New York, and Pittsburgh and claimed, "The First Sleeping Coach Offered to America's Traveling Public." The company and a connecting line provided patrons between New York and Chicago, via Cleveland, these luxury accommodations:

> [W]e have the sleeping coach containing large single and double
> berths seventy-three inches long, equipped with two lights and porter's
> bell together with air cushion mattresses and snowy white linen.

Both upper and lower berths have windows which may be opened or closed and are equipped with adjustable outside ventilators making it possible for the occupants to regulate their supply of fresh air.

A roomy ladies' dressing room and lavatory is built in the rear as well as a complete and compact men's room.

A new electric ventilating system changes the air in these coaches every five minutes and hot water heat maintains an even temperature in the winter time, while electric fans furnish the circulation necessary in the summer time.

Card tables are provided for those who desire to amuse themselves before retiring and ice water is available at all times.[41]

In the 1930s Ohioans began riding Greyhound Corporation buses. This company, which had its origins in northern Minnesota shortly before World War I, expanded rapidly in the late 1920s and forged a transcontinental network. Acquisitions and mergers carried the firm from five million coach miles in 1927 to twenty million two years later. Greyhound's long-distance routes served Ohio well: New York-Erie-Cleveland-Port Clinton-Toledo-Chicago, Pittsburgh-Lima-Fort Wayne-Chicago, Pittsburgh-Columbus-Dayton-Indianapolis-St. Louis, Pittsburgh-Youngstown-Akron-Toledo-Detroit, Pittsburgh-East Liverpool-Youngstown-Warren-Cleveland, and Cleveland-Wooster-Columbus-Washington Court House-Wilmington-Cincinnati.[42]

About the time "hounds" appeared on Ohio roadways, residents could also board buses operated by the state's largest, albeit faltering, electric interurban railways. Several firms, including the Cincinnati & Lake Erie System, Lake Shore Coach Line, and Penn-Ohio Coach Lines, offered substantial service, often replicating or even surpassing the travel opportunities once provided by electric cars. And it would be Greyhound or its principal rival, Trailways System, that frequently absorbed these one-time interurban affiliates and the other larger independents, like Great Lakes Stages, creating by the era of World War II two dominant bus carriers in the state.[43]

Whether using automobiles, trucks, or buses, Ohioans encountered steadily improving roadways. The traditional combination of federal, state, and local financing, including New Deal relief and recovery programs, made possible these advances. By the era of World War II, a network of concrete and "farm-to-market" gravel roads laced the state, at last largely conquering the vicious and viscous mud and solving most related problems. Understandably, speed limits rose, from the posted thirty-five miles per hour in the early 1920s on the Lincoln Highway to fifty miles, common a decade later and by the 1940s in some places "reasonable and proper."[44]

Still, a road utopia hardly existed. Although wartime conditions brought severe rationing of petroleum and rubber and widespread shortages of vehicles and parts, intercity highway travel flourished. Then, after the conflict automobile and truck traffic soared, underscoring the need for road improvements. Employees of the Ohio Department of Highways in 1945, for example, counted more than 222,000 daily movements on Route 3 and U.S. Highway 42 near Cleveland, a volume that at times clogged these arteries and increased the rate of accidents. Although the state worked to eliminate sharp curves, steep grades, narrow pavements, and inadequate bridges, a road crisis confronted Ohio motorists. Since the state embraced a pay-as-you-go approach, relying heavily on modest gasoline and motor vehicle taxes, revenues never generated the money needed to modernize the state system of approximately sixteen thousand miles of surfaced roads.[45]

A host of interest groups, including concrete suppliers, labor unions, oil producers, and truck companies, the so-called "road gang," pushed hard to end congestion on the nation's primary highways by seeking massive federal expenditures on new interstate roads. After nearly a decade of pressure, in 1956 the 85th Congress and President Dwight Eisenhower endorsed the most ambitious public works program undertaken in American history and arguably the most important: the National Defense Highway Act. This statute committed Washington to pay from a Highway Trust Fund 90 percent of the cost of building approximately forty-one thousand miles of toll-free express highways, a task to be completed by 1976. But before interstate highways crossed the Ohio landscape, the state had embarked on its own super, divided, limited-access road project, the Ohio Turnpike.[46]

The same forces that prompted federal action in 1956 explain why in the late 1940s Ohio decided to build a superhighway. Vocal pressure groups, responding to congestion and other inadequacies of east-west trunk highways and wishing to capitalize on plans by Pennsylvania to extend its core turnpike west of Pittsburgh, convinced lawmakers to respond. In 1949 the general assembly authorized creation of the Ohio Turnpike Commission with broad powers of constructing, maintaining, and operating a trans-state turnpike. Financing would not come from fuel and vehicle taxes, but rather from $326 million in state revenue bonds.[47]

Once dignitaries broke ground on October 27, 1952, this biggest building project in Ohio history to that time rapidly took shape. At the peak of construction, contractors employed approximately ten thousand workers, and more than twenty-three hundred bulldozers, graders, loaders, and other machines dotted the staked right-of-way between Pennsylvania and Indiana. On December 1, 1954, the first segment of this 241-mile roadway began operations, extending 22 miles from the Pennsylvania Turnpike to an interchange at Mahoning County Road 18, 9 miles west of Youngstown. The commission rushed this portion to completion in order to reduce vehicle congestion moving to and from the Pennsylvania Turnpike, which had opened in 1951 to the Ohio bor-

In June 1954 a photographer for the Ohio Turnpike Commission captured the work of graders in a deep-rock cut in northern Summit County as the eastern portion of the turnpike took shape. *(Ohio Turnpike Commission Archives)*

Part of the enormous expense of building the Ohio Turnpike involved bridge construction. As part of "Project No.1" the largest set of twin bridges, 2,682 feet in length, rose over the wide, deep valley of the Cuyahoga River. At the highest point, these twin bridges stood 175 feet above the water. *(Ohio Turnpike Commission Archives)*

der. On October 1, 1955, only thirty-eight months after the start of construction, the remaining 219 miles handled its first traffic. At 12:01 A.M., Gov. Frank J. Lausche proudly shouted, "Remove all barricades! Open the gates!," officially marking the debut of the longest stretch of highway ever opened on a single day. As automobiles, buses, and trucks sped along this four-lane divided highway and passed through its seventeen interchanges and terminals, the commission activated its operating infrastructure: restaurants, service stations, maintenance buildings, and radio communications.[48]

From opening day the economics of the Ohio Turnpike were encouraging, and this enterprise rapidly outperformed the state's earlier transportation endeavor, the public canal system. Revenues from tolls, restaurant and service station concessionaire rentals, and other sources

These twin bridges are seen in the fall of 1998 as automobiles and trucks race across the valley of the Cuyahoga River. *(Sally Riede Photograph)*

grew impressively. In 1956 annual income stood at $15,350,966 and thirty years later reached $149,317,707. The turnpike's bond ratings were so strong that in 1996 the commission easily sold $370 million of debt at attractive interest rates for massive betterments, including extensive third-lane construction. From the beginning, the road itself also had a positive impact on business and land values, comparable to canals and railroads of the previous century and a benefit far beyond what toll revenues generated.[49]

The financial prowess of the Ohio Turnpike stemmed from two principal factors, location and leadership. Its strategic position made it an indispensable link between New England, Middle Atlantic, and Midwestern states and the direct avenue between the Massachusetts Turnpike, New York Thruway, New Jersey Turnpike, Pennsylvania Turnpike, Indiana Toll Road, Chicago Skyway, and connecting interstate freeways. The turnpike, moreover, benefited greatly from able, dedicated commissioners who prevented operations from becoming riddled with partisan politics, special-interest control, or financial scandal. The leadership provided by Columbus attorney James W. Shocknessy (1906–1976), who chaired the commission from its beginning until his death on July 15, 1976, contributed mightily to its stellar reputation. "He was not often wrong and those who opposed him found him a lion incarnate, a tenacious infighter with an instinct for the jugular, whose brilliant mind and sharp tongue were his most formidable weapons," observed a colleague at the time of his passing. "But once a battle was done, he bore no grudges. 'Professionals do not bear grudges,' he was fond of saying." The commission appropriately honored the memory of its first chair by naming the roadway the James W. Shocknessy Turnpike.[50]

Soon travelers could use the Ohio Turnpike to reach parts of the burgeoning National System of Interstate and Defense Highways: I-70, 71, 74, 75, 77, and 90, which by 1970 in Ohio were largely finished. In addition, the federal government greatly contributed to the building of expensive urban freeways, most of which were officially part of the interstate system. An illustration is the Third Street Distributor in Cincinnati. This link in I-71, which gave access to the Mill Creek Expressway, Northeast Expressway, and Sixth Street Expressway, was only eight-tenths of a mile long, but when it opened in June 1962 it cost a whopping $26 million. Federal funds later poured into construction of belt, or "ring," and bypass highways around several Ohio cities: Cleveland (I-271 and I-480), Cincinnati (I-275), Columbus (I-270), Dayton (I-675), and Toledo (I-475).[51]

As with the Ohio Turnpike, the economic impact of the interstate system, whether urban or rural, was tremendous. For example, no longer were commercial interests dependent upon rail or water transport; interstates provided viable transportation options. These roads proved invaluable for moving goods at high speeds over long distances. Still, interstates possessed detrimental dimensions. Most of all, they destroyed or damaged a number of cohesive city neighborhoods, fostered suburban sprawl, took out of cultivation thousands of acres of prime farmland, and, until the 1990s, ensured the complete triumph of the automobile over mass-transit and long-distance rail passenger alternatives.[52]

Ohio did much more than pay for its share of federally sponsored roadways, most notably interstates; it continued to upgrade the network of primary highways. In order to make significant improvements, a source of funding other than gasoline and vehicle taxes became paramount. In

1964 a huge boost came when Gov. James A. Rhodes, "Mr. Construction," won voter approval for a $500 million highways bond issue. This money paid for general betterments, including four-lane state highways like Route 11 between Ashtabula and East Liverpool and the governor's pet project, Route 32, the "Appalachian Highway" between Athens and Cincinnati.[53]

Unlike most states, the motorized vehicles that traversed Ohio's highways and byways had a good chance of being locally built, especially before the 1930s, when automobile production became heavily concentrated in southeastern Michigan. Undeniably, the Buckeye State was the cradle of the industry. A renown automotive pioneer was Clevelander Alexander Winton, who left bicycle manufacturing in the mid-1890s to complete in October 1896 the first prototype horseless carriage, and subsequently to launch his own car company. It would be the indefatigable Winton who embarked on several early long-distance test runs. The one that received the greatest notoriety occurred in May 1899, when Winton and a reporter from the *Cleveland Plain Dealer* demonstrated "to the people of this country that the Winton Motor Carriage Company, of Cleveland, was engaged in the manufacture of an automobile which would serve as a means of practical locomotion even to distant points." Winton and his companion left Cleveland City Hall on Monday morning, May 22, and five days later arrived at City Hall in New York City, personally delivering a prophetic message from Cleveland Mayor John Farley: "New York and Cleveland have long been connected by water and by rail, and now they are joined by the horseless carriage route." The 707-mile journey suggested much about the future of the automobile. Other Clevelanders, individuals like Frederick Chandler, Paul Gaeth, Louis Hoffman, Edward "Ned" Jordan, Frank Stearns, and Rollin White, developed their own motorcars and production facilities.[54]

Although in time Detroit eclipsed Cleveland as the Motor City, Ohio remained a leading automobile-producing state. Before oligopoly characterized production, various Ohio communities as far-ranging as Dayton, Norwalk, and Plymouth claimed plants of "independents," frequently more of a cottage rather than a mass-production nature. Yet, Cincinnati and Toledo emerged as significant vehicle-making centers. The former, which at the turn of the century was acclaimed as the largest buggy, carriage, and wagon manufacturing center in the world, became home to several modestly successful automakers, including Enger, Ohio/ Crescent, and Schacht, and a producer of early ambulances and hearses. The latter became identified with Overland and Willys (later Willys-Overland) and its successor firms. Even with Detroit's dominance, the "Big Three," Chrysler, Ford, and General Motors, relied heavily on Buckeye State factories for parts and assembly, especially after World War II. The activities of the Ford Motor Company in the Cleveland area are illustrative. In 1911 the firm began to assemble its popular Model T in the Forest City and three years later embarked on much more extensive production, continuing to make automobiles until the early 1930s. Then, following World War II, Ford launched a nationwide expansion program that resulted in construction of several plants in northeastern Ohio.[55]

When foreign-based vehicle manufacturers recently selected American locations, they did not ignore Ohio. In the late 1970s, for example, Honda Motors of America, a Japanese-owned concern, chose a site near Marysville initially for motorcycle and later automobile production. Later Honda expanded its Marysville facility and made other major investments in the state.

The saga of truck and bus manufacturing in Ohio runs somewhat parallel. For decades Cleveland was "Truck City, U.S.A." The White Motor Corporation, which traced its roots to sewing machines and steam-powered automobiles, by the 1920s had become the nation's premier manufacturer of trucks and buses. After World War II the firm acquired such smaller truck manufacturers as Auto Car, Diamond T, and Reo, but by the 1970s competition from General Motors, managerial shortcomings, and other woes led to its rapid corporate decline, acquisition of its truck operations by Swedish-based Volvo, and its eventual liquidation.[56]

The development of all-weather roads, particularly modern divided ones, and the concomitant age of automobility most likely have had a more profound impact on Ohioans than the earlier canal and railroad eras. Although roads have always been important to the state's citizenry, by the second half of the twentieth century they were absolutely vital. The automobile has excited residents more than any other invention.

Perhaps the greatest physical impact it has had is on the landscape, literally transforming the state to conform to its own needs. The automobile has also fostered massive growth in the bureaucracies of local and state government. Seemingly more and more Ohioans have been employed to maintain roads, patrol them for public safety, and handle such paperwork tasks as licensing and titling of vehicles. If the nineteenth century was the railway age, the twentieth century was the automobile age in the Buckeye State.

2

RIVER AND LAKE

NATIVE Americans were the first individuals who, followed by Euro-Americans, utilized the Ohio River and Lake Erie. These strategic bodies of water allowed entry to a heavily forested region in Ohio that possessed only a limited number of navigable interior streams. The area that is now Ohio did not have a Hudson River, like New York, or a James River, like Virginia, to facilitate *internal* travel. But the Buckeye State's boundary waters were heaven sent. Arguably, had these waterways remained its only major arteries of transportation, the state would have likely continued to develop extensively. Of the two bodies, the Ohio River immediately emerged as the more important.

Beginning where the Allegheny and Monongahela Rivers meet—at what is now Pittsburgh, Pennsylvania, the developing commercial capital of the upper Ohio River valley in the early nineteenth century—the Ohio River stretches for about one thousand miles to its confluence with the Mississippi River at Cairo, Illinois, and then ultimately flows into the Gulf of Mexico near New Orleans. The Ohio and its principal navigable tributaries, which enter mostly from the south, exerted a powerful influence on the orientation and growth of the region. During the frontier phase the stream was the grand road into the West; by the twentieth century it had developed portions of the valley into the "Ruhr of America."[1]

Early Euro-Americans called the beautiful Ohio River La Belle Rivière. Its features made immediate, indelible, and positive impressions. There were precipitous banks, at times ascending several hundred feet from the waterline; broad alluvial bottomlands; tree- and vine-covered islands and islets; and water that ranged from silvery rapids to broad pools, where winds whipped up acres of whitecaps. Then there existed from the numerous bluffs the broad and breathtaking vistas of this great American stream. A woman traveler who in 1811 stopped at the river's edge made these diary entries: "[W]e pass'd on . . . to the pleasant little town of Warren [near Wellsburg], Situated on the banks of the Ohio: which I lately understand Signifies beautiful: & it is rightly indeed named; So beautiful, that it is with real regret, I must bid it an adieu." A few decades later a guide-writer observed, "The Ohio itself, and its principal source, the Allegany [sic], are in a striking manner gentle as respects current . . . except the rapids at Louisville, with not a serious impediment."[2]

Before the transportation revolution the Ohio River provided easy transport, at least when compared to overland travel. Native Americans, afterward joined by explorers, fur trappers and traders, and the earliest settlers, found the canoe a practical way to exploit this strategic waterway. The canoe age, which stretches from time immemorial to the early nineteenth century, involved a variety of craft, most hollowed from logs. Some of the later boats were also modest affairs. Skiffs, or bateaux, for example, were twelve to fourteen feet long, with capacity for two passengers and ability to accommodate several hundred pounds of cargo. Others were significantly larger. The pirogues were thirty-five to forty feet long with room for up to fourteen riders and several thousand pounds of freight.[3]

By the late eighteenth century, the time of the flatboat and keelboat had come in the evolution of river transport. These popular, easy-to-build and inexpensive craft significantly enhanced the travel value of the Ohio River and its tributaries.

Immigrants, most of all, used flatboats. They wanted a cheap and dependable way to reach their destinations downstream and probably had no intention of returning to their previous homes. The typical flat-bottomed vessel, with its straight prow, measured about forty feet in length and twelve feet in width and usually had a roof and various types of oars for steering. Some even sported sails. Since the common, albeit massive, "sweep" oars required two men to operate, families often traveled together. It was, according to one observer, "no uncommon spectacle to see a large family, old and young, servants, cattle, hogs, horses, sheep [and] fowls . . . bringing to recollection the cargo of the ancient ark." For decades these "family boats" or "Kentucky boats" dotted the river.[4]

Flatboats were affordable and usually a good investment. In 1817 they cost about one dollar per linear foot at the headwaters in Pittsburgh, but only one-quarter that price in Marietta, Portsmouth, or some other downstream community. At their destinations owners could sell the lumber locally, recouping some, if not all, of their forty- or fifty-dollar investment. A family might decide instead to convert the vessel into a shelter, perhaps for themselves, their livestock, or something else. The first schoolhouse in Cincinnati, for example, was supposedly built from flatboat timbers, the donation of public-spirited pioneers.[5]

Flatboats also served business needs. Their owners might take on consignment goods to the port of New Orleans, or they might pass from town to town, buying and selling a range of items, typically agricultural products like apples and flour. An English lad, writing from Cincinnati on June 20, 1834, told his parents, "Thare are flat boats that go from hear to New Orleans. Tha can carry 7 and 8 hundred barrell of flower each. A man can get 30 dollours for goin down. It was one of these kind of boat I left Zanesville in, a flat boat, down in 5 weeks from Cincinnati which is 1800 mils." As this young boatman indicated, flatboats appeared on the largest streams (depending on water levels) and mostly ones that flowed into the Ohio River, including Brush, Pine, Raccoon, Symmes, and Whiteoak Creeks and the Hocking, Little Miami, Muskingum, Miami, and Scioto Rivers.[6]

Keelboats possessed a more complex structure than either private or commercial flatboats. As the name implies, they were constructed on keels and contained ribs, much like a ship. These long, narrow craft, measuring about fifty feet in length and ten to fifteen feet in width, sported both prows and "running boards" on each side from end to end to facilitate poling upstream. A roof covered much of the vessel to shelter the thirty to forty tons of freight and the spartan eating and sleeping quarters. The narrowness of keelboats permitted their operation on the larger tributaries of the Ohio. As such, keelboats, joined by smaller flat-boats, appeared on the principal streams in southern Ohio, including the Hocking, Muskingum, and Scioto. When floating with the current, speeds ranged from a few to six or seven miles per hour; but with pol-ing, upstream rates were much slower, likely two or three miles per hour. In that direction keelboat crews considered twenty miles of movement in a day an excellent run.[7]

With commercial craft floating downstream and being poled up-stream, Buckeye State communities along the Ohio River began to de-velop an infrastructure that would expand enormously with the coming of steamboats. Docks, warehouses, and related facilities appeared at bankside. Employment opportunities burgeoned. Farm youth, for ex-ample, found seasonal jobs on the boats or with the support enterprises. For many individuals this was their first wage-earning experience.[8]

Just as steam power revolutionized land transport after the 1830s, nearly two decades earlier it had affected water transport in the trans-Appalachian West. In October 1811, residents of the Buckeye State who lived along the Ohio River had an opportunity to witness an event of enormous historic proportions: passage of the first steamboat, or what Native Americans called "the fire-canoe [that] walked on the waters." The 138-foot *New Orleans,* the forty-thousand-dollar product of the Robert Fulton syndicate, made an epic voyage from Pittsburgh to New Orleans. A few days after the boat chugged by Cincinnati, a local news-paper commented, "The steamboat, lately built at Pittsburgh, passed this town at 5 o'clock in the afternoon [October 27], in fine stile, going at the rate of about ten or twelve miles an hour." Neither this writer nor the populace likely grasped the importance of this nautical event. They did not know that steam navigation, by quickening transportation and cutting distances, would telescope a half century's economic develop-ment into a single generation.[9]

More significant was the subsequent voyage of the *Enterprise.* In 1815 this steamboat made two *roundtrips* from Pittsburgh to Louisville and then proceeded from Pittsburgh to New Orleans, returning in June, against the current of the Mississippi and Ohio Rivers, to its home port. "The celerity and safety with which this boat descends and ascends the current of these waters," observed the *Pittsburgh Gazette* for June 15, 1815, "must be equally interesting to the farmer and the merchant." It

VIEW ON OHIO RIVER MARIETTA O.

About 1910 an unidentified Ohio River steamboat, with its stacks spewing acrid smoke, and a tiny, hand-powered rowboat appear under a massive bridge at Marietta. *(Author's Collection)*

surely was. Within five years the steamboat era had fully arrived on the Ohio River; scores of steamers plied its waters. As boat speeds increased and freight and passenger charges decreased, transport expanded. In 1850 at Cincinnati, for example, more than thirty-six hundred steamers arrived at the public landing. Also, after the 1830s the practicability of the steamboat was enhanced with the debut of the push barge, harbinger of modern river craft.[10]

The steamboats that called at Ohio communities along the Ohio River and its navigable tributaries, most notably the Muskingum River, dramatically differed from those that operated on the major streams and in the coastal waters of the East. In this region two giant side-paddle wheels, powered by bulky, low-pressure engines, moved these large palatial-like vessels. Initially fueled by wood, steamboats were soon using soft coal, the energy source which after the 1840s was followed by anthracite, or "stone" coal. Ohioans and other westerners, on the other hand, saw steamboats that to one commentator "looked like a cheaply constructed, ornate white wooden castle floating on a raft." Most were sternwheelers, propelled by lightweight, high-pressure engines whose compact boilers tolerated muddy river water. Until midcentury they burned wood. Unlike their giant eastern cousins, these western craft featured light-draft hulls and drew only a few feet of water, making shallow-water operations possible or, as one wag suggested, giving them "the ability to navigate on a heavy dew."[11]

The steamboat trade took on various dimensions. Entrepreneurs frequently formed firms to provide scheduled transport to specific destinations. In the early 1850s, for example, owners of the *Malta* offered regular twenty-eight to thirty-hour service between Pittsburgh and Zanesville via the Ohio and Muskingum Rivers, leaving Pittsburgh at 2 P.M. on Fridays and returning at 8 A.M. on Mondays. Other operators employed a "tramp" format, handling freight and passengers wherever and whenever practical. After 1830 all steamboat operations benefited enormously with completion of the Louisville & Portland Canal, which circumvented the extensive falls and rapids on the Ohio near Louisville, Kentucky, thus eliminating an annoying and at times dangerous impediment to navigation. With the river revolution came new jobs, including deck crews, dockhands, woodcutters, boatbuilders, and repairers. Although the industry never employed the numbers associated with steam or even electric interurban railways, many were involved in "steamboatin'."[12]

Strong employment opportunities in the steamboat enterprise occurred in part because of the relatively short life span of these vessels. The wooden hulls and superstructures were subject to destruction by fire, ice, and water. Then, too, there was the element of carelessness. For instance, at times captains overtaxed their engines, often in races with other boats, which led to explosions and fires. Steamboats typically remained in service for only four or five years, although fortunately the machinery usually could be salvaged and installed in replacement craft. The fragile nature of steamers helps account for the building of nearly six thousand vessels from 1811 to 1880 in boatyards along the Ohio River, with Cincinnati, Marietta, and Portsmouth being major construction centers.[13]

Until railroads virtually destroyed passenger travel by steamboat, leaving these vessels to transport freight, mostly bulk commodities, patrons commonly came to expect good and, on occasions, grand accom-

The Lorena, built in 1895 for freight and passenger service between Pittsburgh, Pennsylvania, and Zanesville, steams along the Muskingum River in Morgan County near Malta. Between Marietta, on the Ohio River, and Dresden, north of Zanesville on the Ohio & Erie Canal, the waterway was "canalized" with a series of locks and dams. *(Author's Collection)*

modations. Although the first deck housed the engine, boiler, and other things mechanical, the second deck featured a much more pleasant environment, dominated by the salons and passenger staterooms. The furnishings of these public and private spaces could be attractive, with carpeting, crystal chandeliers, and other accessories. The main salon contained the dining room, bar, and gambling tables, with the latter two often near the bow. The typical steamboat also included a third level, appropriately called the hurricane deck since it was open to the elements. With only the presence of smokestacks and the elevated pilot's house, the view from this part of the boat was mostly unobstructed, giving passengers in good weather a keen vantage spot to observe the passing scenery. But the hurricane deck was not the place for everyone. One English woman strongly objected to "being covered with black sparks, or greased by some horrid invention in the neighborhood of the funnels." Some passenger complained about noise, but others found soothing the regular "paddle, paddle, puff" sounds. Nevertheless, a journey

35

by steamboat was a "modern" experience. "The traveler could be co-cooned completely; a protective, transportation environment encased him," suggested one scholar. "Many travelers knew the country not by what they saw, but by what they were told in the comfort of the steam-boat salons."[14]

Although in the nineteenth century steamboats dominated major boat production along the Ohio River, surprisingly some large nonsteam vessels, designed for the high seas, were also built in the Buckeye State. The *John Farnum* is the best known. This three-masted barque took shape in Marietta for a special mission: to transport food for victims of the Irish famine. In February 1847 the *John Farnum* entered the river, loaded with more than ten thousand bushels of corn, and eventually reached Queenstown, Ireland. After the ship returned to the United States from the Emerald Isle, it spent its remaining years sailing in South American waters for profit rather than mercy.[15]

In the latter part of the nineteenth century, the Ohio River and its feeders seemingly meant little to most Ohioans. As passenger service dwindled, residents thought less and less of river transport; the railway station rather than the public landing became the focal point of community life. Still, cargoes, mostly bulk ones, moved by water. Barges, pushed by steamers, became more common, and the lone steamboat remained active as did the old-fashioned flatboat. The latter craft carried not coal or grain, but a variety of consumer products. A Bellaire-area resident recalled that his father in 1885 bought from a Clarington man a flatboat measuring 24 x 125 feet and set out to sell wooden barrels to area apple growers. "The barrels were delivered at the farm landings along the way, in anticipation of being ready for apple picking time in the autumn. My dad found a ready sale for all the barrels he could furnish." Later in the year, the same flatboat floated down the Ohio to Louisville with a load of apples purchased from streamside farmers. The fruit was then sold from the flatboat's mooring at the central wharf. After the apples were gone, for a modest charge a steamboat pushed the empty flatboat back upstream for a repeat performance the next year.[16]

By the dawn of the twentieth century, Ohio River traffic, especially freight, had declined further. Steam railroads and the new electric interurbans captured much of the remaining shipments, particularly perishables. Yet it would have been wrong for contemporaries to have written the obituary for river commerce.

The era of World War I energized water-borne freight. With America's entry into the conflict on April 6, 1917, a host of technical and logistical problems immediately arose on the home front, most notably from shortcomings in the transport system. Wartime traffic soared and chaos reigned in Atlantic and Gulf terminals. Loaded railroad cars clogged port sidings while shippers clamored for empties. The Woodrow Wilson administration responded to the crisis in land transportation by backing creation of the United States Railroad Administration, one of the most powerful federal agencies ever established. Rail snarls quickly declined, but the volume of business remained high. In order to relieve these pressures, Washington encouraged movement of bulk freight on inland streams, including the strategic Ohio River.[17]

Although the war years were a boon to river traffic, federal officials and particularly officers in the Army Corps of Engineers, realized that additional betterments were essential if this commerce was to prosper. The problem primarily involved maintaining navigable levels of water. The river, of course, would rise and fall according to the whims of nature, overflowing its banks after the winter snow melt and spring rains and drying up in the summer and early autumn, trapping boats in unconnected pools. The solution involved canalization, what had earlier been done to the Muskingum River. The general prosperity of the 1920s, in part, prompted Congress to underwrite construction of forty-six dams and locks by the Corps of Engineers. This public works project, completed in 1929, tamed the once largely free-flowing Ohio by creating a series of impoundment lakes, helping stabilize channel depths and control flooding.[18]

The canalized Ohio River stimulated usage, with chemicals, coal, grain, petroleum products, sand, and gravel dominating shipments. And, to a limited degree, the improved river promoted passenger traffic. Rather than providing scheduled intercity service, steamboat operators recruited leisure travelers. Since the late nineteenth century, cruise boats had operated from Ohio ports, but real growth occurred somewhat later as an increasing number of wage earners sought a refreshing break from their daily routines. Most notably, the Coney Island Company, which

The *Island Queen*, "one of the largest river excursion steamers in the world," annually transported thousands of Ohioans from Cincinnati to the Coney Island amusement park and entertained them onboard with music for dancing and listening. *(Author's Collection)*

ran a popular amusement park upstream from Cincinnati, for many seasons provided boats, including the magnificent *Island Queen,* between the Queen City and the Coney Island Park. These craft not only transported seasonal passengers to and from the park, but also offered cruises for pleasure seekers who had no desire to ride a merry-go-round or a roller coaster. They wanted fresh air, music, and snacks. Although the number of steamboats declined during the Great Depression, a few remained. The *Island Queen,* for one, lasted until it burned in 1947. Even at the end of the twentieth century the heritage of pleasure travel on the Ohio-Mississippi system continues with the *Delta Queen* and the *Mississippi Queen,* operated by the Delta Queen Steamboat Company of Cincinnati and New Orleans.[19]

The continuing demand for good navigation resulted in ongoing improvements to Ohio River navigation. Replacement technologies did much to promote betterments. Most significantly, after World War II powerful diesel-powered towboats, which made coal and oil-fired steamers obsolete, could handle larger and heavier all-steel barges and thus required a deeper waterway and bigger lockage. As a response, in the

1960s, especially, the Corps of Engineers eliminated obsolete dams and locks and installed new ones and made other modifications, creating, under most conditions, a continuous twelve-foot-deep channel. Local politicians, who benefited from "pork barrel" legislation, spearheaded these costly public works. The combination of improved equipment and a better waterway fostered greater usage. An indication of the increasing commercial value of the river is the long-term rise in annual tonnage: 22 million tons in 1930 and 151 million tons in 1977.[20]

Just as the Ohio River remains a transportation asset to Ohio, so Lake Erie and the Great Lakes hold a similar utility. Although these bodies of water were employed less often as a route for pioneers to the Northwest Territory and the early state of Ohio, parallel passenger and freight activities took place. As with streams in the trans–Appalachian West, on the Great Lakes Native Americans and then explorers, trappers, and traders used small paddle craft—canoes, bateaux, and pirogues—for personal and cargo transport. They sought to exploit these vast inland seas, which stretched east and west for a thousand miles and north and south for approximately half that distance.[21]

Next came the sailboat era. By the early nineteenth century scores of masted vessels, predominantly schooners, appeared along Ohio's northern shore, providing both passenger and freight transport. Virtually all of these wind-powered boats hauled freight in addition to any travelers who might seek passage.

Immigrants, who hailed largely from southern New England and New York, however, usually preferred land routes to the Western Reserve and points west. The reasons involved safety, comfort, and reliability. Although a trip over trails and primitive roads could be long and torturous, a journey on Lake Erie involved the real danger and discomfort associated with ubiquitous storms, small craft, and few protected harbors. Also, navigational devices—lighthouses, for example—only slowly started to appear in the early nineteenth century. During inclement weather concerned Ohioans might burn signal fires to mark the shoreline and even prepare to rescue passengers and crew members. The *Cleaveland Herald* of November 4, 1825, printed this card of thanks from a vessel caught in a lake gale:

> The passengers on board [the boat] . . . from Buffalo to Detroit, take this, the only method in their power, to express their thanks to the

inhabitants of Fairport for the solicitude manifested for them on the night of the 1st inst. on which the brig, under the watchful care of a kind Providence and the active exertions of Captain Sherman and his officers, rode out a tremendous gale of 36 hours, off their port. Men who would keep up fires and watch on the beach through a cold and boisterous night, would doubtless have hazarded every danger in assisting us, had the catastrophe occurred which they and we anticipated.[22]

Although the waters of Lake Erie caused mischief and even great suffering and death, they, like those of the mighty Ohio River, possessed their own beauty, inspiring awe, and wonderment in many a viewer. In 1840 the sight of the lake prompted one unidentified traveler to pen the following:

> The Lake when viewed from this place [Cleveland] presents a most grand and picturesque appearance, nothing scarcely can be seen as far as the eye can reach but the blue, or rather greenish waters, interspersed with the white, curling spray of the rolling waves, rising, and sinking alternately and at like intervals. Oh! Grandeur surpassing description! And as Aurora clothed in the mellow tints of eve kisses the unresisting wave and hides her blushing face what thoughts on thoughts crowd on the mind.[23]

As with Ohio River transport the introduction of steamboats on Lake Erie did not cause a rapid decline in the number of other craft, especially sailing vessels. In fact, the era of wind-powered vessels did not wane dramatically until the 1890s. Still, steam engines revolutionized lake transport just as they did on other bodies of water and on land.[24]

On August 25, 1818, the first steamboat on Lake Erie, colorfully named *Walk-in-the-Water*, began to fascinate inhabitants along the largely wilderness shores from Buffalo to Detroit. It measured 135 feet in length with a 32-foot beam, weighed 338 tons, and quartered "about one hundred passengers, in the cabbin, exclusive of the steerage and forecastle, for the accommodation of families." In reality this novel craft was merely an auxiliary-powered sailing boat. In addition to its 30-foot smoke stack, made of iron stovepipe, *Walk-in-the-Water* featured two tall masts with a modified topsail rig. Indeed, the boat was truly a walk in the water, and a slow one at that; nevertheless, it was a harbinger of vessels to come.[25]

The first steamboat on Lake Erie did not last long in commercial service. While it made a number of trips between Buffalo and Cleveland, it wrecked in the autumn of 1821 during bad weather near Buffalo while carrying a full cargo and eighteen passengers. Fortunately, everyone survived the ordeal, although the financial loss exceeded ten thousand dollars. As with most destroyed riverboats, the steam engine was recycled, being placed in the more modern *Superior*.[26]

Soon many of these steam-powered vessels, like counterparts on inland streams, burned coal for power. This switch from wood fuel to "black diamonds" started about 1830 and grew as the superiority of coal became apparent and as local supplies of cheap, suitable wood dwindled. The gradual changeover significantly bolstered freight traffic on the Ohio & Erie Canal; "steamship" coal moved in large quantities from interior Buckeye State mines to the port of Cleveland.[27]

As Lake Erie traffic expanded, ports, particularly Cleveland, Sandusky, and Toledo, experienced an ever-increasing number of steamboats, with these craft making strong gains in the passenger-carrying trade. Bulk freight, grain, and lumber continued to move under sail. Yet passenger growth did not come immediately, largely due to the sparsely developed hinterland and the paucity of safe, improved harbors. But as population increased, river and harbor betterments mounted and such strategic linkages as the Erie, Ohio & Erie, Miami & Erie, and Welland canals opened, the latter in 1828 between Lake Erie and Lake Ontario, steam and sailing vessels proliferated. The numbers are impressive: a single steamboat and 30 to 40 small schooners were recorded in 1825 while 61 steamboats and 211 mostly larger schooners operated a decade later. By the 1840s traffic had become so great that vessels arrived and departed Cleveland around the clock. The city responded accordingly. "On the roofs of the two principal hotels, the American and the Franklin, there are towers, at the top of which a sentinel is kept night and day, relieved every four hours, as a watch to look out for vessels," observed an English visitor. "As soon as noise is given of one approaching, from any direction [including packet boats on the Ohio & Erie Canal], a carriage is sent down to the landing-place for the passengers, and a car for their luggage, from each hotel, to the great comfort and convenience of travellers, who, at whatever hour they arrive, find this accommodation furnished to them without expense."[28]

By the time of the Englishman's commentary, the overall quality of lake steamboats far exceeded those that plied the Ohio River and its major tributaries; they generally resembled ships that sailed the high seas. This came about because of lake conditions, according to Francz Anton Ritter von Gerstner, a German engineer who in the early 1840s visited the eastern part of the United States. "Hence these steamboats require a much deeper draft and much more powerful engines. The larger boats have low-pressure engines, whereas steamboats on the Ohio and Mississippi Rivers are all equipped with high-pressure engines."[29]

By the late 1830s the typical steamboat on Lake Erie was relatively spacious and swift. Gerstner made these comments about the five-hundred-ton, eighty-thousand-dollar *Erie,* which measured 176 feet in length and 27 5/12 feet in width and entered service in 1837.

> Intended primarily for travelers, it has space for 150 cabin passengers and a great number of deck passengers. If need be it could carry as many as 600 persons. It has no separate cargo area, though freight is frequently carried on the open deck. As a rule, steamboats plying the route between Buffalo and Detroit put in at 6 to 8 places to take on the wood and allow passengers to board or disembark. The distance to be covered is 360 miles, and the time required by the *Erie* for this purpose is 26 hours, including stops. Hence the average speed of this ship is 14 miles per hour. On one occasion it covered a distance of 320 miles in 21 hours and 23 minutes, for an average speed of 15 miles per hour. It makes one trip every 6 days from Buffalo to Detroit and back, or 5 round trips a month.[30]

The *Erie* and other comparable steamboats carried a rich variety of passengers. These popular vessels commonly transported immigrants who sought new lives in the West, accounting for the diversity of those on board and paralleling the kind of humanity typically traveling along the National Road and riding coaches of the developing railroads. In 1834 a passenger from Boston, who booked passage on the pioneer *Superior,* made these pointed comments:

> Who can describe a Lake Erie steamboat, a world in miniature, a floating Babel? I embarked in the *Superior* for Cleaveland. It was the last of October; and as the time of discontinuance of lake navigation was fast approaching, I doubtless had a more favorable opportunity to see a real Lake Erie cargo. . . . Two decks and three cabins appeared to be crammed with specimens of every department of nature and of art. Such a heterogeneous group of "human faces divine" could hardly be imag-

ined. Every "kindred and nation and tongue," from Europe, at least, if not from every other quarter of the globe, has sent its delegate. Should the Peace Society push its project for a "Congress of Nations," I would suggest a Lake Erie Steam-boat, on a late passage, as the most feasible point of meeting. . . .

The hardy, country-loving Swiss; the drawling, drudging Dutch-man; the preserving, opinionated Scotsman; and the reckless, roister-ing Irishman, as well as the shrewd and penetrating Yankee, were timbled in admirable confusion, person and effects, upon the narrow area of an upper deck. . . .

But go to the foredeck, appropriated to horses, mules, and oxen—wagons, carts, and coaches; to the forecabin, the resort of the vulgar and the vicious, the intemperate and the profane, with a gaping crowd of wonderers, just out of the center of confusion; go to the deck-cabin, the prison-house of the "women and children," and to the dining-cabin, the sitting-room of the men, to discuss politics, religion, literature, and the wonders of steam. . . . Add the roaring of steam and fire, and the rat-tling of machinery; the trumpeted orders of the captain, and the prompt response of the seamen; and the witness of it all must acknowledge a steam-boat on Lake Erie to be a floating Babel."[31]

Walk-in-the-Water, Erie, Superior and their sister vessels sported side-paddle wheels, but in the early 1840s an engineering breakthrough took place with introduction of the screw propeller. This radical improve-ment made lake steamers more efficient and less clumsy in their dock-ing maneuvers. By midcentury nearly half (118) of lake steamboats used propellers.[32]

Technological improvements continued. In 1861, most significantly, the iron-plated steamer *Merchant* entered Lake Erie. Other sturdy iron vessels followed, in part responding to expanding mineral traffic from the upper lakes, facilitated by the opening in 1855 of the Sault Canal that circumvented the falls in the St. Mary's River between Lake Huron and Lake Superior.[33]

Design changes created a sweepingly different type of lake craft. In response to growing commodity traffic, in 1869 the first bulk freighter appeared. The propeller-driven, wooden steamer *R. J. Hackett,* launched in the major boatbuilding center of Cleveland, sported features that eventually characterized vessels capable of seasonally moving vast quan-tities of cement, coal, grain, iron ore, and limestone. The *R. J. Hackett* was 211 feet long with a cabin and pilothouse near its bow and another cabin and machinery space near its stern. A continuous open cargo hold extended the length of the middle body with hatches, spaced on twenty-four foot centers, covering the deck from cabin to cabin. A year later, the *Forest City*, a carrier of similar design but lacking propelling mechanisms, was also constructed in Cleveland. The two boats operated together as steamer and "consort," or barge, the one always in tow of the other, a common practice for decades in the bulk trade.[34]

Although the *R. J. Hackett* was arguably the prototype of the "freshwater whale"—the long bulk carrier—another boat, also the product of a Cleveland boatyard, claimed a similar distinction. This was the three-hundred-foot propeller-driven *Onoko*, the first iron-hulled bulk freighter. Set afloat in 1882, for more than thirty years this "experimental" craft transported grain and iron ore until a storm sent it to the bottom of Lake Superior.[35]

Enhancements to bulk carriers were ongoing. In 1886, four years after the *Onoko* made its maiden voyage, the first steel-hulled bulk carrier, the *Spokane*, entered service. And the capacities of the ever-expanding steel fleet increased. While the wooden *Onoko* carried a maximum of three thousand tons of cargo, the steel-hulled boats of the early twentieth century accommodated four times the tonnage. Although after 1900 size remained fairly constant, resulting in hundreds of "standard 600-footers," following the Great Depression boats were lengthened. The oil-fired turbine boats of the 1950s, for example, often exceeded seven hundred feet, and later ones, with their automated power plants, ranged up to one thousand feet, having capacities of forty thousand to sixty thousand tons. Channel, harbor, and lock improvements together with efficiency, safety, and cost concerns explain this trend.[36]

The *Edmund Fitzgerald* and the *Stewart J. Cort* were representative of the post–World War II "super carrier." The former, operated from 1958 to 1975 by the Oglebay-Norton Company of Cleveland, measured 729 feet with a 75-foot beam and 39-foot depth and could handle 40,000 tons of taconite (iron) pellets. Understandably the loss of this behemoth and its crew during a November storm grabbed national headlines and led to the boat's immortalization in song. The latter vessel, which shared the Great Lakes with the *Edmund Fitzgerald* for several shipping seasons, was the more imposing. This diesel-powered, twin-screw, 1,000-foot bulk carrier, which first sailed in 1972, could transport for its owner,

This picture postcard, which dates from about 1910, shows lake freighters in the harbor at Lorain. A husky tugboat maneuvers one of the ubiquitous "freshwater whales." *(Author's Collection)*

Bethlehem Steel Corporation, nearly 60,000 tons of taconite pellets and travel at speeds of fifteen to eighteen miles an hour, even faster than the ill-fated *Edmund Fitzgerald.*[37]

Comparing physical appearances of bulk freighters revealed obvious changes over time, but other improvements, less noticeable than length and carrying capacity, also occurred. The list includes double bottoms, stokers, high-pressure water-tube boilers, wireless radios, radar, bow thrusters, and controlled-pitched propellers. Ohio companies frequently perfected or installed these products of new or replacement technologies. The Delta Shipbuilding Company of Toledo in 1945, a year before it was acquired by the American Ship Building Company of Lorain, converted the *E. J. Block* to diesel-electric drive, a pioneering effort on the lakes.[38]

After the spring of 1959 the bigger and better bulk lake freighters, dominant vessels on the Great Lakes, shared the waters with ocean-going ships. On April 25, the mariner's map dramatically changed with opening of the St. Lawrence Seaway. Three new canals with seven locks facilitated navigation for vessels with a draft or a water displacement of twenty-six feet from Montreal to Lake Ontario and their entry to Lake Erie. As a result, several Ohio cities became world ports.[39]

Ocean ship access to the Great Lakes had been a longtime dream of many. The first major attempt to promote a deepwater linkage occurred after World War I with creation of the Great Lakes–St. Lawrence Tidewater Association, strongly backed by the Ohio business interests. Then in the early 1930s a modest triumph occurred. Starting in 1933 small overseas vessels could navigate a series of cramped canals and locks between the St. Lawrence River at Montreal and Lake Ontario and proceed via the twenty-seven-mile-long Welland Ship Canal to Lake Erie and such ports as Cleveland and Toledo. The appearance of these ships stimulated thinking about future possibilities.[40]

Although there were squabbles between Canada and the United States, and the Great Depression and World War II postponed additional action, enthusiasm remained. Rubber executives, for one, liked a report, completed in the late 1930s, that estimated a savings of nearly five dollars per ton on crude rubber sent by water in large ships from the Straits Settlements in Asia to Cleveland and then overland to Akron rather than by sea to New York and then by rail to the Rubber City.[41]

In the early 1950s political and financial roadblocks to the St. Lawrence Seaway melted, and in August 1954 construction of a twenty-seven-foot-deep ship channel from the Atlantic Ocean to Lake Erie began. Once commerce commenced nearly five years later, Ohio ports benefited. Grain, usually the largest outbound commodity, spurred traffic through Toledo. Coal, another leading export, principally aided Sandusky and Toledo. And Cleveland experienced greater activity, not only from inbound iron ore, typically from Brazil, Labrador, and Venezuela, but also in general cargoes. Yet Cleveland did not fully begin to reap the advantages of the seaway until formation in 1968 of the Cleveland-Cuyahoga Port Authority, which brought about physical betterments and international promotion of the facility.[42]

Although the future appeared bright for the St. Lawrence Seaway, troubling times eventually followed. In the early 1980s traffic dropped, and by the late 1990s it had plunged to about half the levels of two decades earlier. Increased competition from deregulated railroads and inland waterways battered seaway shipping. Only coastal ports could handle modern ocean vessels that were too large to negotiate the waterway's network of locks and channels. The container revolution had reshaped the logistics and economics of general cargo traffic, and economies of scale permitted huge, specialized vessels (container ships, dry bulk carriers, and tankers) to displace less specialized, smaller ships. In addition, shifting patterns of world trade, aging facilities, and government red tape have left their negative marks on the seaway. And ice, which annually halts travel, prevents "just-in-time delivery" schedules from January through March. If the new generation of cargo vessels that presently sail the oceans is to reach Lake Erie and other Great Lakes, extensive and expensive rehabilitations must occur.[43]

Many Ohioans lament the negative environmental effect seaway traffic, whether declining or not, has had on Lake Erie. Most of all, concern has come with appearance of zebra mussels, introduced by foreign ships. After leaving the hulls of these vessels, the mollusks have multiplied rapidly, attaching themselves to intake lines and other pieces of equipment. The resulting maintenance costs have been enormous. In the late 1990s marine biologists discovered vast numbers of these pesky creatures on the lake bottom, ending speculation that they gravitated only to solid objects. Moreover, the spread of zebra mussels to inland bodies of water poses additional environmental troubles.[44]

Not only did larger, more efficient lake freighters and then ocean vessels with their unwanted guests call at Ohio ports, but support facilities grew more complex. Over the decades boatbuilding and repair operations expanded. In the nineteenth century small firms predominated and modest-size communities like Conneaut claimed boat works. Between the 1830s and the 1890s, for example, sixty vessels, predominantly schooners, came from this Ashtabula County community. Their design and size were typical of the era and their names reflected the intense individualism of the times, not unlike the named steam locomotives of early railroading: *All Talk*, *Fairy Queen*, *Humming Bird*, *Orarita*, *Star*, and *Zouave*. In the twentieth century larger boat works produced scores of vessels. During World War II, for example, small, oceangoing warships, including minesweepers and net tenders, came from yards in Cleveland and Lorain.[45]

Conceivably the most intriguing, even spectacular, dockside sights

The harbor at Ashtabula bustles with activity, with iron ore from the head of the lakes being transshipped from a freighter to railcars by a giant Hulett unloader. Much of this heavy tonnage traveled to the steel mills of the greater Pittsburgh and Youngstown areas. *(Author's Collection)*

were not the boats themselves but stationary machines—the mighty Hulett unloaders, Ohio-invented and Ohio-built. George Hulett (1846–1923), born in Conneaut and later a Cleveland resident, helped revolutionize Great Lakes shipping. Introduced in the 1890s, his creation was a monster machine with a cantilevered arm and a self-filling, or "grab," bucket for unloading coal and iron ore from lake boats. In less than five hours four of these Huletts and twenty-five men could unload ten thousand tons of ore. Otherwise, it would take twelve hours and two hundred men to remove the same tonnage. These time- and money-saving giants became common in Great Lakes ports until the 1960s, when bulk freighters normally became equipped with much more efficient and economical self-unloaders. Indeed, by the late 1990s historic preservationists were desperately attempting to save the last Huletts, located on the Conrail Railroad docks in Cleveland.[46]

Companies that used Huletts or self-unloaders on their vessels reaped reduced costs and that pleased Ohio transport consumers, who were always looking for better service at cheaper rates. Occasionally, though, these objectives led to rather far-fetched proposals. Perhaps the most notable came in 1949. The Akron-based River-Lake Belt Conveyor Lines, Inc., announced plans to construct a two-way conveyor belt system from Lorain on Lake Erie to a terminal near East Liverpool on the Ohio River. The company claimed that it could economically transport coal, iron ore, and other bulk commodities. About the same time, talk of a Lake Erie to Ohio River barge canal through the Grand, Mahoning, and Beaver River valleys seemed more plausible. But neither the conveyor belt nor the canal progressed much beyond the idea stage.[47]

Paralleling the evolution over time of freight transport, monumental changes in passenger boats also occurred. The most obvious came with the rapid employment of steam, relegating sails to cargo schooners and similar craft, and by the latter part of the nineteenth century metal (iron then steel) rather than wood. As with bulk freighters, but not with riverboats, builders preferred to use the more powerful and less dangerous low-pressure steam boilers.

Not only did boilers of lake passenger steamers differ from those typically found on rivers but service characteristics were dissimilar. The trend toward pleasure cruising was somewhat slower to develop on the lakes; important intercity lake passenger service lasted much longer. Vulnerable to railroad competition, Lake Erie carriers not only responded head-on to their faster rivals, but at times worked with them, coordinating land-water schedules, and this cooperative relationship lasted for decades.[48]

Common to all forms of transportation, consolidation took place in the lake passenger trade. Early on, a winnowing of companies occurred and by the turn of the twentieth century two carriers dominated the Lake Erie market: the Detroit & Cleveland Steam Navigation Company (D&C) and the Cleveland & Buffalo Transit Company (C&B). The former, which dated from 1868, operated principally between Detroit and Cleveland. It owned a variety of wood and later steel-hulled side-wheelers and early on proclaimed to be "The Daily Line between Detroit and Cleveland." By the mid-1920s the D&C operated what were allegedly the largest side-wheelers in the world, the *Greater Detroit* and the *Greater Buffalo*. The latter carrier, started in 1892, developed Cleveland and Buffalo as its core route and began service with two small side-wheelers. In 1913 the company introduced the impressive *Seeanbee*. "She marks the last word in marine architecture." But this commentator wrongly

predicted, "and it is not likely that there will be built in the future anything of her type exceeding her proportions." Still, the *Seeanbee* was a
giant: its five-hundred-foot, four deck, all steel structure accommodated fifteen hundred passengers and tons of mail, freight, and express.[49]

The Detroit & Cleveland and the Cleveland & Buffalo were closely
tied. Not only did they work together on matters of rates and service,
but there existed a "virtual identity of the management." Moreover, the
D&C and C&B controlled the smaller Detroit & Buffalo Steamboat
Company, which began operations in 1901, mostly with Toledo as its
center of operations. Eight years later this firm legally entered the orbit
of the D&C.[50]

Until increased automobile usage and hard times of the 1930s severely
reduced passenger traffic, these boat lines on Lake Erie attracted substantial business. Patrons enjoyed good accommodations, even with a
touch of luxury typified by potted plants, Wilton carpets, and polished
woodwork. Many liked the freedom to roam a much larger area, rather
than being confined to a day coach on a competing rail line. There were
also attractive scheduling features. Individuals, for example, could board
a C&B boat in the early evening, dine peacefully, sleep in comfortable
staterooms and arrive for the business day in Buffalo. Boomed a C&B
brochure in the 1920s: "Spacious staterooms and parlors combined
with the quietness with which the boats are operated insures refreshing
sleep."[51]

Although the Cleveland & Buffalo liquidated in 1939 and the Detroit
& Cleveland lasted somewhat longer, these companies and later ones,
too, found profits from "moonlight" trips. The C&B provided such runs
to Cedar Point and Put-in-Bay. Excursionists especially enjoyed dancing to the sounds of a large orchestra. Even after World War II a streamlined, diesel-powered boat and the first new Lake Erie passenger vessel in
thirty years, the *Aquarama*, sought to carry on this travel tradition. More
successful financially have been the recent Cleveland-based *Goodtime II*
and *Goodtime III*, pleasing sightseers with cruises along the Cuyahoga
River and the Lake Erie shore and to Sandusky and the Erie Islands.[52]

Ohioans have not likely been aware of a vital, nearly invisible dimen-
sion to the saga of transportation on Lake Erie, the role played by the
Lake Carriers Association (LCA). For more than a century this Cleveland trade group has sought stability in shipping and has vigorously

Just as the Muskingum and Ohio Rivers gave Ohioans access to a variety of locations, ports on the Great Lakes often were final passenger and freight destinations. A major passenger, express, and mail carrier on Lake Erie was the "D&C," the Detroit & Cleveland Navigation Company. This "real-photo" card, issued by the firm, proclaims the *City of Cleveland* to be the "largest side wheel steamer on fresh water." *(Author's Collection)*

pursued improvements to channels, docks, harbors, and lighthouses. Early on, the LCA, successor to the Cleveland Vessel Owners Association, embraced self-help to meet its needs, including maintenance of navigation lights at its own expense. Later the association pressured federal lawmakers and agencies to address its requirements. The LCA represents the strong and ongoing Cleveland ties to lake commerce, part of an extensive infrastructure of financial, legal, and other support activities that have resulted in handsome economic returns from this body of water.[53]

Without question, Ohio, particularly the ports of Cleveland and Toledo, remains a hub of lake-shipping activities. The state's historic attachment will continued as long as the Great Lakes and St. Lawrence Seaway serve as commercial highways.

3

"DITCHES"

F OR A noncoastal state, nature has generously engendered transport in Ohio. Two water bodies have bolstered the state's overall
economic health: Lake Erie provides convenient access from points
along the Great Lakes to northern localities, and the Ohio River, part
of the giant Ohio-Mississippi system, gives entrance to southern localities. Although the Buckeye State benefits from major waterways on its
northern and southern extremities, interior sections have fared less
well. Aside from several rivers, notably the Great Miami, Hocking,
Maumee, Muskingum, and Scioto, the approximately forty-four thousand miles of streams that lace the state historically provided only limited transport opportunities; these rivers tend to be relatively short and
exceedingly shallow, particularly in the northern drainage area. Even
once navigable streams possessed limitations: seasonally they might flood
or dry to trickles; sawyers, snags, and sandbars commonly clogged them,
and rapids hindered or at times prevented travel.[1]

Although Ohioans early on exploited their natural waterways, particularly the Ohio-Mississippi route, the majority of residents encountered
enormous obstacles in their efforts to reach commercial markets. This
troubling condition in 1825 prompted Thomas Ewing of Lancaster to
observe: "Vast supplies of the prime necessities of life, the wealth of the

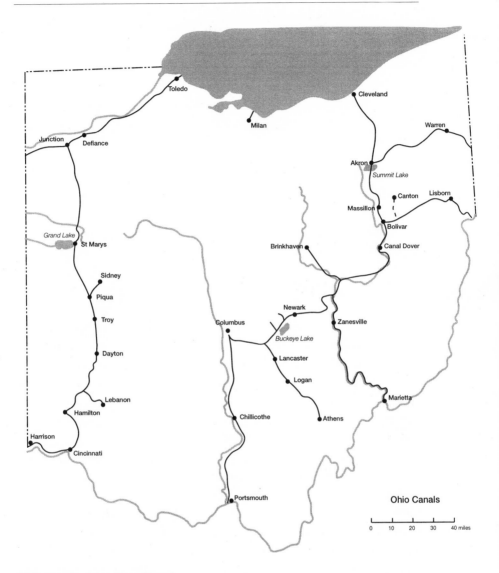

Ohio Canals. *(Art: Sam Girton)*

land, are wasting in our barns, or sacrificed in search of a precarious market." Important products of the infant state, including flour, hemp, potash, and tobacco, were bulky, difficult, and expensive to ship overland to buyers in the East. That great barrier, the Alleghenies, at times made land travel to the seaboard virtually impossible. Understandably, farmers regularly turned their corn into more easily transportable whiskey.[2]

Even those fortunate Ohioans who could tap the New Orleans market experienced difficulties. The distance was long, and these trips, made mostly by flatboats, were susceptible to recurring problems. The oppressive summer heat and humidity, especially as encountered in the lower Mississippi valley, caused foodstuffs to spoil rapidly. Also, commodity prices were fickle because of seasonal surpluses and shortages and the vagaries of deepwater shipping. If residents succeeded in selling their goods at a decent profit, they faced another concern, the threat of robbers. Highwaymen lurked along the popular return paths, most of all the Natchez Trace in Mississippi, and stripped returning travelers of their cash and valuables.[3]

Although Ohio was reasonably well positioned geographically, a water transport utopia hardly existed. If citizens were to exploit fully Lake Erie and the Ohio River for better commercial advantages, human intervention was required. No wonder Gov. Ethan Allen Brown observed in the wake of the Panic of 1819: "Our productions, which form our only great resource, are generally of that bulky and ponderous description, as to need every easement in conveyance, that we can afford." And he added, "Roads and canals are veins and arteries to the body politic, that diffuse supplies, health, vigor and animation to the whole system. . . . Nature strongly invites us to [such] enterprise."[4]

Surely a combination of "internal improvements," public roads and especially canals, offered the best hope for linking Ohio to the nation. "Ditches," as the latter were commonly called, seemed the sensible solution to the conundrum of how to reach distant markets cheaply, reliably, and safely. Perhaps the most popular expectation was that of substantially reduced transportation charges. In the early nineteenth century, freight costs commonly ranged from fifteen to twenty-five cents a ton-mile by wagon but only five cents or less by canal boat.[5]

Ohioans who lived in the newly admitted seventeenth state may have suffered from degrees of physical isolation, but they likely sensed that a transportation revolution was underway. Shortly after the War of 1812 some had observed steam-powered boats on the Ohio River and Lake Erie, and contemporary newspapers told of European canals and ones that had opened in scattered locations in the East. The twenty-eight mile Middlesex Canal, for example, coupled Boston and Lowell and effectively opened up the lower Merrimac River valley to commerce. The harbinger to what became the canal era, however, was neither the Middlesex Canal nor the Dismal Swamp Canal nor the Potomac Canal but the Erie Canal.[6]

Completion in the autumn of 1825 of the 363-mile Erie Canal in New York state marked one of the great engineering achievements of the nineteenth century. The massive complex of locks at the state's western extremity, where the waterway ascended the Niagara escarpment, was internationally acclaimed. This betterment was to canals what finishing the Central Pacific–Union Pacific was to railroads forty-four years later. Although the latter forged a monumental iron road from coast to coast by linking Omaha with Sacramento, the former strategically tied the Atlantic Ocean with the trans–Appalachian West, specifically Albany on the Hudson River with Buffalo on Lake Erie. The Erie Canal, with its practical dimensions of four feet depth, forty feet at the waterline and twenty-six feet width at the base, proved to be enormously profitable. Even before boats traveled through the western section, this transportation marvel had generated approximately $1 million in tolls; its overall cost amounted to about $7 million. By the mid-1820s no knowledgeable observers would seriously challenge the conclusion that the canal readily diffused "wealth, activity and vigor" throughout vast parts of the Empire State, although some initially viewed the undertaking as "Clinton's Folly." Toll revenues flowed into state coffers, making it easy to meet bond obligations and attract additional investment dollars.[7]

Ohioans closely watched the activities of Gov. DeWitt Clinton and his fellow canal backers in New York. Residents of the Buckeye State easily envisioned the advantages an all-water route would offer from their home in the West to the port of New York and intermediate points. The prosperity of the Empire State would surely extend to their locale.[8]

Citizens of Ohio did not remain passive observers to the New Yorkers' triumph. In 1822 and 1823 state-directed field surveys revealed that a river-to-lake artery and a shorter "tap" one were feasible and not exorbitantly expensive. This good news and continued agitation for cheaper transportation prompted the general assembly in February 1825 to agree to a canal-building program. Lawmakers endorsed two projects: the Ohio & Erie Canal, a 308-mile channel from Cleveland, on Lake Erie, south to the Muskingum River, then westward to near Columbus, and finally southward through the Scioto River valley to the Ohio River at West Portsmouth; and the Miami Canal, a 66-mile waterway northward from the Ohio River at Cincinnati to Dayton. The latter proposal, although economically sound, was admittedly designed to win support from southwestern Ohio for a core trans-state canal. And the measure's passage stemmed from other provisions, most notably road appropriations for districts to be bypassed by canals and a progressive tax feature that tied real-estate assessments to property values (it was correctly forecast that land prices would escalate along canal routes).[9]

Even though the young state lacked the ready reserves to finance the estimated $3 million in construction costs, it was largely free of debt. The strong likelihood, moreover, existed for substantial revenues from boat tolls, private gifts, and federal subsidies. Therefore, bond sales at attractive rates, especially to major investors, looked promising.[10]

Using the New York canal experience as the model, the Ohio General Assembly established a canal fund and a Board of Canal Commissioners (after 1836 the Board of Public Works) to finance, build, and operate its projected projects. Fortunately, these sister agencies attracted capable, public-spirited commissioners who contributed immensely to the successful completion of their mandated undertakings. Bond sales supplied the necessary capital, and following a joyous celebration on the Fourth of July, 1825, at Licking Summit near Newark (the second highest point on the route between Cleveland and Portsmouth), construction rapidly took place.[11]

The strategy of state-sponsored canal building worked reasonably well. Ohio embraced the basic New York canal technology and wisely concentrated its resources on the northern part of the evolving Ohio & Erie Canal, thus realizing quickly the primary goal of the project, a low-cost avenue from the interior to Lake Erie and hence an all-water route to the New York market. By the summer of 1827, boats connected Akron with Cleveland, a distance of thirty-eighty miles, and Ohioans could boast of being the first residents of the trans–Appalachian West to have this transport form.[12]

Although difficulties occurred, particularly with several lockage and water-supply endeavors, the Ohio & Erie Canal continued to take shape. In August 1828 the section south from Akron across the Portage Summit, the highest point on the canal, to Massillon opened, and in July 1830 the Licking Summit was reached. Even though spring floods in 1831 disrupted building, the canal was extended to Chillicothe, 250 miles from Cleveland in October of that year. In 1832 a combination of extensive flooding along the Ohio River and a cholera epidemic delayed completion to West Portsmouth until October. At last the $4.3 million waterway, more expensive than planned but less so than any other canal of similar mileage, was finished. Its 151 locks and fourteen aqueducts represented the skill and endurance, even the lives of thousands of workers. The power of human muscle, with axe, pick, plow, spade, and wheelbarrow, had accomplished much. The vision of an inland water route from the Atlantic seaboard to the Ohio valley, which had excited the populace for a decade or longer, had been realized, part of an unending quest for better transportation. No longer would people be bound to the limitations of navigable water.[13]

The Miami Canal, nearly five times shorter than the Ohio & Erie

An important commercial section developed along Water Street in Chillicothe, paralleling the Ohio & Erie Canal. This westward looking view reveals a freight, or "line," boat in the foreground. Water transport greatly benefited this seat of Ross County, which by the mid-nineteenth century supported thriving milling and pork-packing businesses. *(Jack Gieck Collection)*

The *Lady Hamilton*, operated by the Lake Erie & Miami Packet Company, rests in Cincinnati. Even the dirty waters of the Miami & Erie Canal reflect the boat in this late-nineteenth-century urban setting. *(Jack Gieck Collection)*

Canal and with no drainage summits to cross, took shape even sooner. In January 1829 workers, who had begun their toil during the summer of 1825, finished the full length of this $900,000 project, although the terminal lock complex in Cincinnati awaited completion. Two years later the ten locks, which made possible the 112-foot descent to the Ohio River, were finally in place, creating a waterway with fifty-four locks and five aqueducts.[14]

The opening of 375 miles of strategic, well-built, and revenue-generating canals whetted the public's appetite for more. Understandably, those Ohioans who lacked access to these ditches clamored for ones in their home locales. Pressure from representatives of "neglected areas" led Ohio to abandon a rational plan of mainline construction (just as much later some railroads erred with ambitious branchline expansion), and the state truly embraced a "something-for-everyone" approach. By the 1840s, too, a replacement technology, the iron horse, further reduced the viability of additional canals and river improvements.[15]

On the eve of the Civil War a ferrotype (tintype) maker photographed a boat moored in Troy on the Miami & Erie Canal. The industrial-commercial corridor is also captured. *(Jack Gieck Collection)*

The canal expansion was impressive, even though these waterways failed to achieve the financial strength of the initial projects. By far the most substantial undertaking was the Miami Extension Canal. Authorized in 1836, the year Ohio lawmakers voted to expand dramatically the canal network, it became the final segment of the state's second lake-to-river artery. Financing from Columbus, aided by a precedent-setting federal land grant, underwrote this high-priced ditch from Dayton northward through the Auglaize and Maumee valleys to the Indiana-sponsored Wabash & Erie Canal that terminated at Toledo on Lake Erie. The 160-mile extension to the core Miami Canal, with its 103 locks, opened in 1845. Unlike the previous large state canals, engineers concluded that this one required a greater supply of water. Public authorities ordered a massive 17,603-acre reservoir built near Loramine Summit, Lake St. Marys, or Grand Lake Reservoir (Grand Lake St. Marys), at the time allegedly the nation's largest artificial lake, and it was expensive to construct and to maintain.[16]

The Miami Extension Canal bridged the gap between the pioneer Miami Canal and the expanding Wabash & Erie Canal. By 1853 the latter project, underwritten by the state of Indiana, had become the longest single ditch of the canal era, stretching 468 miles from Toledo to Evansville, Indiana. The Hoosier State relied on Ohio to build the pivotal 89-mile section between the Indiana border and Lake Erie, a route that generally followed the valley of the Maumee River. The Miami Extension cost the Buckeye State in excess of $3 million, although the sale of federal lands helped pay construction expenses. The point of connection between the Ohio waterway and Wabash & Erie Canal was Junction, south of Defiance, and this interchange gave both Toledo and Cincinnati access to the developing agricultural lands of northwestern Ohio and northeastern and central Indiana.[17]

Although completion of the Miami Extension Canal created a main-line artery, later known appropriately as the Miami & Erie Canal, several sizable "feeder" or "lateral" canals also joined the two stems, much the way New York and Pennsylvania expanded their canal systems. Early on the eleven-mile "Columbus Feeder" to the Ohio & Erie Canal made the Capital City an inland port, and additional smaller taps were also dug.[18]

One of the major feeder canal projects served the Hocking valley. Its growing population and extensive deposits of coal and salt demanded better transportation facilities. The first portion of what became the Hocking Canal, the Lancaster Lateral Canal, officially launched in 1826 by private commercial interests in Lancaster, opened in 1834 between the Fairfield County seat and the Ohio & Erie Canal at Carroll, a distance of about nine miles. Even though Lancaster residents applauded the advent of canal service, those who lived farther down the valley wanted more direct benefits, namely water access to the Ohio River and ideally a connection with the emerging Chesapeake & Ohio (C&O) Canal, which was then being built toward the Ohio River from Georgetown in the District of Columbia. Backers of the C&O Canal projected their waterway to cross the mountains on either a northerly route to Pittsburgh or a southerly one to a point opposite the mouth of the Muskingum River. But the C&O Canal encountered serious engineering and construction setbacks, and by the mid-1830s its success as a trans-Allegheny route seemed unlikely. It would later stall at Cumberland, Maryland, origin point of the National Road.[19]

Canal enthusiasts in the Hocking valley decided to be pragmatic: they projected an extension of the Lancaster Lateral. The public works program passed in 1836 authorized this scheme and two years later the state bought out the investors of the Lancaster Lateral. At first authorities considered improving the Hocking River to accommodate steamboats, but their "slackwater" navigation scheme, which would have involved dams, locks, and dredging, proved impractical for this meandering and narrow stream. Therefore, construction of a "standard" canal started in 1837, hardly an auspicious time for Ohio to sell bonds because of a national financial panic. Still, the ditch slowly took shape, reaching Nelsonville in 1840 and Athens two years later. This feeder, which stretched fifty-six miles southeastward from Carroll, featured thirty-one locks, an eighty-foot aqueduct, and a price tag of nearly $1 million.[20]

Just as the Hocking Canal fed the Ohio & Erie Canal, so, too, did the Walhonding Canal. In 1836 the state endorsed this waterway, which largely paralleled the Walhonding River, to tap interior sections of Coshocton, Holmes, and Knox Counties. Although by 1841, at a cost of more than six hundred thousand dollars, the canal connected Roscoe (Coshocton) on the Ohio & Erie northwestward with Rochester, it failed to reach either Mt. Vernon on the Vernon River (Kokosing River) or

The crew of the *Maggie Case* pauses on the slackwater section of the Hocking Canal near Logan. The captain, dressed in a dark uniform, stands in the center, and the steersman is near the tiller. The two women are likely their wives. *(Jack Gieck Collection)*

Loudonville on the Mohican River, its two principal destinations. What emerged was a canal and short slackwater segment with thirteen locks that were "twenty-five miles to nowhere," hardly the waterway envisioned by it proponents.[21]

The Miami Canal also had a major feeder, the Warren County Canal. This seventeen-mile ditch more closely resembled the Walhonding Canal than the Hocking Canal. After authorization by lawmakers in 1836, the state absorbed a private "paper" company that had won incorporation six years earlier to link the newly opened Miami Canal from near Middletown with Lebanon, the Warren County seat. Under state control the $217,552 lockless waterway began operations in 1840 but added little to the traffic of the main stem. "It was an empty triumph," concluded historian Harry N. Scheiber, "for it became apparent at once that the canal would perform no substantial economic function: by 1840, several new turnpike roads offered a more direct and economical route from Lebanon to Cincinnati for all but the heaviest freight." Because of road competition, the state made the Warren County Canal a toll-free facility, a recognition of the economic facts of life.[22]

Even though the Warren County Canal contributed virtually nothing to fostering transport, an extensive undertaking, the Muskingum River Improvement, did significantly enhance commercial intercourse. It became the region's preeminent slackwater triumph and one of the nation's earliest complete river "canalization" projects. Included in the state's canal expansion measure of 1836, the Muskingum River betterment created an additional connection between the Ohio & Erie Canal and the Ohio River. What evolved by 1841 were eleven dams and twelve large size locks (36 by 180 feet) and a widened and deepened stream that permitted steamboats to navigate above Zanesville. Public coffers provided more than $1.6 million for the initial construction and later for rebuilding badly designed dams and locks. The state also financed a two-mile "side-cut" canal, a waterway that united the Ohio & Erie Canal at Dresden with the Muskingum River, providing a ninety-one-mile water route between Dresden and Marietta.[23]

Not all projects of the canal era were publicly financed. Ohio had several canals, spearheaded by optimistic entrepreneurs, that were either largely or wholly private endeavors. The longest of these chartered firms was the Pennsylvania & Ohio Canal Company, commonly called the Mahoning or sometimes the Penn Cross Cut Canal. Landlocked residents of the old Western Reserve wanted more than their outlets on Lake Erie and the Ohio & Erie Canal; they sought convenient and cheaper access to the Ohio-Mississippi system and the direct water route between Cleveland and Pittsburgh that a canal from the Ohio & Erie to the "State Works" of Pennsylvania would provide. (By 1850 Pennsylvania claimed the largest canal mileage in the nation, 1,295 miles, 272 more miles than Ohio and 343 miles more than New York.) Such a private waterway would surely stimulate agricultural and coal production, further bolstering, if not ensuring, the region's prosperity.[24]

In time the Mahoning Canal became a reality. Although incorporated in 1827, work did not begin for nearly a decade. Then, in 1841, this 125-mile route opened between the Port of Akron and Pennsylvania's Erie Extension Canal, two miles below New Castle, for a connection to Beaver on the Ohio River, a total distance of 145 miles. Some $450,000 of Ohio funds, made possible by the Loan Act of 1837, which permitted state investments in private sector internal improvements, assisted in creating this alternative route between Lake Erie and the Ohio River.[25]

Ohio invested virtually nothing in the rival Sandy & Beaver Canal Company, which built a largely parallel route to the Mahoning project. As a result, backers, who mostly hailed from communities along the projected path and from Philadelphia, struggled continuously from the time of incorporation in 1828 until completion twenty years later. These hopeful individuals fervently believed that they possessed in their section of the state the better way to link the Ohio & Erie Canal and the Ohio River, specifically a seventy-three mile route from Bolivar in Tuscarawas County to Glasgow, Pennsylvania. At a transportation "convention" held in the fall of 1833 at Warren, champions of the Sandy & Beaver argued that in several ways their proposal would be superior to the Mahoning one. Not only would the projected route through the valleys of the Little Beaver and Sandy Creeks be considerably shorter, it "could be used six to eight weeks longer each year than the northern route." Moreover, the valleys of the Little Beaver and Sandy Creeks contained a clay soil that would allow little water leakage from the canal bed "after proper puddling," and the immediate area contained an abundance of construction materials, including stone, timber, and hydraulic cement.[26]

Cogent arguments did not mean rapid success. Officially started with a gala at New Lisbon (Lisbon) on November 24, 1834, construction moved slowly, and by the time of the Panic of 1837 only about thirty miles of canal and eleven locks had been completed. The intermittent work that continued stopped completely in 1840. With return of better times by the mid-1840s, however, the moribund company reorganized and pushed ahead, completing in 1847 its Eastern Division from New Lisbon to the Ohio River. But the need on the Middle Division to finish two troublesome tunnels, particularly the three-thousand-foot "Big Tunnel" east of Hanoverton, delayed until early 1848 the opening to Bolivar. A related privately financed project, the Nimishillen & Sandy Slackwater Navigation Company, which won incorporation in 1834, never completed its twelve-mile waterway from Canton, seat of Stark County, to near Sandyville on the Sandy & Beaver Canal.[27]

Throughout the long construction period of the Sandy & Beaver investors wanted a buyout from the state, an early desire for "lemon socialism." Instead, public funds went into the coffers of the competing Mahoning route, largely because its backers displayed greater political skill. Still, lawmakers provided the Sandy & Beaver with assistance, granting in its charter the tolls collected from boats that passed through any portion of the Ohio & Erie *if* they traveled at least twenty miles on the Sandy & Beaver. This attractive provision, however, was not enough to make this second northeastern link between lake and river a viable operation.[28]

The Ohio General Assembly showed greater generosity with its support of the Cincinnati & Whitewater Canal Company. Public funds, which amounted to $150,000, went into the stock of this twenty-two mile project, organized in 1837 and begun two years later. The objective was to link Cincinnati with the Whitewater Canal of Indiana, a seventy-six-mile waterway that by the late 1840s ran northward from Lawrenceburg, Indiana, on the Ohio River to Cambridge City, Indiana, on the National Road. Commercial interests in Cincinnati backed this connector; they wanted a second terminus for the Indiana canal, fearing that Lawrenceburgh might displace the Ohio metropolis as the entrepôt for the growing commerce of southeastern Indiana.[29]

What became one of the nation's smallest, but briefly one of its busiest, canals was the three-mile operation of the Milan Canal Company. Chartered in 1827 and opened in 1839, this double-lock "ship" channel connected Milan with the "deepwaters" of the Huron River at Fries Landing and then Lake Erie. Officials wisely designed their waterway to the Port of Milan to accommodate lake vessels. This firm was another example of mixed economy investments; money came from local parties, the town, and the state. The twenty-five-thousand-dollar venture, originally expected to cost only six thousand dollars, helped make Milan, albeit for only a few years, one of the greatest wheat-exporting centers in America, if not the world.[30]

With the flurry of canal construction that began in the mid-1820s and lasted for roughly a score of years, residents of Ohio could take pride with these mostly publicly financed accomplishments. As early as 1828, U.S. Sen. John C. Calhoun of South Carolina correctly concluded: "It seems almost a miracle that a state [Ohio] in its infancy should undertake, and successfully create so great a work." By the 1840s the network of main and feeder canals gave Ohioans the best transport facilities in the Old Northwest and ranked their state high on any listing of internal improvements. Residents could also be proud of their collective ability to withstand the economic hardships caused by the Panic of 1837; unlike neighboring Indiana, for example, the Buckeye State remained solvent, although there were some difficult times.[31]

During the heyday of canal construction, most citizens probably failed to sense that the canal era would be limited. Their principal waterways were built for long-term usage; in fact, they were masterfully constructed. As late as 1840 canal agitation remained unabated. "Canals are proposed from Clinton to Chippeway; from Belleville to Bolivar; from Franklin to New Lisbon; from Mount Vernon to the confluence of Mohican and Vernon rivers; from Lower Sandusky to the mouth of Tyemochte Creek; from Columbus to Delaware; and some others," reported Henry S. Tanner in his *A Description of the Canals and Rail Roads of the United States.* But toward the end of the building phase Ohioans started to encounter the iron horse. While only a limited mileage of railroads appeared from the mid-1830s to midcentury, the decade of the 1850s witnessed an explosion of rail-building activity; laborers had installed only 323 miles of strap and iron rails before 1850, but by 1860 they had laced the state with 2,635 miles of line. By the outbreak of the Civil War more projects were either planned or were under contract. Railroads quickly drew away nearly all the canals' trade in high-value commodities and also competed for bulk items, including coal. Not surprisingly in 1853 the directors of the Pennsylvania & Ohio Canal admitted that "this Canal was constructed at a time when a railroad of any extent was not known. It is probable if there had been a system of railroads of any considerable extent, this work would never have been completed."[32]

As elsewhere, canals in Ohio usually served as the transition between primitive roads and modern railways. When the latter became more than isolated short lines, usually designed to give local communities access to commercial waterways, canals began to decline, at times rapidly. Take the case of the Sandy & Beaver Canal. Even before the first boat traveled the route, railroad fever infected residents of its service area. In 1852, a mere four years after the canal opened, management decided to abandon and liquidate its assets. Severe and recurring water shortages, tunnel-maintenance woes, and mounting debts promoted this draconian action. Soon the bellowing canal horn was replaced by the screeching steam whistle along portions of the corridor. Yet the collapse of the canal hardly ruined the region economically, although some communities lost their vitality and withered away.[33]

The weakest canals, like the Sandy & Beaver, became the earliest causalities. But some arteries remained active for much longer; freight boats, often laden with coal, grain, and lumber, continued to ply their channels. Portions of the Ohio & Erie, the state's premier canal, functioned until the catastrophic floods of Easter week 1913.[34]

But the public role did not remain static. In 1861 lawmakers approved a proposal "to provide for leasing the Public Works of the State." Unfortunately, a poorly designed lease arrangement with the private-sector canal operator failed to ensure proper maintenance of the system; moreover, the annual rental fees were unduly low. However in December 1877, the lessee, faced with declining traffic and other problems, walked away from the contract two and a half years before the expiration date. The state assumed its earlier role as operator, but of a greatly deteriorated property.[35]

The immediate 1861 period not only witnessed the closing of the surviving private canals, but also of large portions of the public ones. The land was sold, frequently to railroad companies who wished to install track on the gentle grades of the canal beds or towpaths, to serve customers who had been attracted to these waterways and to prevent any rehabilitation of these formerly competing arteries.[36]

By the early twentieth century, the large public investment in canals had not become solely memories. Notably, in 1886, the state ceded to the federal government the Muskingum Improvement, and its operation as a commercial waterway continued for decades. "[T]he General Government has so improved the portion between Zanesville and Marietta, 75 miles in length," observed a writer in 1905, "that to-day it is among the best canalized rivers in the United States." In a final effort to maintain the viable segments of the old Ohio & Erie and Miami & Erie canals, during the early years of the century the state made substantial repairs to the northern portions of the former and the southern sections of the latter. Such betterments, however, proved to have only short-term value; in March 1913 biblical-like floods knocked out these functioning units. During the deluge, Akron officials ordered the dynamiting of most of the Cascade lock complex to reduce damage to their

In the twilight of operations on the northern section of the Ohio & Erie Canal, a boat leaves a lock in the Cleveland area. Surely this pleasant day has inspired onlookers to follow the boat's progress. *(Author's Collection)*

city, which ironically had once called itself the "Venice of the West." After the cleanup only isolated segments of the canal system retained any commercial usefulness, not for transport but for industrial water supply.[37]

In retrospect the building of an elaborate canal system might have seemed foolish, but evidence abounds that these waterways served Ohio well, propelling an economic takeoff that became the envy of other states. Every area touched by canals experienced an economic surge, often even during the economically troubled years of the late 1830s and early 1840s. The Pennsylvania & Ohio Canal, for example, fostered a rapid increase of specialized dairy farming and made local coal mining feasible. By 1850 the waterway carried 8.6 million pounds of butter and cheese and 1.4 million bushels of coal. Two years later a whopping 2.9 million bushels passed along the canal. In the late 1840s newly installed blast furnaces in the Mahoning valley produced large quantities of nails and pig iron that became possible by the accessibility of the Pennsylvania

& Ohio waterway. In November 1853, the *Athens Messenger and Hocking Valley Gazette* clearly expressed how the canal era positively affected that area's economy: "The opening of the Hocking Valley Canal was the first movement made towards tapping the resources of our county. It afforded the means of getting to the centre of the State." Added the newspaper: "Business revived, property increased in value, salt wells were sunk, coal mines were opened, farms were cleared up, and vast tracts of good land, before unbroken, were brought into market, and turned to good account."[38]

Without question canals contributed to the economic takeoff of Ohio. Since manufacturers gained better access to both raw materials and consumer markets, the vital ingredients for growth were at hand. The Miami & Erie Canal, for example, accelerated industrial activity in Cincinnati, encouraging production of an array of products, including clothing and soap. On the other hand, consumers could obtain an abundance of less expensive goods not only from domestic sources but from the outside as well, whether sugar from Louisiana or books from Pennsylvania. The products of a burgeoning America were conveniently at hand.

The canal era meant more to Ohioans than better markets, new or expanded industrial activities, and a wider range of attractively priced consumer items; it meant changes in their daily lives. Some of these were both dramatic and long lasting.

The official opening of the canal itself commonly impressed upon residents that a new age had dawned. Communities repeatedly marked the arrival of canal service with celebrations, probably the most elaborate in their histories. A "blow out" at Chillicothe attracted more than eight thousand residents and visitors, and they were hardly disappointed. A parade of ten canal boats, "with flags waving from mastheads," and "delightful music" marked the start of the all-day festival. Speeches followed and so did considerable drinking and eating, the latter being highlighted by "two full grown deer dressed and set on the table in the attitude of full flight." At night scores of large candles illuminated the towpath through town. "The splendor and beauty of this scene," remarked an onlooker, "can be understood only by those who witnessed it."[39]

Even before citizens proudly christened their transport arteries, they had felt their impact. Canal builders frequently were Irish immigrants, often fresh from ditch digging in New York. These notoriously combative and rowdy men, who staved off boredom in their labor camps by fighting, commonly spent their cash wages in "dramshops" and other local places of entertainment. In Akron, for example, Joshua King's Tavern served as the social center for the Irish workers. Their presence typically disrupted many a somnolent village. Also, some of these Irishmen decided to settle along the route, adding a new ethnic and religious element to the local "Yankee or Cavalier" society. In Akron former canal builders occupied a neighborhood nicknamed "Dublin," and in 1844 they organized the community's first Roman Catholic parish—St. Vincent de Paul.[40]

As canal corridors emerged, they created a pronounced difference in the townscapes of Ohio. Although generalizations have exceptions, canal communities, whether new ones like Canal Fulton, Millersport, Port Washington, and Roscoe or established ones like Chillicothe, Dayton, Lisbon, and Massillon, stood apart from "interior" towns and villages. Probably the most apparent differences were the structures that supported canal commerce. Elevators, mills, and warehouses stood along these waterways. Not only did these businesses depend on canal boats for most or all of their incoming and outgoing shipments, but some used canal water to supply their power. Even the orientation of these places was substantially different. Businesses faced the ditches, just as river and lake ports had already created a similar configuration in scores of communities.[41]

Canal towns, too, usually demonstrated greater vitality; canal patrons largely contributed to the hustle and bustle. They needed a variety of services, including hotels, eateries, grocery stores, and livery stables. No wonder the proprietor of the Rising Sun Tavern, located at the corner of Main and Canal Streets in Baltimore, on the Miami Extension Canal, announced in a broadside of the late 1830s that "he still continues to keep a house of PUBLIC ENTERTAINMENT. . . . where he pledges himself that his best endeavors shall *be used* for the *comfort and convenience* of his guest. He has also opened a GROCERY & PROVISION STORE." Such a "house of PUBLIC ENTERTAINMENT" would likely be missing from the streets of a comparable noncanal community, and its usual clientele would probably be less cosmopolitan and secular.[42]

A team of three mules, common on canals in Ohio, pulls a boat along the Ohio & Erie Canal near Independence. The muleskinner controls the animals and the steersman manages the boat, constantly adjusting for the sideward pull of the towline. (*Jack Gieck Collection*)

Canal towns also drew visitors that inland places only occasionally or perhaps never attracted. Itinerant booksellers moved up and down the waterways and peddled their volumes at the various stops: established communities, locks, or wherever people congregated. Similarly, preachers earnestly spread their versions of God's Word and politicians their notions of good government. Since canal towns usually lacked a dominant culture that vigorously defended prudish "village virtues," such worldly diversions as circuses, plays, and other forms of popular entertainment found supportive audiences. As late as 1888, residents of New Philadelphia encountered "a theater pulled by mules." A theatrical troupe of fifteen actors and several musicians, deckhands, and mule skinners reached the Tuscarawas County seat on a small flotilla. The three boats served as a place to live and store paraphernalia, and a vessel could even become a temporary stage. The thespians pitched their tent near the towpath, conducted a local advertising blitz, and then presented one or more performances. "We had comedies and dramas," recalled a participant, "and just about everything the people wanted."[43]

While the appearance of a theater barge was a special occurrence, freight boats and passenger packets were common. The former were highly functional, but hardly products of gifted nautical architects. They generally consisted of two cargo holds flanked by a cabin for the captain and his family and another for the crew. A third cabin, usually situated in the midsection, served as the stable for the spare mule team and for hay storage. Although initially these boats might be nicely painted, they frequently became shabby, especially during the twilight years of the canal era.

Passenger packets, however, sported a style that made them seem sleek, even streamlined, and they were brightly painted and more elaborately decorated. Yet they plied Ohio canals for a much shorter period. The railroad, which was enormously faster, more dependable, and ran year round, easily eclipsed these slow-moving boats that could operate only during the navigation season. Rather than cargo holds, passenger packets contained a sundeck roof under which was a long, low cabin, generally consisting of three compartments: a public area that at night became the sleeping quarters for male passengers, a smaller section for females, and an even smaller one to serve as the women's washroom. Thus fifty to seventy-five passengers carried on these packets were not literally thrown together, and in good weather they enjoyed the additional roof or "promenade" space.[44]

As with trips over the extensive eastern canal networks, the great lengths of the two principal Ohio canals could mean long journeys. Even by traveling at night, it took, for example, at least eighty hours to traverse the Ohio & Erie Canal. A trip could be without incident. In autumn 1847 a female traveler on the Miami & Erie Canal observed: "[L]eft Dayton at 8 o'clock Monday morning on board the packet 'Banner,' . . . not a cloud to intercept the cheerful 23 miles and 7 locks. Paid $5 and a half from Dayton to Toledo. . . . Tuesday at 8 o'clock arrived at St. Mary's distant 65 miles from Dayton. . . . Wednesday found ourselves at Maumee. . . . We got to Toledo at one o'clock." But delays, sometimes for days, could happen. Low water caused by drought, breaks in the bank, and the like disrupted travel; high water could cause even worse interruptions. Congestions at locks, sick animals (packets commonly used faster horses rather than stronger mules), and other unforeseen events also slowed movement.[45]

Toward the end of commercial traffic on the Ohio & Erie Canal a steam-powered launch travels slowly along the historic waterway near Akron. (*Author's Collection*)

Although a trip might be relaxing, with the smooth and even speed of the packet and opportunities to meet interesting fellow travelers and experience the beautiful and uncommon scenes of nature, travelers might find their surroundings less than pleasant. While the sundeck space offered inviting qualities, one traveler, who in the summer of 1839 made the twenty-eight-hour trip between West Portsmouth and Columbus, noted that dangers existed: "When a bridge is approaching, the helmsman gives the warning cry 'bridge,' and woe to anyone who fails to hear or heed the warning and immediately fall flat on the deck, for the space between the deck of the boat and the bottom of the bridge is often no more than 2 feet." In the 1840s a Campbellite preacher, who traveled the Cincinnati & Whitewater Canal from Milton, Indiana, to Cincinnati on the packet *Express Mail*, strongly objected to the overall experience: "Some twenty of us are crowded into the small cabin . . . and of all the miserable stenches from chewing, snuffing, smoking and spitting tobacco, we were ever compelled to witness, this is the nearest beyond the possibility of exaggeration. A good portion of the time, some one is sawing on an old fiddle, while others are whacking down their cards, amid the most horrible profanity imaginable."[46]

It is possible that even disgruntled packet patrons like the Campbellite preacher later in life looked back fondly on their canal encounters. Without question, by the mid-twentieth century that positive, perhaps nostalgic spirit was well entrenched. Individuals, intensely interested in the long-abandoned ditches, formed the Canal Society of Ohio and backed efforts to save scattered aqueducts, culverts, locks, and sections of canal bed. Later a coalition of cyclists, environmentalists, and hikers pushed for preservation of stretches of canal rights-of-way, most dramatically in the state's northeast region. In 1996 eighty-seven miles of the old Ohio & Erie Canal won federal designation as a "Heritage Corridor," encouraging protection of the route between Cleveland and Akron and south beyond the Massillon area to Zoar. In the twenty-first century surely much more of the canal era in the Buckeye State will have been memorialized than the more extensive and recent interurban era, Ohio's other great transitory transport experience.

4

RAILWAYS

T HE ROLE of the railroad in Ohio's past has been monumental, more so than any other transport form, with the possible exception of the automobile and truck. Certainly, few if any would challenge the notion that the railroad has been one of the most formidable instruments of change ever to be created. For generations Ohioans vigorously sought railroad service, knowing that it would forever end any vestiges of isolation. Even in the twilight of new-line construction, residents of southern Ohio appreciated the arguments advanced in 1893 by promoters of the Cincinnati, Dayton & Ironton Railroad who initially sought to build between Chillicothe and Wellston: "[The railroad will] make the farmers rich by providing farm-to-market transportation of all products from feathers for pillows, to eggs for the breakfast plate, from corn for the hogs, to wheat for the mill, from fruit of the orchard to honey from the hives to your breakfast biscuits."[1]

Ohioans have experienced the iron horse virtually since its inception and knew it intimately during the century-long railway age. Although the Buckeye State never claimed a railroad mecca comparable to Chicago or St. Louis, several cities did develop into strategic hubs, and no state possessed a higher density of lines. Ohio started the twentieth century with a mileage of 8,951 and peaked eight years later at 9,581.[2]

Ohio Rail Map (1997). *(Courtesy of the Ohio Rail Development Commission)*

Even before the locomotive *Best Friend of Charleston* and its Lilliput-ian train chugged and clanked along the first primitive miles of the South Carolina Canal and Rail Road on Christmas Day, 1830, helping to demonstrate the practicability of the iron horse, Ohioans were fasci-nated with the embryonic technology. As early as 1826 Eleutheros Cooke

To finance the first railroad that turned a wheel on Ohio soil, backers of the Erie & Kalamazoo Rail Road organized a private bank. This institution, based in Adrian, Michigan, issued paper currency, including these fifty- and one-hundred-dollar notes. *(Author's Collection)*

of Sandusky suggested to fellow residents a publicly financed railroad between their home community and Dayton, connecting Lake Erie with the proposed Miami Canal. It seemed unlikely to Cooke that the legislature would include the Sandusky region in its emerging network of canals.[3]

By the 1830s a railroad rather than a canal appeared to be the practical alternative. The daring visions of an Eleutheros Cooke seemed much less so, and Ohioans forged ahead with the first wave of railway building. As with canals, the tactic was to link navigable bodies of water, or at least interior communities, with waterways. Indeed, the first train to move over Buckeye rails followed such a path.[4]

In April 1833 the Legislative Council of the Territory of Michigan made a monumental decision. It incorporated the Erie & Kalamazoo Rail Road (E&K) to build from the Maumee River (Toledo) to the

Kalamazoo River "by the power and force of steam, animals, or of any mechanical or other power, or of any combination of them." (At that time Michigan claimed dominance from the southern end of Lake Michigan to the southern shore of Lake Erie, but its admission to the union in 1837 resulted in its borders with Indiana and Ohio being adjusted northward, placing a dozen miles of the E&K in Ohio.) In spring 1834 survey work began on the E&K and by late 1835 the construction process had begun. About a year later the pike opened between its two terminals, Toledo and Adrian, a distance of thirty-three miles, but the road never reached its destination to the northwest, 180 miles away.[5]

During the 1830s Franz Anton Ritter von Gerstner, who extensively studied American railroads, described the Erie & Kalamazoo, "Pioneer Railway of the West," as being similar to other contemporary roads. He noted that the company used iron strap rail two and one-half inches wide and five-eighths of an inch thick attached to oak rails and owned two small steam locomotives, which had recently replaced horses. The mixed passenger and freight train handled a score or more of passengers and loads of flour, wheat, and other goods. "A train usually consists of two passenger coaches and 3 or 4 freight cars. The conductor who accompanies the train collects money from passengers who board en route. Two porters accompany the conductor to load and unload freight along the road." In fall 1840 this daily train left Toledo at 8:00 A.M., arrived in Adrian at 11:00 A.M., departed Adrian at 1:30 P.M., and returned to Toledo at 4:00 P.M.[6]

As with other pioneer pikes, a ride on the Erie & Kalamazoo could be a long-remembered experience. Equipment failures, broken rails, derailments, and other problems might delay, even cancel, a scheduled run. In December 1841 a Toledo resident encountered a bad day on the E&K:

> The train left Adrian for Toledo at 7 P.M. and worked its way along over the ice-covered track until we got out of wood and water, when we picked up sticks in the woods and replenished the fire, and with pails dipped up water from ditches and fed the boiler, and made another run towards Toledo. Passing Sylvania, we got the train to a point about four miles from Toledo, when being again out of steam, wood and water, we came to the conclusion that it would be easier to foot it the rest of the way, than to try to get the train along any farther. So we left the locomotive and cars standing upon the track and walked into the city,

reaching there about 2:30 A.M., . . . gratified that we were enjoying the "modern improvement."[7]

Not every Ohioan wanted to travel on a railroad, even when its trains performed properly. Some seemed fully content with canal packets, stage coaches, lake and river steamers, along with horseback riding and walking. Others fretted about the impact of the "machine in the garden." One antirailroad perspective came from the pen of Springfield attorney Samson Mason. "No one can travel on horseback or in a carriage of any description on a railroad, no matter how wide it may be, nor how finished. The steam engines and cars would scare any animal and drive it out of sight." Added Mason, "How long must people wait at the point where the cars start, after they arrive there and are ready to pursue their journey? Is not the whole scheme wild and visionary?"[8]

Although to some "wild and visionary," railroad building in Ohio continued, albeit at a relatively slow pace. By 1840 only forty miles of spindly track served scattered sections of the state, including the emerging Cleveland & Newburg, Fairport & Painesville, Little Miami, Mad River & Lake Erie, and Monroeville & Sandusky City Railroads. The Panic of 1837, which spawned "the great crisis of trade," devastated investors and made politicians leery of spending public funds for railroads or anything else. Neighboring state governments, important backers of the pioneer pikes, rightfully worried about their financial commitments to internal improvement projects and soon Indiana, Michigan, and Pennsylvania teetered on bankruptcy. Foreign investors knew of America's economic woes and stayed away.[9]

Even though hard times greatly reduced major rail expansion, Ohioans, eventually even Samson Mason of Springfield, sensed that iron rails represented the transportation future. It appeared that large chunks of productive territory would always lay frustratingly distant from the nearest navigable body of water or canal; railroads were the only practical way to shatter the isolation. These feelings explain why in the 1840s seventy-six railroad companies won charters from the state, although most remained "paper" affairs, never turning a wheel. Yet, local railroad builders were not certain *how* these potentially powerful arteries of travel and commerce should be fashioned. After all, the 1830s and 1840s proved to be the industry's demonstration period.[10]

Even something as basic as the nature of the roadbed was debated. In what was later considered to be an absurd strategy, promoters in 1836 sought to build a "railroad-on-stilts" along the southern shore of Lake Erie, from "a suitable point on the eastern border of the state" to the Maumee River. Trains of the projected 177-mile Ohio Rail Road would operate on track attached to a massive wooden superstructure, supported by pilings. "Posts at least 10 inches in diameter are driven into the earth in 2 rows," observed a contemporary. "Those in each row are 5 feet apart, center to center, and the distance between the 2 rows is 7 feet 4 inches." Before the Ohio Rail Road floundered, a victim of hard times, cessation of public funding, and allegedly corrupt management, it had installed about one hundred miles of piling and had placed twenty-nine miles of attached superstructure through the Black Swamp between Fremont and the Maumee River.[11]

During the demonstration period the railroad-on-stilts building approach was not unique to Ohio. In the early 1840s the New York & Erie Rail Road (forerunner of the Erie Railway), for one, constructed scores of miles of wooden pilings when it pushed westward through New York's "Southern Tier" of counties. This approach seemed to offer advantages over a graded roadbed. In January 1840 an adviser to the Erie argued: "[A piled roadway] . . . is not liable to rearrangement by frosts; it is not liable to be obstructed by snow; it is free from dangers of a graded road in consequence of the washing of the banks by flood and rains, and settling when set up in soft bottoms, thereby requiring constant expense to adjust the road and replace the earth materials." Proponents contended that "the interest on money saved by building a pile road instead of a graded road will renew the piles, if necessary, every five years." The piling strategy on both the Ohio Rail Road and the Erie failed miserably because of cost and practical engineering reasons. As late as the 1890s some rotting pilings remained near downtown Cleveland as "mournful monuments to a misdirected effort."[12]

Although during the demonstration period "standard gauge" of four feet eight and one-half inches between the rails became common, Ohio experienced significant variations. Unlike roadbed, the issue of gauge was not fully decided until the end of the nineteenth century, well past the experimental era. Probably stemming from the distance between the wheels of the first locomotives delivered to the Buckeye State, a number of local carriers (and also ones in New Jersey) selected four feet ten inches rather than the standard measurements of four feet eight and one-half inches. One of Ohio's important early roads, the Cleveland, Painesville & Ashtabula (later part of the New York Central System), which by the mid-1850s linked the communities of its corporate name, used "Ohio gauge," as did connecting lines to Buffalo, New York. But within a decade or so, these rail widths shrunk by an inch and one-half, greatly facilitating through traffic.[13]

Ohio also claimed hundreds of miles of broad or "Erie gauge," an impressive six feet between the iron rails. Influenced by the wide gauge (7' ¼") Great Western Railway of England, the Erie Railway (née the New York & Erie) had selected this width for its 447-mile line across the Empire State—"Between the Ocean and the Lakes"—that opened in 1851. In the 1860s a principal interchange partner and subsequent affiliate, the Atlantic & Great Western (A&GW), built a six-foot gauge line from Salamanca, New York, where it met the Erie, through Meadville, Pennsylvania, Ravenna, Akron, Galion, Urbana, and Dayton with a wide-gauge connection to Cincinnati. In the Queen City the A&GW linked up with the broad-gauge Ohio & Mississippi Railway, which extended 339 miles west to the Mississippi River at East St. Louis, Illinois, making it possible to traverse the eastern half of the nation and Ohio on a wide-gauge route. Not long after Ohio gauge disappeared, so, too, did Erie gauge, and the question of rail width was seemingly resolved.[14]

As railroads became more common, future generations of Ohioans could easily have identified features of this faster, flexible, and more dependable form of transport. But during the demonstration period what later became the most ubiquitous object along expanding railroad corridors, the depot, was only starting to take on its modern appearance. The earliest railroad officials in Ohio and elsewhere generally did not fuss much about depot buildings or their design. They needed to focus on constructing trackage, providing suitable rolling stock, and recruiting capable workers. Their goals, of course, were to begin operations quickly in order to generate much-needed revenues. This was not easy because they frequently started with limited traffic, in part because of their modest lengths. In order to meet the public's needs, some pioneer roads employed existing community buildings—hotels, stores, taverns, and the like—reminiscent of the way stagecoach firms locally served customers. Railroad patrons used these pre-railroad facilities to buy tickets,

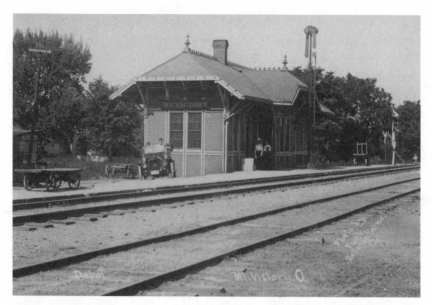

After the Civil War the Cleveland, Cincinnati, Chicago & St. Louis, or "Big Four," Railway erected this ornate, standard model combination depot in the Hardin County settlement of Mt. Victory. By the time of this "real-photo" postcard, the automobile had made its debut, a harbinger of the ultimate demise of the passenger train and the depot itself. *(Author's Collection)*

to send and receive freight, and to await the daily "accommodations." Apparently, the first "depot" on the Erie & Kalamazoo in Sylvania was simply a conveniently situated domestic cottage. Some communities, too, had no depots at all. The problem was hardly of epic proportions; riders could fend for themselves, waiting in a store or tavern. A freight building or shelter, however, might be available, since merchandise—valuable less-than-carload (LCL) freight—required protection from weather and thieves. In the case of Monroeville, southern terminus of the Monroeville & Sandusky City Rail Road, by 1840 the company had "not constructed any *buildings* on the line. The warehouse in Monroeville, which is served by several spurs, was built by private individuals."[15]

In time the maturing railroads created specially designed depots. By the Civil War era they were likely to be "combination" ones that served a community's general transportation needs by providing space for an agent's office, a freight section, and a passenger waiting room. Since Ohio possessed some of America's first depots and continued to erect new and replacement ones, usually of the combination variety, they made the Buckeye State a *zone of transition* between the East and West. By the gilded age of the 1870s and 1880s those structures found in the seaboard East were the more striking when compared with those of the trans–Chicago West. In the former area, depots traditionally were highly individualistic; a large number were not constructed to standardized plans. By the 1880s, moreover, they tended to be the more ornate, with such architectural features as towers, covered pavilions, and decorative gingerbread. Depots farther west, however, reflected the practicability of inexpensive, carbon-copy architecture. These combination structures, which were often erected over a wide expanse of territory, took on their particular styling largely for cost and convenience. A carrier would be uncertain about whether a particular town deserved an expensive depot, and it needed to have a set of depot drawings suitable for various communities sizes, real or anticipated, as lines were built. The Ohio depot scene became a distinct blend of early structures, usually of spartan appearance, later custom built and much more elaborate affairs, and some modest ones from standard plans, usually associated with later line construction.[16]

The phenomenon of "system building," which swept Ohio and much of the nation following the Civil War, helps explain the jumbled depot architecture in the state. The early shortlines nearly always entered the orbits of developing "trunk" roads. Once major carriers absorbed smaller companies, they understandably possessed an array of depot styles. These expanded roads then erected depots, usually replacement ones, to their own plans.[17]

Corporate takeovers led to regional and interregional systems. Railroad finance as a result became oriented more toward large capitalists, mainly out-of-state and foreign, rather than local ones. The former importance of funding from public-spirited residents and township, county, and state governments greatly diminished. By the 1880s four interregional trunk carriers dominated long-distance traffic in Ohio, which flowed heavily east and west rather than north and south because of the prominence of New York City, Philadelphia, Baltimore, Chicago, and St. Louis. For decades much of the state's transportation experiences would be intimately associated with the Baltimore & Ohio, Erie, New York Central, and Pennsylvania railroads.[18]

Yards of the Lake Shore & Michigan Southern (later New York Central System) at Air Line Junction, a few miles west of Toledo, are shown in this photograph from the 1870s. The racks of firewood serve as fuel for the "teakettle" 4-4-0 American Standard–type steam locomotives, two of which are shown. *(Cornelius W. Hauck Collection)*

Each trunk road possessed a complex corporate genealogy, the legacy of purchases, leases, and construction by controlled, albeit separate, corporate entities. The Erie in Ohio is typical. In the 1860s the Erie Railway, which after 1878 became the New York, Lake Erie & Western Railroad and seventeen years later the Erie Railroad, sought to move beyond its core New York route. In its quest to tap the rich traffic potential of Ohio and the Old Northwest, the company mightily strove to control the well-positioned Atlantic & Great Western Railway. In 1865 the A&GW, itself an amalgamation of various lines, opened for through traffic between Salamanca, New York, and Dayton, a distance of 338 miles. In 1867 the A&GW fell into court hands and a year later was transferred by lease to the Erie. Then in 1869 another receiver took control of the A&GW and again leased it to the Erie. Briefly the A&GW regained its independence, but in 1874 the property returned to Erie domination through another lease agreement. In 1880 legal action led to reorganization of this largely Ohio road as the New York, Pennsylvania & Ohio Railroad (NYPANO). But the New York, Lake & Western (Erie) ran NYPANO and with reorganization of the Erie in 1895 the old A&GW finally entered the Erie corporate structure. With stability of the Salamanca to Dayton line, the Erie sought to reach Chicago, already the nation's railroad center, thus forging a through route from Gotham to the Windy City. The company did this by acquiring the assets of a woebegone narrow-gauge road, the Huntington, Indiana–based Chicago & Atlantic Railway (C&A). In late 1882 this subsidiary opened a line from a connection with NYPANO at Marion to Hammond, Indiana, and trackage rights beyond gave it entry into Chicago. The 250-mile C&A featured "airline" qualities, correctly claiming to be the best-engineered right-of-way between Ohio and Illinois.[19]

The fact that a narrow-gauge road, the Chicago & Atlantic, allowed the Erie effectively to become truly interregional was related to the debate over track width that had not been fully decided by the 1870s and 1880s. Shortly after the Civil War a cadre of railroad promoters considered standard-gauge lines to be impractical for certain transportation needs. Instead, they argued that slimmer pikes (usually three feet in width) held several crucial advantages, namely that they were easier and cheaper to build, maintain, and operate. A surprising number of their dreams became reality: between 1871 and 1883 a building boom produced approximately twelve thousand miles of narrow-gauge lines nationally, including about one thousand miles in Ohio.[20]

The nearly two dozen narrow-gauge railroads in Ohio were usually designed to perform the function of originating freight, tapping agricultural, coal, or lumber traffic. In the late 1870s and early 1880s, for example, the Connotton Valley Railway evolved into an important coal carrier from Carroll County and environs to Cleveland via Canton. By being built to relatively high standards for a slim-width road, the Connotton Valley could operate heavy coal and also competitive passenger trains.[21]

Ohio was also the site where promoters dreamed of a much more grandiose form of narrow-gauge operations. They sought to create general transport carriers, linked together, to compete with standard-gauge roads for freight and passengers. The premier effort to forge such a rail alternative was known as the "Grand Narrow Gauge Trunk," a network of several narrow-gauge (3'0") railroads from Toledo to Laredo, Texas, and a narrow-gauge connection to Mexico City, a distance of about 1,600 miles in the United States and 800 miles in Mexico. The Grand Narrow Gauge Trunk also expected to build important appendages to Chicago and Cleveland. By the early 1880s a large portion had become reality, frequently the result of hard-working local promoters who peddled stock and received the support of local taxpayers. In 1886 it was possible to journey continuously 1,581 miles on narrow-gauge lines from Ironton to Sealy, Texas, but likely no one ever did. The Ohio leg on the Toledo, Cincinnati & St. Louis Railway required a circuitous trip from Ironton through Dayton to Delphos and then the road crossed Indiana via Kokomo and Frankfort to St. Louis, Missouri.[22]

By the mid-1890s the narrow-gauge phenomenon, especially the most successful efforts to create a long-distance network, had largely fizzled. The inherent inability to compete with standard-gauge roads along with financial and managerial problems led to an end of construction in Ohio and surrounding states. "The complete downfall of the Toledo, Cincinnati & St. Louis system thoroughly demonstrates the impracticability of the narrow-gauge theory—particularly in the fertile and better regions of the country, when it becomes necessary to compete with standard-gauge roads," aptly editorialized the *Commercial Gazette* of Cincinnati. "[T]here is one thing quite certain—there will not be more narrow-gauge roads built in this portion of the Central States again soon, unless it is some very short road, and then only to fill a 'long felt' local want." The prophecy proved correct.[23]

The narrow-gauge scene in Ohio changed rapidly. By the end of the century most of the weakest companies had failed, although their lines were usually widened, becoming branches of larger carriers. The strongest narrow-gauge roads also converted gauge and joined established roads. The coal-carrying Connotton Valley, for one, in 1888 regauged and subsequently became part of the Wheeling & Lake Erie Railroad, then affiliated with Jay Gould's network of roads. The saga of the last narrow-gauge trackage in the state, a portion of the long-struggling Ohio River & Western Railway, was similar. Opened in 1883, this 112-mile line with its 262 bridges and trestles connected Bellaire and Zanesville via Caldwell and Woodsfield. After a series of corporate

About 1890 a passenger train of the narrow-gauge Cincinnati, Lebanon &
Northern, pulled by No. 2, an Eight-Wheeler built by the Baldwin Locomotive
Works in 1878, waits near Norwood (northern part of Cincinnati) next to the
standard gauge Norfolk & Western. Several railroad employees stand by the
dual-gauge track, which allowed both the CL&N and N&W to serve local
industries. *(Cornelius W. Hauck Collection)*

reorganizations, the Pennsylvania Railroad took control in 1912, later
cutting back the line to Woodsfield, forty-two miles from Bellaire, before
narrow-gauge service ended on Memorial Day 1931.[24]

Whether an Ohio community was served by a narrow- or standard-
gauge railroad hardly lessened the importance of steam cars. The railroad quickly emerged as a vital part of the social and economic life of
residents. In a bustling metropolis or a somnolent village "train time"
meant much to the local citizenry. Recalling his nineteenth-century boy-
hood in Clyde, novelist Sherwood Anderson magnificently captured the
widespread excitement associated with "deepo" happenings:

> As in all American towns of the time the railroad station was a mag-
> net that continually drew our people. There was a passenger train going
> away into the mysterious West at some twenty minutes after seven in
> the evenings and, as six o'clock was our universal supper hour, we all

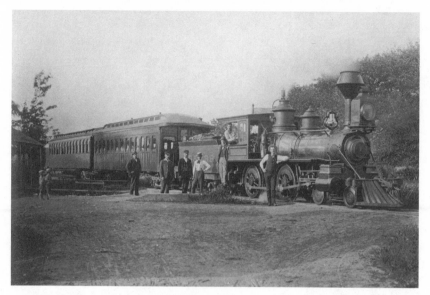

Around 1890 crew members of the evening "accommodation" passenger train on the narrow-gauge Cincinnati, Georgetown & Portsmouth pose at Amelia, nineteen miles out of Cincinnati. Two boys watch the event. *(Cornelius W. Hauck Collection)*

congregated at the station to see the train arrive, we boys gathering far down the station platform to gape with hungry eyes at the locomotive.[25]

Sherwood Anderson and his friends surely sensed how the railroad had shaped their lives and had made for a better, more prosperous home-town. In addition to contributing to both urban and rural development, the iron horse gave Ohioans new options, including where they might live. Just as streetcar lines and later electric interurbans allowed citizens to flee the congestion of teaming metropolitan centers, which were also products of the railway age, the steam carriers opened up suburban areas, boosting populations and economies.

Greater Cincinnati stands out as a premier example. In the late 1880s and early 1890s the Baltimore & Ohio Southwestern Railroad (B&OSW), an affiliate of the Baltimore & Ohio, did much to boom the region. In a lavishly illustrated booklet, *Suburban Homes,* distributed in 1891 by the B&OSW's passenger department, the company promoted communities along its main line to the east of Cincinnati: Loveland, Symmes, Rem-ington, Madeira, Madisonville, Oakley, Norwood, and Bond Hill. "The

In the 1880s two railroad workers at the Baltimore & Ohio Southwestern roundhouse in Cincinnati turn this 4-4-0 American Standard locomotive, with its balloon stack and oil headlight, on the "gallows" turntable, so called because of the structure's appearance. *(Cornelius W. Hauck Collection)*

distance from Loveland to Cincinnati is 24.8 miles. Already there is a double track, sixty-five pound steel rails, as far out from Cincinnati as Madisonville, 13.5 miles, and it will soon be extended to Loveland. Twenty-one towns or villages or city stations dot this distance of twenty-five miles, almost one to each mile." Not only were depots conveniently situated, but "There are twenty trains running each way each day. Nowhere is there such an escape afforded and such relief given from the noise and crowds and smoke and discomforts and temptations of a large city as are afforded and given to these villages along the line of the Baltimore & Ohio Southwestern between Cincinnati and Loveland." And, significantly, "No suburban towns on the lines of great eastern railroads are furnished with better facilities. [And] the railroad stations are pretty and tasteful," a vital promotional consideration.[26]

Ohioans saw the railroad station replacing the stagecoach stop, the public landing, and the canal dock as the gateway to their villages, towns, and cities. The depot was the avenue through which people, freight, mail, and express flowed. Travelers planned their itineraries, purchased their tickets, and awaited their trains. Onlookers greeted and bid farewell to passengers or watched who was coming and going. A town's newspaper editor might assign a reporter to gather newsworthy items for a weekly "depot" or "railroad" column. Similarly, residents made arrangements to send and receive freight. Virtually everything arrived by rail: boxes of bread, sewing machines, window glass, a nearly inexhaustible list of items. Local manufacturers, too, would have the agent bill a carload of outbound goods or a shipment of LCL freight. The postmaster or a representative would drop off and pick up sacks of U.S. mail and packages after passage of the Parcel Post Act in 1913. Agents of express companies, including employees of Adams, American, National, United States, and Wells-Fargo, handled packages until World War I, when the federal government forced creation of the American Railway Express Company, which in the 1920s became the Railway Express Agency and finally, before its liquidation in the 1970s, REA Express.[27]

Much more so than the expressman, the railroad station agent developed a special role in community life. As the official local representative of the company, before the demise of the small-town station, he, and occasionally she, was probably as well known and respected as the physician and preacher. A major reason involved the agent's role as the conduit for incoming and outgoing telegraphic messages. With firsthand knowledge of the cryptic Morse code, the agent was the best-informed person in town. The telegraph carried more than routine railroad business (train locations, switch lists, and the like); it transmitted commercial messages from private telegraph companies, mostly from the largest and most famous, Western Union. (By the turn of the twentieth century the distinctive blue and white porcelain signs that identified Western Union Telegraph and Cable Office were attached to hundreds of Ohio depots.) "In 1916 the telegraph reigned as the world's fastest and most accepted news medium," recalled a veteran agent-telegrapher for the Pennsylvania Railroad in Ohio. "Another five years would elapse before the infant radio outgrew its early gibberish of code and learned to speak and to broadcast the language."[28]

Although the depot and its agent were at the center of local transport activities, a host of businesses that catered to railroaders and railroad patrons were adjacent to the tracks. Since the station served as the official gateway to the community, it made sense for proprietors of hotels, boarding houses, and restaurants to locate nearby. In the Miami County town of Bradford (née Union City Junction), which by the late nineteenth century was a thriving division point on the Pennsylvania Railroad where trains changed crews and equipment was maintained, "hotel row" flourished along the railroad corridor. The Ogden Hotel and Restaurant, for example, stood only a few steps from the depot. Close by, too, were boardinghouses and private homes that accommodated roomers, commonly owned and operated by wives and widows of railroad employees.[29]

In important Ohio rail terminals like Bradford, Collingwood, and Willard (née Chicago Junction) another prominent feature of the railway age was the Railroad "Y." By the dawn of the twentieth century this national movement, which began in 1872 in Cleveland, sponsored more than 175 hotels that annually catered to hundreds of thousands of male railroaders. These widely scattered facilities became popular because they were clean, inexpensive, and conveniently situated. Railroad officials endorsed this division of the Young Men's Christian Association because Railroad "Ys" provided an attractive substitute for saloons, boardinghouses, and other places where employees might drink too much or become too distracted.[30]

Although railroad executives in Ohio and throughout the nation praised the Railroad Y movement, they lacked much enthusiasm for public regulation. Yet corporate leaders had to cope with intervention because of the nearly universal desire by "the people" to regulate America's first big business. Neither in the vanguard of early state regulation nor particularly innovative in approach, state lawmakers in the immediate post–Civil War era established the Ohio Railroad Commission. While sensitive to consumer complaints about rates and services, these bureaucrats did not really throttle the carriers. From an industry perspective, more "damage" came from the Interstate Commerce Act in 1887, which created the Interstate Commerce Commission (ICC), a federal agency that took charge of interstate rates. Early in the twentieth century the ICC became even more powerful when Congress granted it additional authority under terms of the Hepburn and Mann-Elkins acts. Although the ICC came to determine interstate rates closely, intrastate ones remained the prerogative of state commissions. Passage of the Valentine Antitrust Act in 1898 largely solved intrastate rate problems that had caused some concern. A senate committee of the general

A double-headed train on the Big Four races along a section of the abandoned Miami & Erie Canal. When Ohioan Fred Smith took this photograph about 1912 near Lockland, a Cincinnati suburb, neither of these Eight-Wheelers was new. *(Fred Smith Photograph; Cornelius W. Hauck Collection)*

assembly earlier had revealed that freight charges for coal were as great from New Straightsville to Columbus as from Columbus to Boston, Massachusetts! Rather than focusing on rate making, the Ohio commission, however, spent much of its energy mediating complaints about surly agents, unsafe practices, and, most of all, poor-quality depots.[31]

Early in the century a classic case of Ohioans' unhappiness about a local depot occurred in the Huron County town of Greenwich. Although its thousand inhabitants enjoyed excellent access to railroads (the Pittsburgh to Chicago main line of the Baltimore & Ohio, the Cleveland to Columbus stem of the Cleveland, Cincinnati, Chicago & St. Louis ["Big Four," New York Central System], and the Akron to Delphos line of the Northern Ohio), there was dissatisfaction. The B&O and the Big Four offered acceptable depot facilities, but the Northern Ohio clearly did not. When in 1890 a predecessor company of the Northern Ohio built through Greenwich, it erected a modest building in an inconvenient part of town. After the Northern Ohio emerged in the late 1890s, it showed even less interest in the community. The railroad subsequently removed its agent and allowed the depot building to fall into disrepair. The company told patrons to use either the New London station seven miles to the east or the Plymouth stop nine miles to the west. Residents howled. They depended upon the Northern Ohio's two daily trains for personal travel, especially to the nearby communities of Cary, Medina, New London, New Washington, and Plymouth, and for sending and receiving freight, express, and mail over the road and through its strategic connections.[32]

Not surprisingly, Greenwich residents turned to the railroad commission for relief. In a formal complaint filed in late 1907, they charged that the Northern Ohio provided "an old, dilapidated, abandoned and partly destroyed building" and argued that it should be immediately replaced. Seemingly unconcerned about its local image, the company contended that Section 9 of the Ohio Railroad Commission Act did not apply. This provision, in a straightforward manner, stated a carrier's public obligation: "It shall be the duty of every railroad to provide and maintain adequate depots and depot buildings at its *regular stations* [italics added] for the accommodation of passengers, and said depot buildings, shall be kept clean, well lighted and warmed." Lawyers for the Northern Ohio asserted that Greenwich was a "flag" stop and not a "regular station," and therefore this part of the code did not apply.[33]

Townspeople challenged this reasoning. The attorney for Greenwich told regulators that while the railroad might use the flag stop designation in its public timetables, in reality the place was a bona fide regular stop. To prove this point, a postal worker who for eight years had carried the mails to and from the station twice daily testified that trains *always* stopped, regardless of a flag.[34]

In March 1908 the commission decided in favor of Greenwich. The Northern Ohio, the regulators found, had treated the town as a regular station stop. In its ruling, the body ordered that "[T]he defendant should provide a suitable building at said station, and keep the same well lighted for the comfort and accommodations of its patrons . . . and that some person should be placed in charge thereof to receive and receipt for parcel freight . . . and that such person [should] take charge of incoming parcel freight and store the same in the usual and customary way until called for by the owner."[35] Shortly thereafter, the Northern Ohio complied with the commission's verdict. Greenwich got its replacement depot and also a full-time agent. The town's indignation quickly subsided.[36]

Although regulatory prodding explains the new depot at Greenwich, carriers in Ohio willingly spent heavily on major improvements. Before World War I they participated in what became the "second building" of the industry. Companies did so because of an unprecedented demand for freight and passenger services; businesses, factories, and mines flourished and a more affluent and expanding population expected faster, more luxurious trains. A variety of betterments followed: the laying of hundreds of miles of heavier steel rails; installation of modern signaling devices; double-tracking of the busiest routes and a host of rebridging, regrading, line-straightening, and "cut-off" projects. Ohio trunk roads, including the weakest, the "Weary Erie," committed millions of dollars. A documentary pamphlet, "Erie Railroad: Showing Changes from 1901 to 1914 Inclusive," extolled the recent accomplishments of this trans-Ohio railroad: "Bridges: Since 1901, the carrying capacity of Erie Railroad bridges has been increased 31%, and 814 new Main Line bridges have been erected; [and] Automatic Block Signals: In 1901, there were no automatic block signals on the Erie Railroad; in 1914, there are 1,452.2 miles of track so equipped."[37]

The second building, however, added in only a modest amount of new route miles. Often construction involved tapping a mine, serving an industry, or enhancing access to a terminal. Established carriers conducted most of the building, although a few independent shortlines appeared. One of the last railroad projects in Ohio, which largely fits the latter category, was the formation and expansion of the Akron, Canton & Youngstown Railroad (AC&Y). Although chartered in 1907, construction of the core 7.7-mile line did not begin until 1912. Then, eight years later, this Akron-based industrial road dramatically increased its importance through acquisition of the 162-mile Northern Ohio Railway, part of the New York Central System.[38]

Even though the gestation period of the Akron, Canton & Youngstown took place when Akron became famous for rubber products, especially tires, at first this burgeoning industry lacked a tie with the infant carrier. Rather, a Canton cement tycoon, Zebulon Davis, developed the road. Shortly after the turn of the twentieth century he resurrected a defunct two-mile switching company in the Rubber City and used it as the nucleus for a link between the Wheeling & Lake Erie, five miles east of Akron, and the Northern Ohio that entered the city from the west. As a railroad promoter Davis's objective was to extend his property south to Canton, providing his cement works with improved transportation. He also considered a forty-mile eastern extension to Youngstown, "for it will strengthen my position with entrenched steam railroads of northeastern Ohio." A year after the AC&Y opened, a feasibility study warned that construction of additional trackage would be a "grave financial mistake," suggesting that the railroad map of Ohio had finally jelled. Advanced in years and apparently not willing to pursue a potentially risky financial course, Davis sold an interest in the railroad to a legal adviser, H. B. Stewart Sr., but retained stock control. Stewart subsequently invited Frank A. Seiberling, cofounder of the Goodyear Tire & Rubber Company, to invest in the road.[39]

Frank Seiberling, dynamic, resourceful, and exceedingly wealthy, seized the opportunity to buy Akron, Canton & Youngstown securities. He favored the railroad from its inception, for it offered his firm an alternative to routes and services provided by Akron's three principal carriers, the Baltimore & Ohio, Erie, and Pennsylvania. Of special importance to Seiberling's rubber operations were connections the AC&Y afforded between area plants and the automakers of Cleveland and Detroit and later company-owned coal mines near Adena. In time Seiberling bought out Davis's position and orchestrated acquisition of the Northern Ohio (first by lease and then by stock purchase), giving Goodyear a direct route to the Motor City via the Detroit, Toledo & Ironton Railroad at Columbus Grove.[40]

Admittedly, Zebulon Davis and Frank Seiberling failed to achieve the status of railroad "empire builders," but two of their Ohio contemporaries, the "Vans," did. These bachelor brothers—Oris Paxton Van Sweringen and Mantis James Van Sweringen—assembled one of the greatest rail domains in American history and did so from their Cleveland offices.

The Vans began their rise to financial power with shrewd investments in Cuyahoga County real estate. By the early 1900s they became involved in developing Shaker Heights, but to succeed they believed that they needed an electric railway to link their suburban properties with downtown Cleveland. The best way was to use a small segment of the New York, Chicago & St. Louis Railroad, universally called the Nickel Plate Road (NKP). Fortunately for the Vans, the New York Central (NYC), which owned the NKP, was under federal pressure to sell this 523-mile carrier that largely paralleled the NYC's main line between Buffalo and Chicago. The Central president suggested to the brothers that they take *all* of the NKP and they agreed. In 1916 the Vans borrowed heavily and formed a highly leveraged holding company, Nickel Plate Securities Corporation, to provide the appropriate financial vehicle for the takeover. Their strategy succeeded; not only did they obtain a practical route for their interurban, but by the early 1920s their steam railroad prospered. The Vans raised sufficient capital to modernize the NKP, which was nicely suited for competitive freight traffic, and they hired a skilled team of seasoned managers.[41]

The flourishing Nickel Plate whetted the Vans's appetite for more railroads and allowed them to push ahead with acquisitions. With Interstate Commerce Commission approval in 1923, they merged the NKP and two adjoining properties, the Toledo, St. Louis & Western Railroad (The Clover Leaf Route) and the smaller and less robust Lake Erie & Western (*Leave Early & Walk*), creating a 1,700-mile system in the only important *formalized* railroad merger of the twenties. The brothers then purchased from railroad magnate Henry Huntington and his associates controlling interest in the Chesapeake & Ohio (C&O), a thriving 2,100-mile long coal hauler that connected Columbus and Cincinnati with tidewater and also included the Hocking Valley Railway, a Toledo-to-Gallipolis stem with branches into the southeastern Ohio coalfields. Next they acquired a major position in the 2,250-mile Pere Marquette, a mostly Michigan road with a prime Chicago connection, and then bought heavily into the Erie. By the mid-1920s the brothers reigned over more than 9,000 miles of rail line and seriously challenged the region's trunk roads.[42]

The Vans's timing for bringing railroads together was superb. The decade of the 1920s was a period of business consolidation, and not since the turn of the century had political, economic, and social factors created an atmosphere so exhilarating to promoters of vast enterprises. In the case of railroads, Congress, in the Transportation Act of 1920, instructed the Interstate Commerce Commission to prepare a unification plan that would eventually form a limited number of competitive companies of approximately equal financial strength. The scheme never materialized, but Congressional intent unmistakably favored massive, albeit federally supervised, system building.[43]

The transactions of the Vans became progressively complex as they built their empire. They grasped the economic forces at work and controlled their railroads largely through holding companies rather than by formal mergers. In 1924 the Clevelanders dissolved the Nickel Plate Securities Corporation, its original purpose having been served: transferring its assets to other "paper" firms created to facilitate their expansion plans. The Vans embraced this holding-company strategy for several reasons. Such business arrangements gave them control in an extremely leveraged fashion, yet they could attract investors through financial inducements: the Vans held the majority of the voting common stock while others owned nonvoting preferred shares with attractive *fixed* dividends. The brothers also could assemble rail carriers with these mechanisms without federal approval. Similarly, domination of a rail system through holding companies meant that they might later present a formal merger application to regulators as a fait accompli.[44]

In spring 1925 the Vans believed it auspicious to consolidate their affiliated properties. In order to achieve that objective, they required backing from the Interstate Commerce Commission (ICC). The brothers asked the ICC to allow them to merge the Chesapeake & Ohio, Erie, Nickel Plate, and Pere Marquette, but a year later the commission rejected their request. While the Vans's proposal appeared to be in the public interest, financial considerations, most of all complaints from C&O minority stockholders who fervently maintained that their equity in a strong road would be diluted by the weaker carriers, especially the Erie, led to the adverse decision. The Vans, however, continued to use holding companies to circumvent the ICC, to generate additional capital, and to make further rail acquisitions.[45]

Undaunted by the earlier commission decision, the Vans returned to that body in February 1928 and asked to merge the Chesapeake & Ohio with the Erie and Pere Marquette. But fifteen months later the ICC authorized only a C&O–Pere Marquette union. Once again concern about the financial condition of the Erie precluded a full consolidation. Frustrated, but still anxious to expand their empire, the Vans in January 1929 formed a master holding company, the Alleghany Corporation. This firm immediately absorbed all of the brothers' railroad assets, providing them with personal control, while its capital came from bonds, notes, and nonvoting stocks.[46]

Then, suddenly, the growth of the Vans's Cleveland-based empire stopped. Following the stock market crash of October 1929 the deepening national depression devastated real-estate and railroad investments, the brothers' principal businesses. By 1933 portions of the Vans's railroad assets had fallen under control of court-appointed receivers. Yet, the relatively stable Chesapeake & Ohio kept the brothers' stack of financial cards from collapsing totally. The Vans were also able to transfer funds from one company to another, to refinance some loans, and to negotiate payment deferrals. In 1935 a restructuring of assets through formation of another holding company, the Midamerica Corporation, also helped. But soon thereafter both brothers died of natural causes. After their deaths, the largest unit, the Alleghany Corporation, became the domain of another financial wizard, Texan Robert Young. The C&O star still shone, and it burned even more brightly as the national economy rebounded dramatically after 1938. That year the weary Erie, however, went bankrupt, although it emerged in the early 1940s from court supervision. Both carriers continued to run their operations from the office complex opened in the late 1920s and early 1930s by the Vans in the heart of Cleveland, Terminal Tower and the Midland Building.[47]

The Great Depression adversely affected not only the Vans's empire but holdings of Ohio's other carriers. The giants—Baltimore & Ohio, New York Central, and Pennsylvania—saw their equity values plummet and barely kept out of bankruptcy court. Some of the smaller Buckeye State roads, however, were not so fortunate. The Akron, Canton &

On August 30, 1939, the *Interstate Express*, Train No. 151, running over the New York Central's main line between Chicago and New York City, grabs a drink of boiler water at the track pans near Stryker, forty-five miles west of Toledo. This speedy way of "taking water" represented the best in railroad technology of the day. *(John F. Humiston Photograph)*

Youngstown, for one, entered receivership in 1933 and remained there until its reorganization eleven years later.[48]

More long-term damage of Ohio railroads occurred because of the increased popularity of automobiles, buses, and trucks. Since the 1920s use of these motorized vehicles, which rolled over ever-improving roadways, had risen dramatically. The state's railroads, large and small, started to seek ways to end their financial losses, especially resulting from poorly patronized main- and branch-line passenger "locals" that could not compete with cars and buses for short-distance travel. When state regulators objected to these "takeoffs," companies often reduced the financial bleeding in other ways. An important counterresponse was the introduction of self-propelled gas-electric motor cars—popularly, even affectionately, called doodlebugs. These units, common on the Baltimore & Ohio and Pennsylvania, usually had ample space for passengers, mail, and express;

World War II had recently ended when Baltimore & Ohio Train No. 56, Motor 6044, was "being worked" at the station in Marietta. A Railway Express Agency truck stands near the weathered, multistory depot. This "doodlebug" linked Marietta with Parkersburg, West Virginia, and provided the railroad with relatively low-cost passenger operations. *(John F. Humiston Photograph)*

some, too, could pull coaches, trailers, or even an occasional freight car. Doodlebugs proved to be much more economical to operate than conventional steam-powered trains because of reduced fuel consumption and labor costs, accommodating riders and mail and express business that might exist in considerable quantity.[49]

A more drastic, yet "permanent" solution to the matter of modal competition involved retiring the weakest lines. However, this was often difficult because of strong public opposition to abandonments, reflected in the decisions made by state regulators. Yet from the pre–World War I years to the mid-1930s railroads removed nearly one thousand miles of low-density trackage. But from then on, unlike neighboring states, Ohio had a remarkably stable rail network, largely explained by its extensive industrial and mining base. Between 1934 and 1954 only 170 miles disappeared from the rail map.[50]

Efforts by railroads in Ohio to retrench, whether through passenger-service cutbacks or line abandonments, abruptly ended with America's entry into World War II. By early 1942 Ohioans, who previously had left flanged wheels for rubber tires, rediscovered railroad schedules, depots, and trains from the lowliest branch-line locals to the finest intercity runs. "I recall people pushing and shoving to get on trains in Akron during the war years," recalled a local resident. "Some of them couldn't tell the difference between A.M. and P.M. in the timetables, but they learned pretty fast if they wanted to leave town." Carriers warned Ohioans to expect less-than-perfect equipment and to accept inconveniences. "The number one responsibility of all transit is to meet the increasing demand for essential rides," announced the Erie Railroad in June 1943. "Comfort and convenience are playing second fiddle now. Transportation, like everything else, is dedicated to Victory."[51]

Companies found it difficult to cope with wartime traffic. They faced chronic shortages of equipment, both freight and passenger, and qualified workers. Hundreds of Ohio railroaders rallied to the colors, often joining special military railroad units, and many more enlisted or were drafted. Roads hired high-school youth and women and people of color, brought veteran personnel out of retirement, and urged employees to toil beyond their normal hours. In August 1942 a reporter for the Associated Press, who rode a sixty-car oil train from Texas to Rhode Island, which crossed the Buckeye State on the Erie, caught the temper of the times when he described a stop in Marion:

> The oil's going through. It's a gigantic effort that compares with the great sagas of our pioneer days. It's the toughest kind of work, because railroads are short-handed, like every big outfit. That means hours up to the limit of Interstate Commerce Commission rules, a quick flop and bath, and back again for a new assignment. . . . Railroaders are working the hours it takes to move the freight that's got to move.
> This conversation, in the Marion, O., yards of the Erie, is typical.
> "Yay, Smitty, How y'doing? Playing the horses lately?"
> "Playin'em hell. I'm the horse. I've had one day off since April."
> "Ya big sissy. What's a day off? I don't remember."[52]

The return of peace seemingly promised a bright future for Ohio rails. In the immediate postwar America most companies enjoyed robust financial health, having plenty of cash and credit to repair or replace war-worn track and equipment and also to modernize. New postwar depots in Akron, Toledo, and Youngstown symbolized this optimism, just as building Terminal Tower in Cleveland and Cincinnati Union Station represented industry confidence prior to the Great Depression.

The vast majority of the state's roads soon spent heavily on a variety of betterments, and most of all, they embraced a revolutionary type of technology replacement, the diesel-electric locomotive. This sleek motive power was faster, cleaner, cheaper to operate, and traveled farther between refueling and maintenance than the steamers. By the mid-1950s it was becoming difficult to find an iron horse, except perhaps on the Nickel Plate Road, one of the last regional citadels of steam. The NKP did not fully dieselize until the end of the decade.[53]

In the post–World War II years, however, Ohioans had no trouble discovering diesel-powered "streamliners." The state's trunk roads understandably publicized their luxury passenger service. One illustration is the Baltimore & Ohio's promotion of the *Capitol Limited,* a premier train that linked Chicago with Washington, D.C., stopping in its trans-Ohio journey at Deshler, Willard, Akron, and Youngstown. The company extolled its leadership in intercity travel: "First Air-Conditioned! then Diesel powered! then Streamlined!" In a 1949 folder the B&O described features of its new *Capitol Limited:* "A continuation of the same high standard of service, including Private Bedrooms, Drawing Rooms, Compartments and Section Sleepers; Colonial Dining Car, Lounge Car, Sunroom Observation Car; Radio; Train Secretary, Valet, Maid-Manicure. Air-Conditioned, of course—and Diesel-Power makes the ride so smooth it's like gliding!"[54]

Attractive name trains on the Baltimore & Ohio, Erie, New York Central, and Pennsylvania notwithstanding, the rail companies failed to protect the passenger sector. The increasing popularity of commercial aircraft, particularly jets by the early 1960s; residents' longstanding love affair with automobiles, faster and more luxurious than ever, which they could drive over the Ohio Turnpike; and the developing network of interstate highways, mostly doomed long-distance passenger trains, just as they had already doomed local and branch-line trains. The shrinkage became striking. As the decade of the 1950s began, the Pennsylvania listed in its public timetables for Ohio seventy-four inter- and intrastate trains; ten years later the company ran forty-six, and in 1970, on the eve of Amtrak, the National Railroad Passenger Corporation, the combined Pennsylvania *and* New York Central (now Penn Central) operated just twenty. Although Amtrak, which began officially on May 1, 1971, "saved" the intercity passenger trains, this quasipublic corporation provided

The *Fast Flying Virginian*, Train No. 43, stands on June 22, 1947, in the massive Cincinnati Union Station. This popular steam-powered Chesapeake & Ohio name train ran between the Queen City and Norfolk, Virginia. *(John F. Humiston Photograph)*

Although after World War II many Ohioans raved about their fast, sleek stream-liners, still some endured poky mixed passenger-freight trains. On June 23, 1951, under the conductor's watchful eye, the Akron, Canton & Youngstown Railroad unloads a passenger at New London on the train's 161-mile trans-state journey between Akron and Delphos. *(John F. Humiston Photograph)*

Ohioans with even fewer opportunities to travel by rail: Amtrak stopped at only six Buckeye State stations. The Public Utilities Commission of Ohio, successor to the Ohio Railroad Commission, was responsible for another train; it ordered the Erie Lackawanna Railway (the enlarged Erie) to dispatch during the business week a commuter run between Cleveland and Youngstown.[55]

Some diehard Ohio rail travelers welcomed the appearance of Amtrak. Although the new trains carried "heritage" equipment, namely rolling stock from former passenger carriers, particularly the Burlington and Santa Fe, the quality was often better than what the New York Central, Pennsylvania, or Penn Central had used in their last days. And Amtrak made a concerted effort to provide the best possible service; indeed, it expanded modestly the scope of its Ohio operations. Unquestionably, during the twilight years some railroads in private hands seemingly went out of their way to annoy patrons. The president of the Erie Lackawanna, Gregory Maxwell, for one, noted the deterioration of even the name trains. "I took the *20th Century Limited* just before it disappeared and it was an awful experience. I got on the train in January in Cleveland for a meeting in Chicago. Well, the toilets in the Pullmans had all frozen and there were broken pipes with water standing in the corridors. The dining car people ran out of food. I think that I had only soup for dinner." Concluded Maxwell, "There was clearly a desire to discourage the public so that the case could be made to have the train dropped."[56]

Dieselization, coupled to passenger train cutbacks and a growing number of feeder-line abandonments, which the Transportation Act of 1958 facilitated, financially aided Ohio railroads. But in an increasingly competitive transportation environment the industry required much more. Railroad leaders, whether from their offices in Cleveland or elsewhere, became intrigued with the possibilities of substantial savings from corporate mergers.[57]

Soon merger madness took hold. One of the first major unions nationally, and one that attracted interest in Ohio, involved the pairing of the 940-mile Delaware, Lackawanna and Western, the faltering "Road of Anthracite," with the Cleveland-based Erie. The new corporate couple became the 3,188-mile Erie-Lackawanna Railroad (EL), and it met the public officially on October 17, 1960. Two even larger mergers of roads serving Ohio followed. In 1963 the Chesapeake & Ohio officially took control of the ailing Baltimore & Ohio, and a year later the Norfolk & Western acquired the Nickel Plate Road and leased the Wabash. But the merger that grabbed headlines came on February 1, 1968, with creation of the Penn Central Transportation Company, a carrier that dominated rail transport in the state.[58]

Hopes for a successful Penn Central quickly turned to dross. At first patrons believed that the firm would stabilize, even improve, transport; but, alas, that did not happened. Poor management, increasing modal competition, and rising inflation doomed this nineteen-thousand-mile rail giant. In less than two years the company, with its operations in chaos, went bankrupt. Then in 1973 Penn Central trustees told a federal court that the railroad could not be reorganized on an "income basis"; instead, they proposed liquidation.[59]

Penn Central, unfortunately, was not the sole railroad serving Ohio to encounter severe financial troubles. A year earlier extensive damages caused by Hurricane Agnes in New York and Pennsylvania forced the Erie Lackawanna into bankruptcy, and concern grew that it, too, might not endure.[60]

Although Ohioans had access to excellent highway transport, railroads remained vital for the economic well-being of a diverse business base. They were especially important to steel and heavy manufacturing, even with the sting of developing Rust Belt conditions.

A new day dawned for railroads in the Northeast and the Old Northwest on April 1, 1976, with the debut of Conrail. Federal interventions made the difference. Passage in 1973 of the Regional Rail Reorganization Act (3R Act) provided the framework for formation of the Consolidated Rail Corporation (or Conrail), a quasipublic entity that assumed control of much of the Penn Central, Erie Lackawanna, and several other failed carriers.[61]

The appearance of Conrail had a mixed impact on Ohioans. Most of all, the new firm dispatched trains on most key arteries. The steel industry in the Mahoning Valley, for example, continued to receive its raw materials and ship its metal products. But there was redundant trackage and facilities, and some rail patrons for good reason grumbled about the restructuring. Of note, service became radically altered to some Ohio communities on the old Erie mainline west of Akron. Since Conrail did not need most of this trackage, it abandoned segments and sold other pieces to shippers or newly formed shortline carriers. Such corporate banners as the Ashland Railway and the Spencerville & Elgin Railroad flew over scattered portions of ex-EL track. Conrail, too, did not want the old EL diesel shop in Marion. Quickly its thirteen-hundred member workforce, which was mostly reassigned to other Conrail units, shrunk markedly, even though employees, civic leaders, and others battled to save these high-paying jobs. Their MONEY (Marionites Opposed to the Negation of the Erie Yards) grassroots crusade collected thousands of signatures on petitions to lawmakers objecting to any downgrading, but their cause found few supporters outside the community.[62]

Yet it was statewide rail cutbacks and the threat of more that prompted Ohio politicians to act. In 1975 state lawmakers created the Ohio Rail Transportation Authority (ORTA) to oversee trackage that might be acquired from dismemberment of the Penn Central and Erie Lackawanna. Ohio, therefore, sought to join such other states as Michigan and Vermont as a rail owner. Then with additional "mega-mergers"—notably formation of CSX in 1980, which included the Chessie System (C&O–B&O), and Norfolk Southern (NS) in 1982, which contained the Norfolk & Western—more lines in Ohio became unwanted. And passage in 1980 of the Staggers Act, which brought about partial deregulation of the rail industry, made it easier for companies like CSX and NS to dispose of surplus trackage. In order to protect businesses, thus saving jobs and tax revenues, portions of unwanted lines were retained for shippers under ORTA supervision. In the 1990s the state remained active in the rail sector, assisting public and private entities in acquiring threatened trackage.[63]

An illustration of the impact of ORTA and the effects of mega-mergers can be seen in the emergence and expansion of the Coshocton-based Ohio Central Railroad. This carrier, launched in 1987, initially operated a one-time appendage of the Norfolk Southern (née Wheeling & Lake Erie) in Coshocton, Stark, and Tuscarawas Counties and a former Erie-controlled industrial-switching firm in Mahoning County, the Youngstown & Austintown Railroad. Later the Ohio Central acquired trackage that once had been part of the Baltimore & Ohio and Pennsylvania systems. By the mid-1990s the Ohio Central achieved status of a "mini" rail conglomerate, controlling not only its original properties but also the Columbus & Ohio River Railroad, Ohio & Pennsylvania Railroad, Ohio Southern Railroad, and Warren & Trumbull Railroad.[64]

ORTA did more than seek retention of vital local rail service; it also had responsibility for creating a state master plan for high-speed rail. Inspired by "bullet" trains in Japan and elsewhere and the energy crisis of the mid-1970s, in 1980, ORTA completed its study that recommended a six-hundred-mile and $8.2 billion "top-of-the-line" system that would connect twelve cities; namely, Akron, Cincinnati, Cleveland, Columbus, Dayton, Elyria-Lorain, Mansfield, Middletown, Springfield, Toledo, and Youngstown. Two years later voters faced a ballot request for a one-cent sales tax increase earmarked for high-speed rail, but they defeated the referendum by a two-to-one margin. Yet as the *Columbus Dispatch* editorialized, "We think the electorate was rejecting the method of financing such a program and not the concept itself."[65]

Disappointment at the polls did not stop proponents of high-speed rail. In 1986 lawmakers created the Ohio High Speed Rail Authority, an

This modern scene of railroading in the Buckeye State shows a Norfolk Southern Corporation freight barreling through Hamilton on heavy steel rails resting
on knife-sharp rock ballast. Behind the two diesel-electric locomotives, one at-
tired with the older Norfolk & Western livery, are several "pigs," truck trailers on
flatcars. *(John F. Humiston Photograph)*

independent agency within the Ohio Department of Transportation,
and experts once again studied the matter and sought to develop support for 125–175 mph rail passenger service. The focus continues to
center on the potentially most popular route, the Cleveland-Columbus-
Cincinnati corridor.[66]

When rail lines were abandoned, leaving nothing but naked grades,
some Ohioans believed that the public might continue to benefit from
these former transportation arteries. The state became a national leader
in the rails-to-trails movement. The concept lacked complexity, namely
conversion of abandoned rights-of-way into surfaced trails, perhaps
using the original rock or cinder ballast for hiking, biking, horseback
riding, cross-country skiing, and snowmobiling. These rail trails, because
of their engineering, offered gentle grades and easy access for all types
of recreation enthusiasts. By the 1980s a national Rails-to-Trails Conservancy and many state affiliates were operational, including the Ohio
Rails-to-Trails Conservancy. A decade later the Buckeye State boasted

more than two dozen rail trails, one of the largest numbers nationally. They ranged from units that measured only a few miles in length, like the one-and-a-half-mile Little Miami Bike Route in Clark County, to much longer ones, typified by the sixty-three-mile Wabash Cannonball Trail in Fulton, Henry, Lucas, and Williams Counties. These former paths of the iron horse also have been "banked," available, if necessary, for use again as freight or high-speed lines.[67]

Although the nature of railroading has changed strikingly in the post–railway age, Ohioans still require flanged wheels for their economic well-being. Once more, the state's strategic location and diverse agricultural, commercial, industrial, and mining base explain why citizens continue to have access to approximately six thousand miles of trackage, making Ohio a rail bastion.[68]

5

THE ELECTRIC WAY

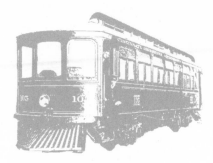

O HIOANS attending the Columbian Exposition in Chicago in 1893 joined other visitors who marveled at the magnificent buildings and grounds. These Buckeye fair goers found exhibits that depicted the four centuries of progress since the discovery of the New World by Christopher Columbus. Wide eyed, they gazed at displays showcasing the potential of electricity, the wonderful new power source. The Court of Honor with its Electricity Building immediately captivated them. It was even possible to reach these popular attractions via the Columbian Intramural Railway, "The First and Only Electric Elevated Railroad in the World." A fare of ten cents paid for a ride into the future.[1]

Even before the gates to the Chicago gala opened, the potential of electricity was becoming widely known. For decades news reports had chronicled a series of exciting developments. In 1844 the telegraph became the first important application of electric energy. Then during the 1870s several extensively publicized inventions appeared, including the stock printer (printing telegraph), telephone, and lightbulb.[2]

The new electrical age involved more than such marvels as the telegraph and incandescent lamp. Newspapers and magazines also described attempts to harness electricity for transport. In midcentury inventors

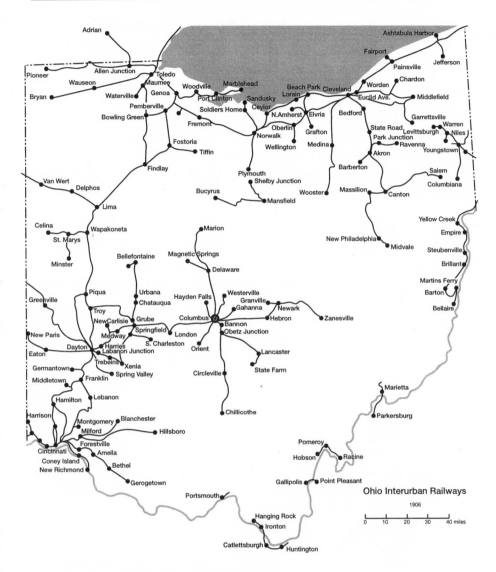

Ohio Interurban Railways. *(Art: Sam Girton)*

sought to make battery-powered motors propel railcars, but by the 1880s a consensus emerged that the potential of battery power was limited. Attention turned to how electric generators as a central power source might be used. Overhead wires or third rails were judged as practical ways to distribute current to vehicles. Even though the principle was simple, working out details for dependable operations at first baffled even the most gifted engineers. Nevertheless, breakthroughs soon occurred. In 1888 Frank Sprague, a determined and talented Naval Academy graduate, used electricity to power the rolling stock of the local street railway in Richmond, Virginia. He specifically demonstrated two valuable innovations: a spring-loaded electric motor and adoption of five-hundred-volt direct current (DC). On May 4, thirty cars handily traveled over city thoroughfares, harbinger of a national trolley frenzy. Moreover, Sprague's triumph set a pattern for a revolution in urban transportation, and by the 1890s additional research demonstrated the feasibility of long-distance, intercity electric lines. In 1896 a system of three-phase alternating current (AC) transmission was perfected that significantly reduced voltage losses; refinements continued, most notably the efficient change by rotary converters of AC to DC power.[3]

Trolley enthusiasts in Ohio quickly took advantage of the technological advances. By the 1890s large and small communities rapidly replaced their animal and cable car operations with electricity. But Ohioans also backed construction of prototypes of the electric interurban. On December 28, 1889, the seven-mile Newark & Granville Street Railway, in reality a rural trolley, opened between the two central Ohio towns of its corporate name. Later this company gained the distinction of being the first electric line to become part of a general network of interurbans. The Buckeye State witnessed other pioneer roads. In 1892 an eight-mile electric carrier made its debut between Canton and Massillon, and a year later a nearly twenty-mile line began operations between the Soldiers' Home in Sandusky and downtown Norwalk under the banner of the Sandusky, Milan & Norwalk Railway.[4]

Although the severe depression of 1893 to 1897 retarded most intercity electric projects, the return of prosperity encouraged expansion. Growth, however, was stimulated by more than a greatly improved financial climate. Potential patrons liked what they had read about or had occasionally seen. Their enthusiasm is understandable. If a community or region lacked adequate steam railroad service, an interurban could solve the problem. Traction routes would give farmers, villagers, and others convenient access to the socioeconomic opportunities offered by urban centers, and merchants, bankers, and other business people could profitably tap a larger trading area. When in operation, electric

The motorman (left), conductor (center), and likely another interurban company employee stand along car No. 9 of Ohio's pioneer Sandusky, Milan & Norwalk Railway, which in 1893 opened its 19.5-mile line between Sandusky and Norwalk. No. 9 is a "combine," carrying baggage, express, mail, and passengers. *(Krambles Archive)*

lines maintained frequent passenger service; cars often ran on hourly schedules while steam roads typically dispatched only one or two trains daily, which might arrive at inconvenient hours. Moreover, interurbans, unless operated on a "limited" fashion, would stop at farmsteads, road crossings, or virtually anywhere. An early Lake Shore Electric Railway public timetable provided these pertinent instructions: "Passengers wishing to stop cars should signal the motorman with arm extended horizontally across the track by day and a light swung across the track by night at a distance of not less than 1,500 feet from approaching car." The company reassuringly added, "The motorman will answer with two short blasts of the whistle, signifying that he sees and understands you."[5]

Other factors contributed to the immense popularity of interurbans. Electric cars were sleek and clean, producing "no cinders, no dirt, no dust, no smoke," a common annoyance for riders of soft-coal-burning steam trains. Interurbans were also potentially fast. If roadbed and operating conditions permitted, they could accelerate within seconds to

A large wooden car of the Lake Shore Electric Railway pauses in front of its convenient storefront station in Huron. Express and freight shipments are being "worked," and a "drummer" (traveling salesman), bags in hand, leaves the trackside area. *(Author's Collection)*

sixty or more miles per hour. Since interurbans commonly used city streets for access into urban terminals, high speeds were restricted to stretches of private rights-of-way. Yet this seeming liability offered still another advantage. Since city centers were the destination of most travelers, cars that stopped on the public square or similar downtown locations were more convenient than steam trains that might use a station blocks, even miles away from the commercial district, necessitating additional travel time and requiring patrons to use hacks or streetcars or to make long walks.[6]

Interurbans could carry more than passengers in a comfortable and efficient fashion. All companies provided express and package service. At times these items were transported in the "baggage" compartment behind the motorman's seat or in specially designed "box motors," in reality electric boxcars. Some carriers handled carload freight, which might be interchanged with steam roads, depending upon physical conditions of the electric road's track and equipment and the steam railway's willingness to accept such business. The public also welcomed the usually cheaper passenger fares, especially appreciated after years of widespread discontent with steam railroad charges.[7]

This new mode of transportation, with all of its advantages, was most

About 1925, employees of the Toledo, Bowling Green & Southern Traction Company attend to a freight train at the car barn area in Bowling Green. Box motor No. 300 is attached to a freight trailer belonging to "The Lima Route," the Western Ohio Railway. Trolley freight equipment came in a variety of types and sizes. Car No. 300 is really nothing more than a motorized baggage car, yet it is capable of pulling a short train of freight trailers. *(Krambles Archive)*

popular because travel by horse-drawn buggy and wagon had severe limitations, even for relatively short-distance trips. The network of poorly built and maintained roads was vulnerable to adverse weather conditions. Even with the coming of the automobile and motortruck, highway travel remained primitive. It would take years for the good roads movement to lift Ohio out of the dust and mud. That fact largely explains why farmers typically donated land for interurban rights-of-way and why, too, the Columbus, Delaware & Marion Electric Railroad could argue in 1903, "The novelty and luxury of riding on the traction cars has now become a necessity with rural populations."[8]

Less obvious to citizens, promoters sensed the possibility of enormous profits and wished to be part of this burgeoning industry. This incentive, for example, explained why Ohioans Henry Everett and Edward Moore, who in the mid-1890s built the Akron, Bedford & Cleveland, the "Alphabet Route," became major players in Midwestern interurban development. "Mr. Everett and Mr. Moore," commented an Akron newspaper in 1902, "knew that their pot of gold was awaiting them not at the end of a rainbow but under a trolley pole." Surely the price of electric railway stock would advance rapidly and presumably pay regular and handsome dividends. There also existed the financial windfalls from the sale of electricity along the route to commercial and residential users. After all, electric power had to be generated and transmission lines and electric substations built.[9]

Moreover, the opening of a traction road caused land prices to increase, even soar, often to the personal benefit of backers. The possibility of easy access to jobs or markets made housing along these arteries desirable, explaining brisk sales of lots in "electric" or "interurban" subdivisions. Also, promoters might acquire real estate for construction of an amusement park, picnic grounds, dance hall, or similar public-use facilities. Once in operation, these places generated additional income, both from admissions and car fares.[10]

Some Ohio traction firms vigorously promoted benefits of a "clean trolley ride in the open country." In 1903 the Cincinnati, Georgetown & Portsmouth Railroad suggested that "To the city bred, the delight of the ride through the villages and hills of Hamilton, Clermont and Brown Counties, is equaled only by their surprise to find that many acres of the finest fruit farms and the great tobacco belt of Ohio fairly touches the gates of their home city." Continued this copywriter: "Again the whirl of machinery is far behind and lo, 'tis the primitive log cabin and plodding oxen, with the small clearing, surrounded by great forests, and at once you seem to view a scene familiar to your father's father." An interurban supposedly made possible a journey into a promised land, a Garden of Eden, where the hustle and bustle of the modern world were largely unknown or forgotten.[11]

From an operations perspective the financial picture appeared rosy. Electric equipment sported superior qualities when compared to steam power. Significantly, traction cars and locomotives initially cost less, and, in time, a used market further reduced these capital expenditures. Electric rolling stock, moreover, usually could be converted inexpensively from passenger to express or freight usage. Receiving extra life from old equipment meant avoiding payments for modern units. Mechanically these pieces of rolling stock contained fewer moving parts than did iron horses; they boasted a much simpler and hence more easily re-

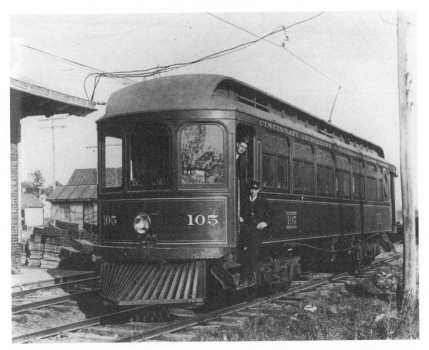

About 1910 the two-person crew, motorman (left) and conductor, of a heavy-weight wooden car of the Cincinnati, Georgetown & Portsmouth Railroad Company await their orders at the station in Bethel. *(Krambles Archive)*

pairable design. Since electric motors required neither coal nor water and had no fires to be banked and ashes to be removed, firemen were not required. Crew sizes generally were much smaller for interurbans—a motorman and conductor—rather than the four or more employees demanded for a steam passenger or freight train.[12]

Much of the Ohio environment, both natural and artificial, proved ideally suited for construction of intercity electric railway construction. The setting goes far to explain why by 1916 the Buckeye State possessed 2,798 miles of interurban lines, the most of any state and nearly 20 percent of a widely scattered national network of 15,580 miles. Indiana, with the second greatest mileage, fell short of Ohio by nearly a thousand miles. With exception of Ohio River counties, most all the topography was flat or gently rolling and the interior streams were relatively small and shallow, greatly reducing construction and maintenance costs. The state, moreover, was densely settled in many areas. The federal census

of 1900 counted 4,157,545 residents, making it the fourth most populated state after New York, Pennsylvania, and Illinois. Ohio was also a
prosperous place. That same document ranked the Buckeye State fifth
in manufacturing, with 345,869 individuals creating a plethora of products worth approximately $830 million (the national total stood at about
$11 billion). These prosperous and productive residents commonly lived
in closely spaced towns and cities. Ohio furthermore possessed several
robust urban centers and a well-developed countryside. Even the less
agriculturally rich southeastern section was dotted with coal-mining
camps that contributed to the state's over-all wealth.[13]

Exploiting the interurban-building potential in Ohio paralleled national trends. The boom largely occurred in three intervals: following
the depression of the 1890s and before the brief Panic of 1903; between
1905 and the "Bankers' Panic" of 1907; and from 1908 to about 1912.
The last Ohio interurban built, the Cleveland, Alliance & Mahoning
Valley Railway, opened in 1912 between Alliance and Ravenna and three
years later finished its construction.[14]

Although many interurbans in America were not built to standards
employed by steam railroads, most in Ohio were substantially constructed. Certainly they equaled a steam branch line. Around 1910 the
engineering firm of Westinghouse, Church, Kerr and Company studied
the Toledo, Fremont & Norwalk Railway, a sixty-two mile road that
connected Toledo, via Fremont, and Norwalk. It concluded that the
carrier "approximates steam road construction and is well adapted to
high-speed operations." The report specifically commented: "The track
consists of 70 and 75 pound rails of standard A.S.C.E. section laid upon
standard cedar ties, spaced 2,640 per mile. Six-bolt, 44-inch angle
splice bars, Harvey hold-fast grip bolts and Goldie patent spikes are
used. The ballast employed is crusted limestone and gravel; the former
being used upon the western and the latter upon the eastern portions
of the route."[15]

The forces that made Ohio the heartland of the electric interurban
may not have produced a network that resembled a piece of fancy lace,
but lines in some parts gave that impression. The most heavily built sections skirted the shores of Lake Erie and roughly followed the old
Miami & Erie Canal. Contributing to this density were companies like
the Cleveland, Painesville & Eastern; Lake Shore Electric; Northern

PUBLIC MEETING!

A Meeting will be held at AMMON'S HALL in

GEORGETOWN

THURSDAY,

JULY 21, 1910

(AT 8 O'CLOCK P. M.)

For the purpose of discussing the practicability of building an

ELECTRIC ROAD

With Terminals at

UNION AND VERSAILLES

Connecting Phillipsburg, Georgetown, and other intervening
Towns. All persons interested in the proposed improvement
are requested to be present.

COMMITTEE

A 1910 poster promotes an electric interurban thirty-mile line between Union in Montgomery County and Versailles in Darke County. This project, which never progressed beyond the talking stage, lacked the population base for sustained profitable operations. *(Author's Collection)*

Ohio Traction & Light; Stark Electric; Cincinnati, Dayton & Toledo Traction; Dayton & Troy Electric; Toledo, Bowling Green & Southern; Toledo, Fostoria & Findlay; and the Western Ohio. Although the southeastern region had the lightest concentration, interurbans still appeared, connecting such communities as Athens and Nelsonville, Beverly and Marietta, and Jackson and Wellston.[16]

Even the extensive interurban building that took place in Ohio failed to reveal fully the immense popularity of this transport form. Literally hundreds of miles of what might best be described as "paper" roads were also proposed. In the prime north central section, for example, promoter after promoter sought to realize electric dreams. One enthusiast, Frank Ohl, labored to link Fostoria, Upper Sandusky, and Marion, but failed in spite of several incorporations. Even some established and, for the industry, well-heeled firms stumbled as they tried to expand. The Northern Ohio Traction & Light Company (NOT&L) is an example. Through a series of mergers and construction, the company created one of the region's largest and most important interurban networks. Although the NOT&L wanted to reach the Ohio River city of Wheeling, West Virginia, it stalled at Uhrichsville, about fifty miles short of its projected southern destination.[17]

As with virtually every technological advancement, some resistance developed to interurban mania. Just as downtown business people would later object to superhighways that spawned suburban shopping malls, some feared that electric cars would whisk away customers to larger trading centers. In 1897 Oberlin merchants, who were content to rely upon the steam trains of the Lake Shore & Michigan Southern and who likely sold clothing, dry goods and other nonperishable items, blasted local efforts to secure an interurban to Cleveland. "RUIN!," proclaimed the headline of a handbill they distributed, "Follows in the Wake of the Electric Railroad! *Elyria* has Three Steam Railways and Two Electric Roads. Result, Six Big Business Failures recently and Five of them within Three Days. *Oberlin* has one Steam Railway and No Electric Railroad. Result, One Small Failure in Twenty-five years." In Wooster commercial interests fussed about a traction line interfering with horse-traffic patterns. They argued that electric cars would make it unsafe for farmers to drive their teams and wagons into town, especially on Saturdays, the busiest trading day of the week. Although the concerns advanced by these protesters may have been illogical or exaggerated, they nevertheless felt threatened. Fortunately for shoppers who wished to patronize out-of-town stores, where selections would be greater and prices lower, the electric way came to Oberlin and western Lorain County. By year's end, cars were rolling over the thirty-three miles of electrified track between Oberlin and Cleveland via the Cleveland, Elyria & Western Railway, subsequently part of Ohio's second largest interurban, the Cleveland, Southwestern & Columbus Railway (CS&C). And this same carrier would also later serve Wooster and northern Wayne County.[18]

Officials of steam railroads, who generally ignored the initial development of the automobile and truck, early on also marginalized the threat posed by electric cars. But by 1905 or so their attitude changed; competing interurbans were capturing a substantial volume of short-distance passenger, express, and less-than-carload freight business. Steam officials took little solace in the argument advanced by traction men that "the habit of traveling is being developed among people who formerly seldom traveled at all, and that this fact, combined with the fact that steam railways have been made more accessible through connection with electric lines, leads to the conclusion that steam railway systems will ultimately be benefited, if they are not already deriving benefit."[19]

Options for steam road managers to oppose the "Electric Way" were limited. An early response, one born out of anger or desperation, was to impede interurban construction. As plans for a juice road took shape, a steam railroad might refuse to allow it to cross its property, a ploy that usually led to expensive and lengthy litigation or even physical confrontation. When construction workers of the Ohio Central Traction Company (later part of the Cleveland, Columbus & Southwestern) reached Crestline, fisticuffs erupted, pitting traction workers against ones rushed in by the Big Four (New York Central System) and Pennsylvania railroads in a futile attempt to prevent installation of a crossing. If the interurban won, which it almost always did, custom required that it (the newest road) assume the financial burden of installing the crossover or "diamond" rails, and perhaps the cost of erecting an interlocking tower, and then maintaining this facility in perpetuity. Actually in the long run these arrangements proved a silver lining to steam roads, helping sap the strength of their upstart competitors.[20]

A somewhat more realistic response was to attempt to meet traction competition. A few companies increased their service, either with additional conventional steam trains or with experimental self-propelled gas-mechanical railcars. Costs and reliability problems with the latter rolling stock doomed most of these efforts.[21]

Another way to manage upstart interurban challengers was for steam roads to acquire them. Although the New York, New Haven & Hartford, for one, aggressively gobbled up traction lines in southern New England, only a few carriers in Ohio purchased their electric rivals. The Hocking Valley Railroad owned the eighteen-mile Wellston & Jackson Belt Railway, and the Wabash Railroad controlled the eighty-eight-mile Toledo & Western Railway. Perhaps the magnitude of these investments prevented such actions. Also, Ohio steam roads, unlike those in the Northeast, depended more on freight than passenger traffic.[22]

Had some traction promoters fully realized their electric fantasies, steam road executives would surely have had reason to panic. They might have been forced to buy off such dangerous competitors or to electrify their principal arteries (so-called "heavy traction"), a response several Eastern steam roads were then pursuing. The only widely discussed, albeit remote, threat to the steam giants in Ohio came with the Chicago–New York Electric Air Line Railroad, the most ambitious interurban project ever seriously attempted in the United States. Incorporating under the laws of Maine in August 1905, backers of the Air Line sought to build a double-track speedway that would slice through the northern part of Ohio and whose completion would make it possible for passengers to travel the 750 miles between its two great urban terminals in only ten hours. Financed heavily through investor clubs, including several in Ohio, and energized by a splashy monthly publication, *The Air Line News,* construction efforts began in 1906. Enormous building costs, the Panic of 1907, and poor, even corrupt management killed the scheme; the Air Line never became more than a short interurban that connected the Indiana towns of Goodrum and La Porte.[23]

Failure of the pie-in-the-sky Air Line to bring high-speed interurban service to Ohioans hardly had an impact on them. The hundreds of miles of operating electric lines, though, intimately affected residents for twenty or thirty years and in some cases longer.

The opening of an interurban meant much to Ohioans. Remarked a Seville resident, who knew well the Cleveland, Southwestern & Columbus: "Shoppers can take advantage of Cleveland sales; farmers can expect their produce to arrive in city markets in good condition; and everybody can enjoy an outing to a motion-picture show." Just as Oberlin merchants had feared, farm, village, and town residents boarded cars for urban centers, where they shopped, dined, and relaxed. City retailers might refund part or all of the price of a roundtrip ticket if the cus-

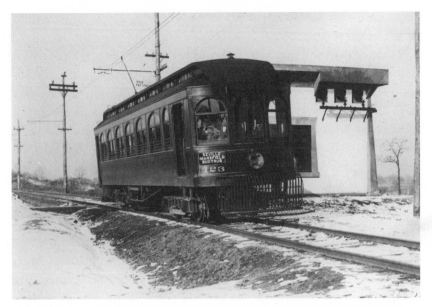

About 1909 a new wooden car of the Cleveland, Southwestern & Columbus Railway passes a combination electrical substation and depot at the crossroads village of Polk, located between West Salem and Ashland and sixty-two miles from Cleveland. *(Krambles Archive)*

tomer made a major purchase; for example, a bolt of cloth or a suit of clothes.[24]

Although Ohio agrarians had long been oriented toward commercial markets—waterways and steam railroads had largely ended subsistence and semi-subsistence farming—the coming of intercity trolleys greatly aided specialized agricultural development. Interurbans commonly handled perishables, including seasonal shipments of fruits and vegetables. A few roads, the Sandusky, Norwalk & Mansfield Electric Railway for one, transported grain and livestock. But milk producers, in particular, benefited from the radial pattern of electric roads, which tended to coincide with the milk sheds of metropolitan centers, and dairy farmers took advantage of the convenience and speed of this transport form. Frequent schedules avoided the need for refrigeration of this perishable commodity. These factors made milk traffic a vital source of freight revenues for many roads. For example, the Cleveland & Eastern Traction Company, which linked Chardon, Garrettsville, and Middlefield with the Forest City, depended upon this business to generate about a third of its annual revenues.[25]

Satisfied milk shippers were only one segment of the population who found interurbans to their liking. The traveling salesman, the ubiquitous drummer, quickly discovered that for similar reasons electric cars were ideal. He could travel conveniently and cheaply from town to town, conducting business along the way. In 1904 carriers organized the Ohio Interurban Railway Association, a trade group that evolved into the Central Electric Railway Association (CERA). A major objective of this organization was to attract a business clientele, and it did so in a variety of ways: coordinated interline and limited services; consolidated maps and timetables; and, most of all, mileage coupon books that offered deeply discounted fares. In May 1913 the Ohio Electric Railway, the state's largest interurban, could advertise: "C.E.R.A. 1,000 Mile Book, $17.50. Good for bearer, or two or more persons traveling together, over 2,500 miles of Interurban Lines in Ohio and Indiana, including divisions of this Company."[26]

What Ohioans most likely remembered about the interurban era was how it affected their leisure time. Although the forty-hour week and paid annual vacations postdated the heyday of interurban usage, Ohioans still could leave their work routine if only for brief periods. Cars often carried berry and flower gatherers, fishermen, hunters, picnickers, and sightseers. At the turn of the century, a booklet published by the Cincinnati, Lawrenceburg & Aurora Electric Street Railroad (CL&A) noted that in season "the sound of the hunter's gun could be heard during the day, and the evening 'runs' into the city [Cincinnati] carried many hunters with bags well filled with almost every kind of small game." Although these patrons pleased CL&A management, casual travelers occasionally caused concern. Officials of the Cleveland & Eastern surely appreciated extra passengers on their last run of the evening from Cleveland, but they strongly objected to these riders, eager mushroom pickers, tearing off boards from their wooden waiting shelters and burning them to keep warm during the chilly, overnight hours. These reckless individuals were awaiting the early morning appearance of highly coveted fungi.[27]

The most popular destination for pleasure seekers was an amusement park or "resort." Virtually every company served at least one of these attractions and a few smaller carriers; the Columbus, Magnetic Springs & Northern and the Toledo, Port Clinton & Lakeside relied heavily on this tourist traffic. Even the largest firms, which developed a diverse business, aggressively promoted trackside attractions. Readers of the May 1915 public timetable of the mighty Northern Ohio Traction & Light Company learned that "Summer's charms are nowhere more delightful than in the beautiful lake-region of the Summit watershed," and the road proudly listed eight amusement parks and resorts along its routes. One was Silver Lake: "Among the best known of Ohio's popu-lar summer playgrounds. Very accessible from all points. One mile from Cuyahoga Falls, also reached by Akron city cars in summer. Silver Lake Chautauqua offers annually a program of great excellence. Gaylord Inn serves special meals for parties."[28]

If residents of northeast Ohio who lived along the lines of the Northern Ohio Traction & Light wished to venture beyond their home road, they might select one of several resorts that abutted the shores of Lake Erie, what one journalist called "Ohio's Riviera." The Cleveland, Painesville & Eastern Railroad, for example, ballyhooed Willoughbeach as "the ideal park for picnics, reunions and outings," which it served with its Shore Line Route. "Small summer houses, rustic bridges, several arbors, and an almost unlimited number of lunch tables are scattered about in localities well shaded by grand old trees." There was much more: "The dining hall is in charge of a competent caterer, the service is first-class at reasonable rates. Meals, lunches, and refreshments are served at all times. New swings have been added for the free use of children." As commonly was the case, owners of Willoughbeach complied with residents' strong "dry" sentiments. "[T]he park is operated on a strictly temperance basis, no intoxicating drinks are sold within twelve miles of the park, thereby eliminating the undesirable element."[29]

Interurban executives knew that resorts were good for their balance sheets. They sensibly promoted them by more than merely describing their physical features. The Cleveland, Southwestern & Columbus creatively boasted its Chippewa Lake Park in Medina County as a place for Ohioans to find renewal. "At this resort the busy man or woman finds restoration of strength and buoyancy of brain which are required to meet successfully the demands of modern life." This was an imaginative ploy and one that responded well to the personal pressures felt by residents of a rapidly industrializing and urbanizing state.[30]

Since the electric interurban quickly became a vital part of the lives of thousands of Ohioans, concerns developed when service declined or other problems arose. Take the case of a complaint made in 1909 to the Ohio Railroad Commission by several patrons of the Columbus, Magnetic Springs & Northern Railway about unacceptable station facilities in the Union County spa community of Magnetic Springs. An inspector for the commission investigated and concluded: "I took personal note of the station, which is located about one-fourth mile from the village store, at which point tickets are sold. The building consists of a frame shed about 10 x 12; there is one bench in the building for patrons. I also noticed the room is in a very unsanitary condition and unfit for passengers; also is not heated." The general manager of the road admitted that poor conditions existed but explained that "the company was in very straightened financial condition." Pressure from the commission, however, led to the track being extended into the community and the depot being relocated. The company then extensively remodeled the structure and, according to the commission, "the improved condition is satisfactory to the public."[31]

The halcyon years when shoppers, drummers, and pleasure seekers filled electric cars began to fade after World War I. In Ohio and the nation, too, heretofore marginally profitable roads revealed that they were vulnerable to automobile and truck competition. Even before the war some traction personnel publicly admitted that construction may have been too extensive. "We have some parts of the road that never should have been built," opined a Cleveland, Southwestern & Columbus executive in 1912. But by the early 1920s not only had the volume of motor vehicles soared, but the general condition of the state's roads had markedly improved. The automobile was coming of age. When Ohio-born President Warren G. Harding proclaimed in 1921 that "the motor car has become an indispensable instrument in our political, social, and industrial life," he stated the obvious.[32]

As the decade of the 1920s progressed, the weakest interurbans failed and the healthier ones fought for survival, usually through innovative efforts. The most notable were in the area of express and freight handling, where imaginative efforts had been long standing. In 1905, for example, the Dayton, Springfield & Urbana Railway (DS&U) inaugurated "night owl" newspaper delivery. A special car handled early morning Dayton papers; after leaving the Montgomery County capital the motorman threw off bundles at stations and road crossings along the line and made his last drop-off in downtown Springfield. Since every Ohio road, like the DS&U, hauled less-than-carload freight and packages, these services were expanded or upgraded after the war. The largest companies focused on interline freight movements and improved terminal facilities. In 1928 the Northern Ohio Traction & Light, Penn-Ohio Public Service Company, and the Lake Shore Electric Railway launched the Electric Railways Freight Company to operate efficiently their various freight services. Akron-to-Detroit tire shipments, in conjunction with the electric Eastern Michigan–Toledo Railroad, were especially lucrative. Earlier, in 1926, the Penn-Ohio had opened a modern freight house in Youngstown, and a year later the Northern Ohio had completed a similar facility in Akron. Speed and just-in-time delivery frequently allowed these roads to attract shippers who willingly paid a premium price for this freight service.[33]

Although a financial flop, the Lake Shore Electric (LSE), acting on its own, caught the public's eye in 1931 with introduction of the short-lived "railwagon" scheme. The LSE purchased six ten-ton truck trailers that could be hauled on specially designed flatcars. This pioneer piggyback arrangement made it possible for shippers to receive better service, since their goods did not need to be reloaded from truck to train to truck. Announced the company: "Co-ordinated highway-railway freight service. Express Freight Service at Truck Rates. Railwagons—semi-trailers that travel equally as well over the highway as over the railway—are now in operation between Cleveland and Toledo over the Lake Shore Electric Railway System." Unregulated truck competition, relatively high charges, collapse of connecting interurbans, and a deepening national depression ended this bold experiment. But two other Midwestern interurbans, the Chicago, North Shore & Milwaukee Railway and the Chicago, South Shore & South Bend Railroad, which served the Windy City and its environs, prospered with their versions of piggybacking.[34]

Passengers also saw noticeable changes after World War I. Several interurbans acquired lighter, smoother riding, and faster cars, commonly built by either Cleveland's G. C. Kuhlman Car Company or the Cincinnati Car Company. In 1927 the Northern Ohio Power & Light Company, successor to the Northern Ohio Traction & Light Company, distributed a richly illustrated folder, "A Deluxe Electric Line Chair Car Service," which described Kuhlman cars, assigned to its *The Northern Ohio Limited*: "Lighted Steps Provide Against Accident; Individual Plush Seats That Make Riding a Comfort; Rubber Flooring Helps Eliminate Noise and Adds to Sanitation; Wide Windows Give Passengers a Splendid View; [and] Lighting That Makes Reading Easy."[35]

The epitome of rolling stock modernization, however, came in 1930 shortly after the formation of the Cincinnati & Lake Erie Railroad (C&LE), an amalgamation of several failing Ohio interurbans that earlier had been part of the Ohio Electric Railway. Headed by Thomas Conway Jr., a former professor of finance at the Wharton School of the University of Pennsylvania, the C&LE bought twenty lightweight, high-speed cars from the Cincinnati Car Company. Ten were coaches and ten were coach-observation cars. Commented the editor of the *Deshler Flag*: "The cars are so constructed that there are no blind partitions to shut off any part of the view. One can look safely too, as both the front and rear ends of the car are completely enclosed with glass of the non-shatterable type, and flying glass and splinters are a thing of the past. Big, comfortable, low sitting, individual chairs with individual head rests greet one upon their first entrance to the car." Added this journalist, "The observation compartment is especially well equipped. Big comfortable overstuffed davenports and chairs make for very comfortable riding. Large clear glass in the windows gives a clear view from any angle. A writing desk is placed on each side of the aisle and two small tables with small table lamps finish out the luxurious fittings." These replacement cars rode well and, understandably, were popular with riders. To introduce the new C&LE and its equipment, Conway staged a much heralded publicity race on July 7, 1930, near Dayton between car No. 126 and a rather slow biplane. Not surprisingly, No. 126 outdistanced its aerial competitor; the sleek Cincinnati-built car attained a speed of nearly one hundred miles per hour.[36]

Less spectacular than the Cincinnati & Lake Erie's Dayton race, yet also associated with aviation, was one of the more imaginative passenger-generating schemes attempted by an interurban firm. Beginning on

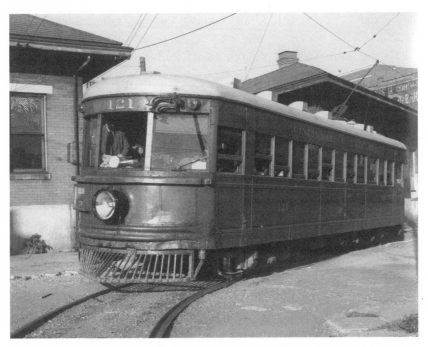

It's close to the end of the line for Ohio's renaissance interurban, the Cincinnati & Lake Railroad. On September 22, 1937, Car No. 121 awaits a highball at the company's Lafayette Street station in Toledo. *(Krambles Archive)*

May 5, 1928, the Cleveland, Southwestern Railway & Light Company offered its riders at selected stations the convenience of purchasing tickets for connecting flights on Stout Airlines. This early commercial air carrier linked Cleveland with Detroit and later Chicago. Unfortunately, few travelers opted for a joint interurban-air journey. In addition, this creative company briefly sold excursion tickets for a fifty-mile sightseeing flight from Cleveland in a Ford Tri-Motor airplane.[37]

A much more common response to modal competition involved some type of coordinated interurban and bus service. Representative was the arrangement employed by the Toledo & Indiana Railroad. This interurban, which had opened between the Glass City and Bryan in 1905, never reached the Hoosier State or any important western terminus, although it made several attempts to do so. But from the mid-1920s to the early 1930s this resourceful carrier offered patrons bus connections from Bryan to Defiance, Bryan to Hicksville and Fort Wayne, Indiana, and

Bryan to Montpelier and Edon, providing them with more popular destinations.[38]

Neither innovation by the spunkiest Ohio interurban firm nor self-promotion efforts like those employed by the Fort Wayne–Lima Railroad in 1929—"To and from the shopping centers, no time lost looking for a parking place, punctures, police stickers,"—could save the industry. Keen modal competition together with the crippling depression of the 1930s led to the junking of most interurbans by decade's end. The last of the big companies to fold were the Lake Shore Electric (May 14, 1938) and the Cincinnati & Lake Erie. Its Springfield-Toledo line closed November 19, 1937, and the remaining service ended on May 31, 1939. Clearly, though, Thomas Conway's efforts to make the C&LE a viable operation proved impressive considering the nature of the business. And in both cases, bus subsidiaries, launched a decade or so earlier, continued to shuttle passengers along most former rail routes: the Lake Shore Coach Company and the C&LE Bus Company (later C&LE Transportation Company) carried on the interurban tradition.[39]

Although the story of Ohio's interurban era was one of frequent financial failures, the state benefited enormously from this form of transport. The impact on development was considerable. The interurban served as that transitional link between the steam railroad and the internal combustion vehicle; the electric intercity car expanded personal mobility that would be more fully attained with the automobile. But Ohio's interurbans were at times more than a convenient, comfortable, and economical means of travel. A number of firms profitably entered the commercial power business, advantaging thousands of customers. For example, the availability of electricity allowed the Frank Dill family of rural Miner to acquire in 1916 the first electric cookstove to be used in an Ohio farmhouse, the power being supplied by the Scioto Valley Traction Company. Interurbans required that generating plants, substations, and transmission lines be built and maintained. Excess electrical capacity could be sold, and interurban companies early on promoted such sales. The cover of the Northwestern Ohio Railway & Power Company's spring 1916 timecard carried a typical example of such efforts: "We are supplying current in any quantity. Make application to Superintendent or General Manager for rates, etc." Indeed, commercial elec-

Abandonment is only about a year away for the Lake Shore Electric, one of the last great interurbans of Ohio and the Midwest. Car No. 143, running "express," is arriving from Norwalk at Ceylon Junction, west of Vermilion. *(Krambles Archive)*

tric operations in some cases saved interurban investors. And this service provided numerous places with essential electric power.[40]

Unlike some interurbans, especially those in California, Iowa, and Texas, companies in Ohio almost universally failed to develop the capacity to handle steam-railroad freight cars. Street running, sharp curves, and building obstructions hampered such designs. So, there was little movement by Buckeye State interurbans into carload interchange freight operations. The Youngstown & Southern Railway (Y&S) and the Toledo & Eastern Railroad (T&E), née Toledo, Port Clinton & Lakeside Railway, were notable exceptions. The former company generated a brisk inbound coal business using standard interline railroad equipment. In time this interurban converted to diesel-electric power and was absorbed by the (steam) Pittsburgh & Lake Erie Railroad, which also became a fallen flag, and ultimately fell into the hands of independent investors. In 1948 the Y&S was the final Ohio firm to discontinue passenger service. Although the latter interurban in 1939 stopped carrying passengers, it remained an active freight hauler. Reorganization in 1945 by an Alliance scrap dealer led to a small but active electric shortline. Carloads of coal, dolomite, and other quarry products sustained this company until abandonment in 1958. The life span of this electric road, which totaled fifty-four years, was truly exemplary.[41]

Like the canal era, today not much remains physically of Ohio's once-robust interurban enterprise. Tiny segments of a few carriers continue in operation, and occasionally abandoned rights-of-way can be detected, especially after a skiff of snow or their presence is marked by utility pole lines. A few stretches have become biking, hiking, or nature trails. Occasionally, too, a knowledgeable observer can spot a former interurban depot, electrical substation, or bridge abutment. Ironically, present-day commuters, who seemingly encounter more frequent traffic snarls, follow some of the routes once served by that expected wave of the future, the electric interurban railway. Arguably, this eulogy to the end of service on the Cleveland, Southwestern Railway & Light Company ("Green Line") is more than nostalgic; it suggests a possible setback for public travel in the Buckeye State:

> Oh, the trucks and the buses
> and the automobiles
> Have killed the merry rumble of the
> "Green Line" wheels.
> They grabbed up her fares;
> on her freight they fed—
> Shed a tear, Old Settler,
> The Green Line's dead.[42]

6

URBAN TRANSIT

A S URBAN areas developed in Ohio in the nineteenth century, the central walking city began to fade. Residents who previously lived near most of their daily destinations started to find public transport alternatives. Crowding, crime, and pollution made living away from the city more attractive. Early on some urbanites thought that the omnibus would solve transport problems. This type of vehicle was essentially a stagecoach, modified to handle additional passengers and usually pulled by a team of spirited horses. Unlike liverymen, who offered hack service on call, omnibus owners operated their vehicles over dedicated routes with announced schedules. By 1849 Cleveland had its first omnibus line, and soon others appeared. But the relatively small carrying capacity, the difficulty of moving through mud or snow, and the strain on animals, not only in bad road conditions but on hills, limited the usefulness of this form of mass transit.[1]

A better idea involved horses and occasionally mules hitched to street *railway* vehicles. These animal-car lines used an omnibuslike car, albeit a larger one, that traveled on iron wheels along metal strap or iron rails laid in public streets. The relative ease of movement permitted faster speeds, four to six miles an hour, and less stress on horses. Patrons, too, appreciated a more comfortable ride, although cars were usually diminutive affairs with no heat, hard seats, and minimal lighting.[2]

The simple technology, ease of construction, reasonable capital costs, profit potential, and public need account for the popularity of animal-powered street railways. Adjoining or nearby property owners also appreciated the increase in land values that generally accompanied the appearance of a street railway. By the mid-1870s the five horse-car companies that operated along the streets of Columbus, for example, had encountered no citizen opposition to either their initial line construction or extensions. The opposite reaction occurred; residents enthusiastically welcomed these transport arteries. From midcentury on, the inhabitants of scores of Ohio communities could take these vehicles, perhaps riding them between their residential neighborhoods and commercial centers, railway stations, factories, churches, cemeteries, or other destinations.[3]

Common characteristics of animal-car operations were the profusion of independent companies and their generally modest operational scope. What occurred in Toledo is typical. Between 1862 and 1875, *six* separate horse-car firms served this expanding manufacturing, port, and trading community. In February 1861 the city council granted the recently incorporated Toledo Street Railroad Company permission to build from the boundary between Manhattan (North Toledo) and Toledo along Summit Street, thence by Ottawa Street and Broadway to the Lake Shore & Michigan Southern Railroad. On May 27, 1862, service began; cars departed every half hour. A decade later citizens could take the new equipment of the Adams Street Railway Company that rolled from Summit Street, along Adams Street and Ashland Avenue, to Bancroft Street. Soon cars appeared on Collingwood Avenue. Another contemporary firm, the Toledo Union Street Railroad, built from Summit Street to Detroit Avenue. In October 1873, a fourth firm, the Metropolitan Street Railway, opened primarily on Lagrange Street, and by 1883 it had reached West Toledo. Another carrier also made its debut in 1873, the Monroe Street Railroad Company, which operated from Summit Street to Auburndale. Then in 1875 the Erie Street and North Toledo Railroad Company began service. Its first line occupied portions of Cherry, Erie, and Summit Streets; subsequently its cars also ran along Division, Erie, Lafayette, Monroe, Superior Streets and Nebraska Avenue to City Park Avenue. Expansion followed and by the early 1880s

Toledo claimed a sizable network of horse-car lines. Because of the expense and inefficiency of separate car barns and other facilities, the need of many riders to transfer between companies and the lack of any major competitive advantages for the public, consolidation became a predictable course. In 1884 the process began with creation of the Toledo Consolidated Street Railway Company, and eleven years later a final union of surface lines took place.[4]

Horse-car lines, whether in Toledo or elsewhere, possessed some distinct negatives. As a major part of a firm's investment, horses cost about $125 to $200 each and were good for an average of only four years of active service. Moreover, they were susceptible to injury and death. In the 1870s a respiratory and lymphatic disease—Epizootic Apthnae, or the "Great Epizootic"—struck the eastern United States, killing thousands of animals. In the case of the West Side Railroad in Cleveland, for example, the company suspended operations in early November 1872 when eighty-nine of its ninety-three horses contracted the ailment. Fortunately, the death toll was low and within a few weeks the epidemic had mostly run its course, allowing transit activities to return to normal. Then there was the nuisance of animals on public thoroughfares and the greater concern of health risks. A horse dropped about ten pounds of feces daily and periodically discharged large quantities of urine. These wastes slickened streets and produced offensive odors. More troubling, horse feces caused tetanus; any skin abrasion exposed on these streets enhanced the chance of a deadly illness. Then, too, there was the challenge of the disposal of manure from stables. Most firms responded by selling it; manure sales could generate meaningful income. The noxious smell of the manure pits regularly brought complaints from nearby residents, and despite the use of various disinfectants, the problem was never solved.[5]

Fear of recurrence of the Great Epizootic and the other troubling aspects of animal propulsion prompted street railway executives to seek replacement technologies. In their quest they considered the method of overland transportation: steam. After the Civil War several locomotive builders, including the giant Baldwin Locomotive Works of Philadelphia, produced small steam locomotives for the metropolitan market. These "steam dummies" were downsized versions of standard road locomotives disguised as horsecars (and hence the common nickname),

By the era of World War I, Middletown possessed one of the last horse-car lines in North America. A somewhat forlorn horse waits with the small four-wheel car at the Cincinnati, Hamilton & Dayton Railway (Baltimore & Ohio System) station. *(Krambles Archive)*

which pulled powerless trailers or were part of a combined engine-coach unit. The public fretted that these hissing contraptions would scare horses and cause general mayhem, perhaps explaining why by 1890 only 7 percent of the national street track mileage (221.8 miles) were dummy lines. That not so far-fetched worry accounts for why one, if not the first, steam dummy experiment in the country, which occurred in 1860 in Cincinnati, quickly ended. Within twenty-four hours the tiny six-horsepower, coke-burning locomotive caused two serious horse-related accidents.[6]

Ignoring the obvious drawbacks to steam-dummy locomotives, several Ohio communities used them. Between 1866 and 1897 Cincinnati had three operations, including the Cincinnati & Columbia Street Railroad that served the Mount Lookout section. Cleveland also claimed three such carriers, two opening in 1868 and the other seven years later. The Lake View & Collamer Railroad, Newburgh & Cleveland Railroad, and Rocky River Railroad were more suburban operations than truly intracity ones and therefore somewhat less offensive to urban dwellers.

And Columbus and Canton residents briefly encountered the steam dummy. In October 1873 land developer Samuel Doyle opened a small steam-dummy road from Columbus to North Columbus to boom his "Doyle's Summit Street Addition." His operation proved to be financially unviable, and a year later service ended—equipment sold and track removed. In Canton the Lakeside Street Railway, which opened in 1887 and "operated only from May to September, being a summer road," owned an engine. It survived longer, closing in 1890.[7]

Although there may have been some nostalgia associated with the steam dummy, Ohioans hardly mourned its disappearance. Owners of the Mount Lookout dummy, likely capitalizing on that feeling, held on New Year's Day 1898 a widely publicized "Cremation Service" in which a steam-dummy car was burned and its ashes scattered along the right-of-way of the replacement electric trolley. In the black-bordered broadside that announced the public "funeral," with its accompanying fireworks and refreshments, the text told of a transport anachronism:

> The old oaken dummy, the iron bound dummy,
> The steam leaking dummy, on its trembling old rails,
> It sputtered and rumbled o'er bridges and gullies
> While to keep to its schedule it signally failed.
> With dogs and with cattle for speed it did battle
> And shrieked till the forest resounded with noise,
> But its age was against it, its rivets were rusted
> No longer it's classed as one of the boys.
> So here's to the past of the old oaken dummy
> And peace to its ashes, when it ends its career.
> Though fast, there are others much faster than it was,
> And Electrics will carry the poor dummy's bier.[8]

Before the time of the trolley an improved technology was the cable car, which largely coincided with the appearance of the steam dummy. Steam was still used, but not on moving transit vehicles. Rather, powerful stationary steam engines propelled wire-rope cables that traveled through underground conduits. Cable or "grip" cars, not dissimilar from animal cars, were attached by retractable mechanical devices to the steadily moving cable, allowing for constant speeds of eight to fourteen miles per hour. Introduced in 1873 to conquer the hills of San Francisco, cable lines by the early 1890s appeared in most major American cities.

The leading one was Chicago, which claimed three companies, collectively owning eighty-two miles of track and more than seven hundred grip cars.[9]

Predictably cable transit came to a wealthy and growing Ohio. Although initial capital costs were much greater than for animal car lines, there existed some attractive features. Speeds were faster; steep inclines could be overcome; operations were clean and environmentally friendly. Significantly, too, long-term costs were lower; horses, most of all, did not have to be purchased, housed, fed, or kept healthy. And another advantage existed in wintry weather: cable cars did not depend on adhesion, making operations easier in ice and snow. Chiefly for these reasons transit promoters in Cincinnati and Cleveland, the state's leading metropolises, adopted this technology and opened several cable car routes.[10]

Cincinnati was ideally suited for grip cars. Its sizable population, which stood at 296,908 in 1890, and its rugged terrain above the central business district contributed to the construction of three routes. Between 1885 and 1886 the Mount Adams & Eden Park Railway opened nearly four miles of line between the downtown and Blair Avenue, along Gilbert Avenue, McMillan Street, Madisonville Road, and Woodburn Avenue. Two years later the Vine Street Cable Railway, a division of the Cincinnati Street Railway Company, installed a four-mile line between Fountain Square (downtown) along Vine Street, Jefferson, and Ludlow Avenues and suburban Clifton. The last cable route in the Queen City, which began service in 1888, was the 4.5-mile Mount Auburn Cable Railway, which linked the central business district to Main Avenue (Avondale) along Auburn Street, Highland, Burnet, and Rockdale Avenues. Although this company used an inferior cable system when compared to the earlier two projects, initially it prospered. However, after a fire in 1892 destroyed its powerhouse and much of its rolling stock, the Mount Auburn Cable Railway entered bankruptcy.[11]

Cleveland had only a single cable car company, the relatively long 9.2-mile Cleveland City Cable Railway. Yet this firm constructed two lines, one that operated on Superior Avenue from the downtown union railway station and the other on Payne, Lexington, and Hough Avenues. The former opened on December 17, 1890, and the latter soon thereafter.[12]

Even though cable car operations in Ohio lasted for only a decade or

Mt. Adams Incline Plane, Cincinnati, O.

The rugged terrain of Cincinnati prompted the construction of both cable car and incline plane lines. This turn-of-the-century postcard is of the incline facility at Mount Adams. *(Author's Collection)*

so, they held some importance. Most significantly, they served as a *transition* between animal and electric cars, being superior to the former but inferior to the latter. Furthermore, grip service not only accommodated commuters dependably and frequently—the Vine Street Cable Railway had 325 daily scheduled trips—but pleasure seekers benefited as well. Cable cars, for example, served the zoo in Cincinnati and the major league baseball park in Cleveland.[13]

On January 7, 1888, a new urban transit form, the electric trolley, officially made its successful debut on the twelve-mile Richmond Union Passenger Railway in Virginia. These prototype streetcars were propelled by electric motors that received current directly from an overhead copper wire connected to the car by a pole with a moving metal wheel. The technology borrowed and perfected by inventor-promoter Frank J. Sprague offered much: it was faster, less expensive to install, more versatile, and easier and less costly to maintain than the cable car. Simply stated: electric trolley cars were vastly better engineered and rendered cable cars as obsolete as horsecars.[14]

Although the Richmond experiment made its mark in the history of urban transit, what was likely the *first* electric-powered streetcar to carry *revenue* passengers in the United States took place on the East Cleveland Street Horse Railway. The date of the company's inaugural service was July 26, 1884. The electrification system utilized an underground conduit similar to the vault that cable car railways employed, but this particular approach worked poorly. Since motormen had difficulty controlling the speed of cars, the owners soon abandoned electricity for predictable animal power.[15]

After the trolley era dawned, this new public conveyance quickly spread. Almost immediately Ohioans sensed the worth of electric traction. Within a year of Sprague's Richmond triumph, the Akron Street Railway Company, for one, acquired the replacement technology, and by the autumn of 1888 the modest horsecar system, which operated on Howard and Main Streets through the commercial district, was no more. This route and new ones that followed sported a cobweb of electric overhead wires, and "dear ol' Dobbin went to a farmer's field or the glue factory." By August 1891 the firm boasted fifteen route miles and employed 175 workers.[16]

Although not much larger than an animal or cable car, this early electric car, which belonged to the Norwalk Consolidated Electric Railway Company, pleased patrons because of its speed and generally pleasant riding qualities. *(Author's Collection)*

The rapidity with which the conversion process occurred was breathtaking. By 1900 it was impossible to find a steam dummy or cable car line in Ohio and difficult to locate an animal one. Strangely, though, Middletown, with a 1910 population of 13,152, as late as World War I still had a mule operation, surely one of the last on the continent. Isaac Silverman, who owned the tiny (one-mile) Middletown Street Railway Company, maintained five mules and two cars. Fortunately, residents of this bustling community had access to the intercity electric cars of the Cincinnati, Hamilton & Dayton Railway and to local bus or jitney service.[17]

The attractiveness of electricity as a transport power source also led to the rise of the interurban and the appearance of a host of companies, including "paper" holding firms. In this process "juice magnates," represented by several Cincinnati and Cleveland businessmen, bought up horsecar lines, electrified them, and extended their trackage into the surrounding environs and perhaps constructed bona fide intercity railways. And, too, they swiftly discovered that excess power could be profitably sold to commercial and residential customers. By 1910 it was common for an interurban railway to own a city transit system and also to provide local electric power. For example, the Northern Ohio Traction & Light Company, one of the state's most important interurbans, operated street railways in Akron, Canton, and Massillon and also generated electricity for the area.[18]

If there existed a "typical" electric street railway among the more than sixty that appeared in Ohio, it might be the Chillicothe Electric Railroad, Light & Power Company. Launched in 1894 as the Chillicothe Electric Railway & Lighting Company, the 6.25-mile system linked the commercial hub to the depots, ballpark, and the Pickaway County Fairgrounds, the latter two destinations being seasonally important sources of fare-box income. The firm's eight trolley cars rolled over fifty-six-pound (per yard) steel rails laid mostly in public streets. During the street car era the financial picture was good; in 1907, for example, the company generated gross earnings of $72,591 and incurred operating expenses of $52,685. Its bonded debt stood at a manageable $75,000. By World War I the restructured company was no longer locally owned but instead was controlled by the Ohio & Western Utilities Company, affiliated with a New York City–based syndicate, and the firm's Chillicothe trackage had shrunk to 4.5 miles. In 1929 the owners junked the trolleys, automobiles having inflicted the mortal wound. Still, public transit continued in Chillicothe; Public Transport, Inc. operated replacement bus service. Significantly, the profitable electric-power business remained, a great financial solace to investors.[19]

Residents of Chillicothe and other Ohio places with trolleys found that convenient and affordable public transport gave them new opportunities for enjoying their limited leisure time. The modern weekend had yet to be "invented" and would not become common until after World War II. Yet it was possible "to take the car" to a variety of pleasure spots: amusement parks, baseball fields, Chautauqua encampments, dance halls, fairgrounds, and picnic groves. And during sunny, warm weather most street railways used open-air "summer cars." The Cleveland Electric Railway even had a special "City Touring Car"; fun-seekers paid twenty-five cents for a two-hour trip in this largely open trolley.[20]

Just as street railways handled pleasure riders, several of the larger systems provided funeral cars, appropriately lettered and painted in a somber fashion and with ample room for the casket and a party of

After 1900 the trolley car had became commonplace on the streets of Ohio
cities and towns. Here an electric car rumbles over the Rocky River bridge west
of Cleveland. *(Author's Collection)*

mourners. Between 1899 and 1923 the Cleveland Electric Railway operated two of these distinctive pieces of rolling stock that whisked patrons
between church and cemetery.[21]

Ohioans found some problems with electric traction companies and
at times expressed their unhappiness toward them. During the crippling
depression of the 1890s, concerned citizens lashed out against various
acts of "corporate arrogance," charging that quasipublic businesses,
particularly street railways, did not pay their fair share of taxes. In their
rush to attract capital to trolley projects Ohioans often gave promoters
extremely attractive franchises, ones that might exempt them from
property assessments. Owners paid either a modest annual franchise fee
or a small percentage of gross revenues. Then, too, patrons fussed about
fares, often demanding three or four cents per ride rather than what by
the 1890s had become the standard nickel charge. These concerns,
which fueled the fires of progressive-era reform, led to clashes between
the public and traction firms, most notably in Cleveland where early
in the twentieth century Mayor Tom L. Johnson battled, albeit unsuccessfully, for municipal ownership in order "to achieve justice for the
people."[22]

Employees, too, often felt anger toward Ohio trolley companies. Most traction workers hardly had ideal jobs. There was, of course, the thrill of the trolley; motormen and conductors met a wide variety of their fellow citizens, some of whom were in a festive mood. And on a pleasant day there was the delight of rumbling down a tree-lined street or into the nearby countryside. But generally companies paid poorly, expected long stints in daily service, and stubbornly opposed unionization. Even "green country lads," who worked cheaply and did not form unions, altered their behavior. Strikes occurred and at times management made adjustments, including pay hikes and union recognition. Occasionally disputes turned nasty. When motormen of the Cleveland Electric Railway in 1899 struck for higher wages, violence ensued. At first workers and their supporters threw stones, even bombs, at those trolleys that were still running. Then strikers placed dynamite and nitroglycerine on the tracks, blowing up rails and damaging cars. Peace finally returned, but the settlement satisfied neither labor nor management. And what was probably the most serious labor disturbance in the history of Columbus erupted in the summer of 1910, when nearly six hundred employees of the Columbus Street Railway, Power & Light Company "hit the bricks," demanding union recognition, collective bargaining, a pay raise, and time-and-a-half pay beyond the standard nine-and-a-half-hour workday. Dynamiting of cars and tracks and fights between union men and strike breakers led to intervention by the National Guard. After more than three months of unrest, the union surrendered and peace returned.[23]

As with long-lasting forms of mechanical transport, technological betterments evolved. In the case of electric streetcars, during the early part of the twentieth century Ohioans encountered larger pieces of rolling stock, and, at times, noticeably so. Beginning about 1912 riders in Columbus could board monster double-deck trolleys. Although the concept was not new, these super cars, with their capacity of 171 sitting and standing passengers, that appeared on the busiest streets of the capital city were "low-floor" ones, featuring a stepless first level. After a few years the Columbus Railway, Power & Light Company, like the few other firms nationally that tried this equipment, concluded that these "battleships" were not particularly successful and soon retired them. Officials found that while the double-deckers increased passenger-carrying capacity without a corresponding increase in labor costs, they were extremely slow to load and unload.[24]

There were other important changes. A nationally significant improvement originated in Cleveland. Peter Witt, who served as the city's traction commissioner from 1911 to 1915, designed a more efficient trolley, the "pay-as-you-enter," or "Peter Witt," car. He arranged for front entrance and center exit, with passengers paying either when leaving or before passing to the rear section. Devoting the front area to unpaid passengers lessened annoying delays.[25]

As more Ohioans acquired automobiles, demand for streetcars dropped. Even if individuals did not own a tin lizzie, they found nontraction travel options. In the late 1910s and early 1920s enterprising motorists solicited passengers along trolley lines for a nickel, a "jitney," cash fare. Operating only when and where there was business, these jitney drivers in their touring cars made no attempt to provide the scheduled, all-day service that corporate franchises and regulatory bodies required of traction companies; rather, they simply skimmed off the "cream" of the peak-hour business. The jitney craze hurt fare-box receipts, and traction firms in the Buckeye State and elsewhere fought back as best they could. Although they could not prevent increasing automobile ownership, they pushed hard for corrective legislation and enforcement, actions that largely solved the problem.[26]

Adding to the woes of streetcar companies were the rapidly increasing costs of labor and materials, particularly during the era of World War I. Firms in Ohio reacted in various ways. Many pushed hard for substantial fare increases, but franchise agreements usually required city council approval, which might be difficult or impossible to obtain. Others focused on reducing the number of runs and abandoning money-losing routes. One response that helped stabilize some companies was the Birney safety car. Developed in 1916 by Charles O. Birney, an engineer for the Boston-based Stone and Webster Company, a major streetcar and interurban concern, these short, single-truck, and light-weight trolleys required only a single operator. And they featured a "dead-man" safety device, whereby a circuit breaker was automatically cut out when the motorman's hand left the controller handle, thus setting the air and stopping the car. Birneys were money savers and they were reliable, but patrons found them slow and rough riding.[27]

Although the Birney car was better suited to smaller operations and the less patronized lines of major traction firms, a strikingly successful streetcar appeared on the rosters of Ohio's big city systems, the PCC car. In 1929 a group of street traction executives formed the Electric Railway Presidents' Conference to create a standardized streetcar design of radically improved appearance and performance. In the mid-1930s the Presidents' Conference Committee (PCC) car took to the rails and soon these popular streamlined beauties strengthened the fleets of surviving companies. The PCC cars were high capacity, rapid accelerators, comfortable, and amazingly quiet, explaining their enthusiastic acceptance by riders. It is understandable that the last trolley operation in the state, the Shaker Heights Rapid Transit Company, which in 1975 joined the Greater Cleveland Rapid Transit Authority (RTA), used these practical pieces of rolling stock from the early 1950s until the end of its corporate existence.[28]

Coinciding with introduction of PCC cars were trackless trolleys, also called trolley buses or curbliners. This hybrid transit vehicle received power from an overhead wire but used rubber bus tires. Transit operators found that their most attractive feature was the end of expensive track construction and maintenance, and motorists liked not encountering annoying rails in the pavement. In the 1930s several Ohio systems and scores nationwide acquired this state-of-the-art equipment. Clevelanders, for example, saw them on their streets from 1936 to 1963. Dayton residents, however, continue to have access to several of the few remaining trolley bus lines in America. Because of fuel and environmental concerns, Dayton in the 1980s replaced its fleet of trolley buses with new ones, likely ensuring this form of urban transit for the immediate future.[29]

But neither PCC cars nor the more widely used trackless trolleys prevented the bus, first gasoline and then diesel powered, from gaining dominance on Ohio city streets. Although transit buses during their early stages of development were diminutive and not too dependable, by the mid-1920s national manufacturers, led by the White Motor Company of Cleveland, built practical ones that effectively competed with streetcars. These internal combustion vehicles were more versatile and usually less expensive to operate than trolleys, even trackless ones. Initial cost, road worthiness, and passenger comfort also contributed to their popularity. While the hard times of the 1930s and the war years of

Part of the fleet of motor buses operated in the 1920s by the Northern Ohio Traction & Light Company await their assignments. From the roll signs, the company has dedicated them to serve Akron's Mill and Howard Streets route. *(Author's Collection)*

the 1940s, the later characterized by shortages of fuel, parts and tires, slowed or halted the conversion process, the return of peace and prosperity created a market for better buses. Still, these vehicles lacked the charm of trolleys—in the words of a Cincinnati resident, they were "a very sterile form of mass transit."[30]

The purchasers of fleets of shiny new buses likely were not privately owned transit companies. Although before World War I traction interests had battled reformers who advocated "gas and water socialism," by the 1920s and 1930s the seemingly unending financial problems prompted many owners to rethink their long-standing position. Ultimately the result was that within less than a half century, investor-owned transit firms had disappeared. In time, taxpayers, supported by generous federal and state grants, accepted "lemon socialism," namely community acquisition of financially troubled private transit firms. If service was going to continue, public ownership was the only option. Even with more automobiles on city streets, there was a social consequence; if transit operations ended, the poor, minorities and elderly, most of all, would be on their own to find other ways to travel about their hometowns.[31]

What took place in Akron illustrates the transformation of private transit operations into public ones. The locally based Northern Ohio Traction & Light Company (NOT&L), the mighty electric interurban and utility, dominated mass transit in Akron and its suburbs. In the early 1920s the firm decided that any new routes would be served by buses rather than trolleys. The appearance of jitneys and bona-fide independent bus firms worried the company and, "determined to maintain its hold on the transportation business in this locality," it purchased several upstart bus operations, including Zeno Brothers Transportation Company, an aggressive, hence annoying, competitor. As a result of restructuring, by 1930 the power operations of the NOT&L had found a corporate home under the banner of the Ohio Edison Company and the interurban had been sold off and shortly would be abandoned. But the controlling force, the gigantic holding company, Commonwealth & Southern Utilities, headquartered in New York City, decided to place the Akron and suburban operations under its subsidiary, the Transportation Securities Corporation. The latter entity controlled what was known as the Akron Transportation Company (ATC), which by the late 1930s dispatched trolleys, trolley buses, and buses to serve the greater Rubber City locale. In 1938 the firm began to retire its streetcar routes, and by 1941 all were gone except the Akron-Kenmore-Barberton line. On March 23, 1947, the remaining segment, the trackage between Main and Mill Streets in Akron and the Kenmore "Loop," closed. Four years earlier the federal government had forced Commonwealth & Southern to divest itself of its transit activities, and in the process ATC was sold to investors associated with Equitable Securities of Nashville, Tennessee. In 1945 another group, United Transit Company, which also controlled transit operations in Youngstown and several out-of-state cities, took charge. By the early 1950s ACT operated ten trolley bus and thirty-two gasoline bus routes. A decade later the trolley buses had been retired and the firm's health was rapidly failing. The fatal blow came in the late 1960s when a bitter strike erupted between management and workers, forcing suspension of service and killing the company. In time, the cities of Akron, Barberton, and Cuyahoga Falls acquired the assets of ACT

The last run of a streetcar in Akron is about to take place on March 23, 1947, from the Kenmore carbarn on Kenmore Avenue on the city's south side. *(Author's Collection)*

and returned buses to the streets. The Metro Regional Transit Authority (Metro) gradually modernized the system, including several upgradings of its fleet of diesel-powered buses and making it services countywide.[32]

Buses remain the backbone of Ohio's transit systems. But the largest municipalities have either considered, attempted, or created a heavy-duty network of commuter rail service. In the 1920s Cincinnati embarked upon a publicly financed rapid transit system, especially designed to accommodate interurban cars. By 1923 eleven miles of subways, graded rights-of-way, overpasses, and stations, which extended from downtown north and east, had been completed. Yet the Rapid Transit Commissioners delayed installation of electrical equipment and double-track rail until the entire right-of-way was finished. Inflation, politics, and growing automobile usage, however, stymied completion. Except for designating portions of the subway as public bomb shelters during the cold war years of the 1950s, tax dollars went to waste.[33]

A happier story occurred in Cleveland. Although not equal to the "heavy traction" systems found in the Greater Chicago, New York, and Philadelphia regions, the Forest City built a quality network of electric rapid rail, the envy of many a city. While the Cleveland Transit System, the public entity that since 1942 had run the transit operation, busily removed and paved over streetcar rails, it planned its new rapid transit lines. In 1951 the green light came when the Reconstruction Finance Corporation in Washington, D.C., approved a nearly $30 million loan for construction. Work began the following year.[34]

Since Cleveland had developed on an east-west axis, the system contained two distinct parts, ones that developed somewhat differently. Service on the eastern line, which tied Terminal Tower on Public Square with Windermere in East Cleveland, began in March 1955. This 7.8-mile artery appeared first because it could share the track of the Shaker Heights Rapid Transit from downtown to approximately East 35th Street. Also, there were available sections of a never-railed right-of-way that years earlier had been readied by the Van Sweringen brothers. The shorter western component, designed to cover the 5.3 miles between Terminal Tower and West 117th Street and Berea Road, opened in August 1955. Two western mainline extensions eventually followed: initially the two miles between West 117th and West 143rd Street in 1958 and a decade later the four miles to Cleveland Hopkins Airport. But a proposed downtown subway loop, which voters endorsed in 1953 by ratifying a $35 million bond levy, never materialized. Local opposition to public transit, which glorified the superiority of the automobile, prevented construction; the authorized bonds were never sold.[35]

Nevertheless, Clevelanders gained access to the most modern urban rail transit system in the region. Although projected usage was not reached, riders appreciated the roomy, quiet, and fast rapid cars. Travel time dropped markedly. If a patron boarded a car at West 117th Street to Terminal Tower, it took only twelve minutes—thirteen minutes less than by the former trolley. And those who used feeder bus lines did not seem too unhappy with their required change of transit equipment.[36]

Even though in the 1960s public transit declined in popularity, the shocking impact of gasoline shortages in the 1970s promoted a rethinking of alternatives to the automobile. Ohioans did not witness the building of *new* "light rail" systems (contemporary nomenclature for trolleys), as did, for example, Buffalo, New York; Portland, Oregon; and San Diego, California. However, they did discuss the concept. Significantly, this sentiment led to major rehabilitation of the Shaker Heights Rapid Transit. In 1975 the Greater Cleveland Rapid Transit Authority (née CTA) took control of the quasi-interurban with its fleet of PCC cars from the City of Shaker Heights and subsequently updated trackage, stations, and rolling stock, effectively converting the property into a modern light-rail facility. These same forces led to construction of a substitute for the ill-fated downtown Cleveland subway, the 2.2-mile Waterfront rail line. This extension, which opened in 1996, linked Tower City (Terminal Tower) with East 9th Street and the North Coast Harbor via the popular "Flats" entertainment area, locations with chronic shortages of parking.[37]

Although most Ohioans prefer the freedom and flexibility that driving their own automobile provides and continually demand more and better expressways, there are signs that urban transit may enjoy a rebirth, albeit less extensive than in the pre–tin lizzie era. Congestion, even gridlock, on city streets and concomitant concerns of air pollution, road safety, operating costs, and the aesthetics of the car culture may well spark the dramatic growth of urban transit. Already public agencies are planning for the future. In 1997 Akron's Metro, for one, acquired the out-of-service former Erie Lackawanna mainline between Akron and Kent and placed it in a rail "bank." In the next century students at the University of Akron and Kent State University may take to the rails rather than to the roads between their campuses, joined by hundreds of thousands of other Ohioans seeking different destinations. Indeed, as the technology of the leading historic form of urban transit, the electric trolley, became not a fact of everyday life but only a remembrance, it might seem surprising that contemporary perceptions have changed. More Ohioans, joined by their fellow Americans, consider trolleys (light-rail vehicles) not as conveyances that have become outmoded and uneconomic—and therefore have died a deserved death—but as quite the opposite, as something altogether superior to what displaced them.[38]

7

AIRWAYS

LICENSE tags in North Carolina proudly proclaim "First in Flight," but it is Ohio, not the Tar Heel State, that can rightfully claim that honor. Only because of favorable wind currents on the sand dunes at Kitty Hawk, North Carolina, did the Ohio bicycle makers turned aeronauts Orville and Wilbur Wright of Dayton make their historic flight there on December 17, 1903, rather than in their home state. Much of the brothers' subsequent testing of improved heavier-than-air machines, including the world's first practical airplane, the Wright Flyer III, centered at Huffman Prairie in Greene and Montgomery Counties. Beginning in 1998 Ohio license plates fittingly declare: "Birthplace of Aviation."[1]

Virtually everyone acknowledges that the Wright brothers fathered powered flight. Still, their early triumphs did not mean the immediate dawn of modern aviation. Not until 1911 did an airplane fly across the United States, and then this exploit required nearly seven weeks with numerous forced landings. Indeed, until about the time of World War I, Ohioans and their fellow Americans considered "aeroplanes" to be mechanical curiosities and aviators to be daredevils or madmen. Residents received their firsthand knowledge of these fragile, unstable craft and their brave, resourceful pilots from air shows and stunting exhibitions.

The *Sunday Cincinnati Enquirer* of July 14, 1911, for example, reported that two pilots in their biplanes "thrilled the throngs" when they flew above the nearby Coney Island Amusement Park. "The two airmen reached altitudes of 2,000 and 3,000 feet; they remained in the air thirty-five minutes at a time, and attained speeds of up to 60 miles an hour, doing figure-eights and loops." The *Enquirer* observed that this performance was the first time Cincinnatians had seen "real aviation" and that "thousands availed themselves of the opportunity."[2]

Even the first commercial air freight shipment fits the entertainment category. This historic happening not unexpectedly occurred in Ohio and involved the Wright brothers. In October 1910 Columbus businessman Max Morehouse, whose Morehouse-Martens Company operated the Home Dry Goods Store, the city's premier emporium, contacted the Wrights to learn if "a bolt of ribbon" might be flown from Dayton to Columbus (it would earlier be dispatched from Columbus to Dayton by electric interurban!) to publicize the store's annual fall sale. The Wrights agreed. The big day took place on November 7, when a Wright Company pilot, Philip Parmalee, in a "Model B" biplane delivered two hundred pounds of silk cloth to a makeshift landing strip in the capital city before an estimated crowd of three thousand people who had paid handsomely to witness this event. Morehouse's five-thousand-dollar payment to the Wrights was a good investment: the airplane show and the store sale generated a tidy profit. And everyone surely agreed with the pilot when he told reporters, "It was a dandy trip."[3]

A similar story is associated with the earliest delivery of U.S. mail by airplane in Ohio. Although nationally this was not the first such event, it nevertheless was one of the pioneer endeavors to use aircraft for mail transport. In July 1912 the postmaster in Cincinnati allowed "birdman" Paul Peck to fly sacks of picture postcards from the amusement park at Coney Island to the nearby post office in California for cancellation and transfer to a rail connection for the Queen City. Soon several of these flights took place and recipients treasured their souvenir cards marked "U.S. Official Aerial Mail." Again, novelty rather than a viable and on-going commercial venture characterized this episode.[4]

What transpired during the formative years of the age of winged flight resembled a much earlier phase in aeronautical history, hot-air balloon ascensions, when only the most venturesome took to the skies.

Even though the first recorded free-ballooning triumph in the country had occurred shortly after the American Revolution, the decade of the 1830s marked the start of this widely popular activity both nationally and in Ohio. In 1834 the Buckeye State's pioneer aeronaut, Thomas Kirkby, arrived in Cincinnati, probably from Baltimore, to enhance his pocketbook by demonstrating his ballooning skills. On November 27 Kirkby planned to stage such an event from a hastily erected amphitheater. With admission money collected, equipment readied, and the crowd anxious, only frustration and failure followed. The inability of the hydrogen-gas-generating apparatus, which used large quantities of acid and iron scraps, to fill fully the balloon bag thwarted liftoff. Kirkby, however, hoped for a better day on November 28. The audience reassembled, and when the ascension again failed, anger spread. Fortunately, the aeronaut, the mayor, and police officers averted a "riot" by convincing spectators that these unsuccessful efforts to fly had not been fraudulent. Everyone dispersed peacefully after learning that in a few weeks another ascent would be scheduled. Finally, on December 15, "the largest [crowd] that we have ever seen in this city" anxiously watched Kirkby enter the suspended car and eventually soar upwards, his balloon resembling a "brilliant star" as it reflected the late afternoon sun. The balloon and Kirkby disappeared into the east, landing unceremoniously about an hour later in a tree in neighboring Clermont County. Kirkby decided to repeat his "beautiful and sublime spectacle," largely because he wanted to recoup his losses from his November attempts. The aeronaut scheduled his next ascension for Christmas Day, but inclement weather postponed the flight until December 27. Kirkby's final ascension in Ohio went reasonably well; he floated into the heavens before a modest but excited crowd and landed thirteen miles away in a soft, plowed field near the Clermont-Hamilton County line.[5]

In the spring of 1835 the amazing flight of Richard Clayton, a watchmaker from Cincinnati, overshadowed the path-breaking achievements of Kirkby. On April 8 Clayton sailed in his airship, the *Star of the West*, 350 miles from the Queen City to Monroe County, Virginia, in nine and one-half hours, and in the process established a world-distance record for free ballooning. Clayton did not stop with this success. On July 4, 1835, he cast off with the usual balloon equipment and also with a small quantity of U.S. mail; his goal was the Atlantic shore. The appearance of two holes in the silk balloon fabric forced a landing in Pike County about one hundred miles from Cincinnati. Both Clayton and the mail were safe, the latter being transported to the post office in nearby Waverly. Nevertheless, this shorter-than-expected journey became the first balloon-mail experiment in American history.[6]

In subsequent years other balloonists departed from Ohio localities, most to entertain audiences at circuses, fairs, and similar events, the role later performed by early aviators. One notable exception to this pattern involved the memorable flight of T. S. C. Lowe. On April 20, 1861, Lowe departed Cincinnati on what he expected to be the first leg of a trans-Atlantic flight. He found himself instead in South Carolina, where Yankee-hating residents quickly captured him, making Lowe "the first prisoner of the Civil War." Fortunately, Lowe did not die or rot away in a Palmetto State jail; he quickly won his freedom and returned to the Buckeye State and later had a distinguished career as the "chief aeronaut" of the Army of the Potomac.[7]

Although the technology of ballooning for decades remained rather static, the special needs of World War I resulted in a raft of improvements. The Akron-based B. F. Goodrich and Goodyear companies employed the latest betterments in their production of observation balloons and blimps (nonrigid airships) for the military. After the conflict Goodyear remained involved in lighter-than-air craft, forming in 1924 a subsidiary firm, the Goodyear-Zeppelin Company. The results were impressive: construction of an air dock in Akron that was the world's largest building without interior supports and rigid airships that inspired awe because of their size, elegance, and long-distance flying capabilities. These behemoths were used by the military and also for commercial passenger service until the deadly crash in 1937 of the *Hindenburg* at Lakehurst, New Jersey, destroyed public confidence in these craft.[8]

Just as the Great War stimulated improvements in lighter-than-air craft, it similarly led to better airplanes. Streamlined designs, stronger structural components, and more powerful engines greatly enhanced flying. Attractive contracts from the federal government helped to underwrite these technological advancements. By war's end thousands of planes had been produced for the military, whether in service or stored in warehouses.[9]

Both technological betterments and surplus equipment gave impetus to commercial aviation. One entrepreneur, Inglis Uppercu, a New Jersey engineer turned airline promoter, believed that the time was right for regularly scheduled passenger flights. Using modified F-5L ex-Navy seaplanes, with accommodations for a dozen occupants, Uppercu in 1920 formed the Aeromarine Sightseeing and Navigation Company and set out to demonstrate the comfort, reliability, and safety of air travel. Initially, the upstart firm flew riders between New York City and nearby summer coastal resorts and then, operating as Florida–West Indies Airways (later Aeromarine–West Indies Airways), it started roundtrip flights between Key West and Cuba. The latter operation received a crucial financial boost when the Post Office Department awarded the company its first international airmail contract. In 1921 Aeromarine began service between Miami, Bimini, and Nassau.[10]

The encouraging results of Aeromarine's formative years prompted expansion. The Uppercu company turned to the Midwest, creating its Great Lakes Division between Cleveland and Detroit. Again using seaplanes, which landed on Lake Erie and the Detroit River, Aeromarine operated only a summer schedule, transporting more than four thousand riders during July and August 1922. Public demand had become so great that a second daily flight was added.[11]

But all was not well at Aeromarine. In 1923 declining revenues, operational problems, and two plane crashes in the Caribbean forced Uppercu to retrench, although service continued on the Great Lakes Division. During that summer Aeromarine's "flying boats" transported over five thousand passengers between Cleveland's lakefront and Detroit's riverfront. Then, in early 1924, Uppercu decided to shut down the airline and to focus instead on building intercity buses and custom bodies for Cadillac.[12]

The Aeromarine saga, nevertheless, was more than a footnote to the aviation history of Ohio. The company's Great Lakes Division demonstrated a potentially profitable local market. The small capacity of Aeromarine aircraft and the absence of U.S. mail contracts, however, had precluded success until larger planes and postal subsidies appeared.

When domestic airmail service began in the United States in spring 1918 between New York City and Washington, D.C., it was the U.S. Army and not private carriers who were involved. Soon thereafter the Post Office Department expanded the Army's role by creating a transcontinental air route. Although taking shape in several stages, on September 8, 1920, veteran pilots from the Great War flew the mails between New York City and San Francisco through Cleveland, Chicago, Omaha, Cheyenne, Salt Lake City, and Reno. The strategic location of Ohio allowed "aerial mail" deliveries to and from the Forest City.[13]

Under the best conditions, operating open cockpit airplanes was challenging. Most of these aircraft were obsolete de Havilland D.H.4's, originally designed for wartime reconnaissance missions. As in the war, bad weather delayed or canceled these high-priority airmail flights. Even when the Department of Commerce later installed a national network of navigational beacons or "guide lights" for night trips, pilots still needed to be quick witted and eagle eyed. In 1921 the Division of Air Mails of the Post Office Department published a set of instructions to assist flyers in navigating their runs. Those directions for flights from Cleveland to Bryan suggest how these aviators traversed the Buckeye State.

Miles

0. *Martin Field, Cleveland.*—Fly a little west of south for nearly 10 miles or about seven minutes flying and then due west, thus keeping over good emergency landing fields. The country between Cleveland and Chicago is divided into sections, section lines running due north and south and east and west. For the first 15 miles the lake shore is only a few miles north of the course.

20. *Elyria, Ohio.*—Five miles north of the course. Five railroads radiate out of Elyria.

37. *Vermilion.*—Two miles north of the course. On Lake Erie. The New York Central Railroad follows the shore line of the lake from Vermilion to Sandusky.

55. *Sandusky.*—Five miles north of the course on Sandusky Bay, a large irregular body of water crossed by the New York Central Railroad. Continues due west from this point, following the east-west section lines.

112. *Maumee River,* which you cross about 5 miles northeast of Grand Rapids and 5 miles south of Waterville. Waterville is on the east bank of the Maumee and Grand Rapids is on the south bank of the river where it turns east and parallels the course for 7 miles.

130. *Detroit, Toledo & Ironton Railroad,* crossed at right angles. Wauseon is 7 miles north of the course and Napoleon is 5 miles south, both on the above-mentioned railroad. By flying about 11 miles north from the point where the Maumee River is crossed and then due west

the New York Central four-track railroad will be picked up just before reaching Bryan.[14]

Airmail operations steadily expanded. In 1922, for example, the Post Office Department established airmail service between Cleveland and Cincinnati. By the mid-1920s the distribution system was on a solid footing. Businessmen, most of all, willingly paid the premium for airmail postage, knowing that most planes on long-distance routes could easily beat the fastest mail trains.[15]

After 1925 aviation in Ohio and elsewhere changed strikingly. In February 1925 Congress passed and President Calvin Coolidge signed the Contract Air Mail Act, popularly called the Kelly Act after its sponsor, Rep. Clyde Kelly of Pennsylvania. This measure energized commercial air transport because it authorized the postmaster general to determine air routes and to pay private carriers to fly mail over them. No other nontechnological event so directly encouraged firms; soon passengers were transported along with sacks of mail.[16]

Coinciding with the financial injections from federal mail contracts, airplane manufacturers in America and Europe were constantly improving their products. As the decade of the 1920s progressed, all-metal, enclosed cockpit, multiengine, single-wing craft appeared. In 1929 a Ford Motor Company promotional brochure, titled "Now That Everyone Can Fly," cheerfully observed: "Completed, a Ford tri-motor all-metal monoplane weighs almost four tons and is capable of carrying a useful load of more than three-quarters of its own weight—at an air speed of from 70 to 155 miles per hour." And the explanation continued: "With a capacity of carrying up to 15 passengers with their baggage at a normal cruising speed of 125 miles an hour, the Ford tri-motor is standard equipment on many of the passenger air transport routes not only in the United States but also in Central and South America."[17]

Ford not only emerged as a leading producer of airplanes but also entered the commercial air market. Under the corporate banner of Ford Commercial Air Lines, the company on July 1, 1925, inaugurated daily trips between Cleveland and Detroit. Significantly, it was the first domestic carrier to start contract operations with the Post Office. Although Ford subsequently left the passenger business, it remained an important supplier of its reliable and versatile planes to firms that served Ohio communities, ending its aircraft manufacturing in 1932 because of the

Great Depression and competition. Indeed, until the early 1980s the tiny Island Airlines, based in Port Clinton, operated a Ford 4-T Tri-Motor "Tin Goose," a veteran of more than a half century of service.[18]

One pioneer Ohio commercial carrier with a close connection to Ford was Stout Air Services. Operations began in August 1926, and before the company sold out in June 1929, Stout had assumed Ford's passenger and express business, flying four Ford-Stout 2-AT's and two Ford 4-AT Tri-Motors. At the end of its corporate life before joining United Aircraft and Transportation Corporation (later United Air Lines), Stout operated two daily roundtrips between Cleveland and Detroit and Detroit and Chicago. The firm tapped the business market between these Midwestern metropolises, providing competition with the premier passenger trains of the New York Central System. Patrons on the "Detroit-Cleveland Division" departed from the Consolidated Air Travel ticket office on Superior Avenue in Cleveland in a Stout car for the newly opened Cleveland Municipal Airport. The 9:15 A.M. and 4:45 P.M. flights spent one hour and forty minutes in the air and cost passengers eighteen dollars for a one-way ticket and thirty-five dollars roundtrip, including ground transportation. (The New York Central priced a one-way rail coach ticket at approximately nine dollars.) A company vehicle met the plane at Ford Airport in Dearborn for locations in downtown Detroit.[19]

Stout and other infant airlines needed to convince the traveling public that "air voyages" were safe, comfortable, and dependable. The task was considerable, in part because of some widely publicized crashes, excessive cabin noise and vibrations, and service disruptions due to mechanical and weather problems. Still, the airlines ballyhooed their service. In a public timetable of April 1, 1929, Stout described its equipment in a reassuring way:

> Until you actually see the great Ford-Stout tri-motored all-metal transport monoplanes which fly the Stout Airlines, it is almost impossible to conceive the mighty strides that have been made in recent years in airplane building.
>
> A roomy cabin, completely enclosed, in which you may ride in the same clothes you wear on the street! Clear plate-glass windows which may be opened if you wish. Restful chairs from which you gaze at the wonderful scene below. No glare from the sun, for the wing above you acts as a welcome shield. *The cabin is heated in cold weather!*

The Flight Engineer who always accompanies the pilot will cheerfully answer questions, furnish you with a magazine or newspaper, and draw your attention to scenes of particular interest or beauty.

The planes, pilots and mechanics are licensed by the Aeronautics branch of the Department of Commerce, and a rigid daily inspection of equipment insures maximum dependability at all times.[20]

By the late 1920s, more first-time passengers boarded commercial flights like those offered by Stout and technological advances occurred at an impressive pace. Nonetheless, pilots still found extended night trips difficult, even with beacons, particularly over mountainous terrain. To rectify this problem, a number of air carriers arranged with steam railroads for coordinated operations, specifically: "The night by train—The day by plane."[21]

What is usually acknowledged as the first transcontinental air-rail service began on June 15, 1929, and made Cleveland an integral part of a sixty-seven hour journey between New York and Los Angeles. The Universal Aviation Corporation offered well-heeled and time-conscious travelers this arrangement: departure at 5:00 p.m. from Grand Central Terminal on New York Central's *Southwestern Limited* and arrival at 6:05 A.M. in Cleveland; departure at 7:10 A.M. aboard Universal's *Skyliner,* a fourteen seat Fokker F-XA, for Toledo, Chicago, and Kansas City with arrival at 5:20 P.M. in Garden City, Kansas; and departure at 6:10 P.M. on Santa Fe's *California Limited* for an arrival approximately thirty-nine hours later in the City of Angels.[22]

Although Universal, Kohler Aviation Corporation, Rapid Air Lines, and several other regional carriers offered additional air-rail arrangements, the most acclaimed plane-train venture involved an agreement between Transcontinental Air Transport (TAT); the *Lindbergh Line,* joined by Maddax Air Lines; and the Pennsylvania and Santa Fe railroads. Starting on July 7, 1929, these companies offered a forty-eight hour cross-country air-rail travel package. Again, because of its key location, Ohioans received this service. Westbound travelers stepped into Pennsylvania's special *Airways Limited,* which departed New York City's Pennsylvania Station at 6:05 P.M. After dinner, a night's slumber, and breakfast, these pampered patrons detrained at 7:55 A.M. in the newly completed Port Columbus station, seven miles east of the capital city, and walked under a canopy from their Pullman car to the airport terminal

The reverse side of this 1931 postcard announced: "Port Columbus, America's greatest air-harbor, can be reached within 15 minutes from the center of Columbus. It is a two million dollar public utility owned by the City of Columbus, and is the eastern terminus of the T.A.T. Airways System. Port Columbus contains 640 acres of perfectly level terrain and has two 100 feet wide cement runways. It is fully equipped for all night operations." *(Author's Collection)*

and an awaiting TAT Ford Tri-Motor for the second leg of their journey. "With a thrill of anticipation you take your seat in one of the ten comfortable chairs which line each side of the tastefully decorated interior," exclaimed a TAT folder. The 8:15 A.M. departure placed passengers at a landing field near Waynoka, Oklahoma, at 6:24 P.M., after stops in Indianapolis, St. Louis, Kansas City, and Wichita. Travelers returned to the rails; a Pullman on the Santa Fe's *Missionary* departed at 11:00 P.M. for an 8:20 A.M. arrival at Clovis, New Mexico, and transfer to the TAT terminal at Portair, New Mexico, and resumption of the air journey. The TAT plane lifted off the ground at 8:10 A.M., stopping three times before touching down near Los Angeles at 5:22 P.M., with connections for San Francisco by Maddox Air Lines. The best all-rail time exceeded eighty hours, not including layover periods.[23]

Several factors explain why the carefully conceived and executed transcontinental plane-train experiment was short lived. The fare of more than three hundred dollars hurt ridership, especially with the onslaught of the Great Depression. The air portion of the cross-country ticket averaged sixteen cents per mile, about double the first-class air rate *after* World War II. Moreover, the fixed costs were enormous, prompting TAT nearly to hemorrhage in red ink. Financial considerations, coupled to better aircraft and guidance equipment, soon eliminated the need for overnight rail trips. Airplanes could bind the nation without a railroad partnership.[24]

A financially less risky intermodal arrangement was the coordinated air-water journey. These trips, aimed at well-heeled and adventurous travelers, usually involved one leg by plane and the other by boat. In a 1932 public timetable, Transamerican Airlines, an affiliate of Cleveland-based Thompson Aeronautical Corporation, lauded coordinated service with the Detroit & Cleveland Navigation Company (D&C). The airline offered roundtrip passage between Cleveland and Detroit: one way via a speedy Keystone-Leoning amphibian and the other by an unhurried D&C steamer.[25]

Ohio continued to be a place where aviation experiments occurred. The activities of Pittsburgh entrepreneur Clifford Ball illustrate this phenomena. In 1925 Ball won the Post Office contract to carry mail between Cleveland and Pittsburgh, and on April 27, 1927, his Clifford Ball, Inc., flew the first cargo of cards and letters between the two cities.

Ball's operation quickly became one of the few profitable mail routes in the nation. If, however, his fledgling company had to make stops between its terminals, its slim time advantage over Railway Post Office runs would disappear. In order to maximize profits and to remain competitive, the carrier tried a daring idea, a "pickup trap" for sacks of mail from a low-flying plane. In the summer of 1929, preliminary trials took place at Youngstown, the principal city between the Ohio and Pennsylvania metropolises, and the relative success led to regular ground mail retrievals. But mechanical problems forced temporary suspension of this service and further experimentation followed. Subsequently Clifford Ball resumed airmail pickup, but in nearby Beaver Falls and New Castle, Pennsylvania, although service to both Niles and Warren was considered. The company then decided to abandon the practice; it failed to generate enough mail volume to justify its considerable costs. Although Ball soon sold his airline to the Pittsburgh Aviation Industries Corporation, the mail-pickup concept would later be employed by Pittsburgh-based All-American Airlines along its route over the mountainous terrain of the Keystone State.[26]

When in late 1929 Clifford Ball, Inc., became Pennsylvania Airlines, the firm operated a single route: Cleveland to Washington, D.C., with a stop in Pittsburgh, although soon adding one in Akron. The company's economic health depended heavily on its mail subsidy. Other carriers that served Ohio also relied on their contracts with the Post Office Department. By the early 1930s mail routes coincided with commercial passenger ones.[27]

In addition to Pennsylvania Airlines, three other commercial carriers dominated Buckeye skies in the 1930s. All of them operated extensive mileage, reminiscent of the long-haul orientation of contemporary railroad and bus companies. American Airways offered service between Boston, Cleveland, Columbus, Cincinnati, and Fort Worth and Chicago, Indianapolis, and Cincinnati. Transcontinental & Western Air, successor of TAT, flew between New York, Columbus, and Los Angeles and New York, Columbus, and Chicago. And United Air Lines, a recent amalgamation of Boeing Air Transport, National Airlines, Varney Air Lines, and Pacific Air Transport connected New York, Cleveland, Toledo, and Chicago.[28]

During this time period the significance of mail contracts did not diminish. Although for a brief period in 1934 the government canceled these subsidies because of alleged influence peddling by lobbyists with bureaucrats and politicians, Congress rapidly passed the Air Mail Act of 1934 that restored contract operations. This legislation contained safeguards to assure competitive bidding. Fortunately for companies, aircraft became larger, faster, and safer, characterized by introduction in the mid-1930s of the Douglas DC-2s and DC-3s. Such planes increased the likelihood that passenger revenues alone could underwrite much or all of a flight. "The advent of the DC-3 marked the beginning of the end of profitless air transport operations," concluded aviation historian R. E. G. Davies, "and a real chance to escape from dependence on mail payments to make up the difference between operating costs and passenger revenue." The industry, too, mostly benefited from establishment in 1938 of the Civil Aeronautical Authority. This government agency, later reconstituted as the Civil Aeronautics Board (CAB), not only had extensive powers to regulate aviation but also to adjust airmail payments to the needs of different operators.[29]

The Civil Aeronautics Board created a remarkable degree of stability in Ohio aviation. For decades, several major carriers dominated the local skies, most notably American Airlines, Trans World Airlines (née Transcontinental & Western) and United Air Lines. Yet in the early 1940s the CAB decided to bring commercial aviation to a number of small cities. "Local service" carriers would provide these flights rather than "trunk" ones. These operations became "feeders" to large cities, allowing passengers to connect with major lines. This federal policy, especially after World War II, resulted in additional firms and expansion of air service.[30]

The quintessential local service feeder that flew in Ohio skies was Lake Central Airlines. Founded as Roscoe Turner Aeronautical Corporation in 1947 and two years later renamed Turner Airlines, this Indianapolis-based company took the Lake Central moniker in 1950. During its twenty-one years of corporate life before it joined Allegheny Airlines, Lake Central developed an extensive network of routes across the Buckeye State. Although in the early 1950s the carrier connected only Cincinnati with communities in Illinois, Indiana, and Michigan, a decade later it served more Ohio places than any other company. Lake Central's growing fleet

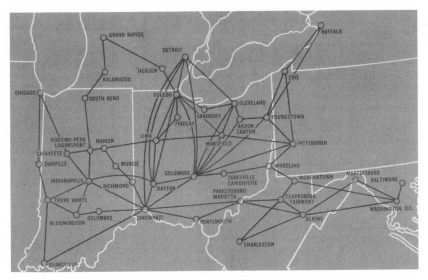

By the early 1960s the feeder carrier, Lake Central Airlines, covered Ohio like a morning dew. No other airline has ever provided such extensive service to the Buckeye State. *(Author's Collection)*

of Convair 340 prop jets paid daily visits to Akron-Canton, Cleveland, Columbus, Dayton, Findlay, Lima, Mansfield, Parkersburg-Marietta, Portsmouth, Sandusky, Toledo, Youngstown, and Zanesville-Cambridge. Lake Central performed the way that the Civil Aeronautics Board had intended, and by the 1960s it was one of thirteen major national local service carriers, a list that included Allegheny, Bonanza, Central, Frontier, Mohawk, North Central, Ozark, Pacific, Piedmont, Southern, Trans-Texas, and West Coast airlines.[31]

A carrier might remain small yet tap a successful niche market. TAG Airlines (originally Taxi Air Group) represents this genre. Launched in 1955, the little firm operated only between Cleveland and Detroit, that historic route of Aeromarine, Ford, and Stout. In spite of intense competition, TAG prospered, largely because of its frequent, fast service and its use of convenient downtown airports, Lakefront in Cleveland and City in Detroit, both only a few minutes from prime business locations. "If I had to get to Detroit in a hurry from Public Square, I'd take the TAG commuter flight," recalled a satisfied Cleveland executive. "I didn't have to drive myself or take some airline that would waste time by landing out in the suburbs." By 1963 TAG annually carried about thirty-five thousand passengers. Unfortunately, in early 1970 service abruptly ended in the wake of a tragic crash in Lake Erie.[32]

Although during the era of regulation airlines started up and failed, like TAG, and merged, as with Lake Central and Allegheny, commercial aviation remained reasonably stable. However, after 1978 conditions changed abruptly with deregulation and the demise of the Civil Aeronautics Board. Since carriers were no longer required to fly fixed routes and to serve designated communities, they rapidly abandoned money-losing and marginally profitable operations, concentrating instead on the most promising markets. In the process these companies emphasized "hubs" where they could best direct their business. Rare among the states, Ohio became the flight centers for several airlines; airport hubs have operated or continue to operate in four cities: Dayton with Piedmont Airlines until that company's acquisition by U.S. Air (née Allegheny); Cincinnati (Greater Cincinnati Regional Airport at Covington, Kentucky) with Delta Air Lines; Cleveland initially with United and later with Continental Airlines; and Columbus with America West Airlines.[33]

While changes at hubs have occurred, greater volatility has reigned with upstart airlines that sought to fill voids left by the larger carriers. Since 1978 a plethora of companies have appeared and disappeared, including such "fallen flags" as Aeromech, Air Toronto, Air Virginia, Central States, Freedom, Sundorph, and Wright. Some, in fact, have had histories that can be measured in months rather than years. The candidate for Ohio's least successful carrier in the era of deregulation is surely Liberty Airlines. This Swanton-based firm began operations in mid-1982 between Chicago and Toledo. Soon the company's two vintage Convair prop jets added the Akron-Canton Airport to its schedule. Although Liberty sought to exploit a niche left vacant by United, it quickly entered the corporate graveyard, leaving behind unpaid bills and unhappy customers.[34]

The Liberty opposite is Comair. Headquartered in Cincinnati, this commuter airline in the mid-1970s began operations with limited service to Akron-Canton, Cleveland, Detroit, Michigan, and Evansville, Indiana. But aggressive management and a close relationship with Delta Air Lines resulted in the spectacular expansion of Comair. By the late 1990s its fleet of modern jet aircraft served scores of communities, often with frequent daily flights, from its principal base at the Greater Cincinnati Regional Airport and another one in Orlando, Florida. Along with ASA, Business Express, and Skywest, Comair became the "Delta Connection."[35]

By the end of the twentieth century aviation in Ohio had progressed fantastically from the time of the Wright brothers. Arguably the most notable betterment and monumental example of replacement technology began in the late 1950s with introduction of jet-powered commercial aircraft. These planes meant greater speed and range. The trunk carriers that served the state quickly entered the jet age. Capital Airlines, for one, successor to Pennsylvania and Pennsylvania Central airlines and later part of United, which by 1958 served Akron-Canton, Cleveland, Toledo, and Youngstown, proclaimed itself in September of that year to be the "World's No. 1 Jet-Prop Airline," with its fleet of Vickers Viscounts. A few years later Capital bragged of its purchase of nonprop jets, Boeing 720s. Although feeders often flew propeller craft, including the enduring DC-3, into the age of deregulation, the growing used market for jets, particularly prop jets, allowed virtually every commercial flight to and from the state by 1990 to be jet powered, either by straight or prop jet.[36]

As airplane service commonly increased and ticket prices generally decreased, more Ohioans flew. Nearly universally they preferred large jets. Ohioans, too, expected their airports to be able to accommodate flights in an efficient and safe manner, and this meant adequate runways, the latest radio and radar equipment, weather forecasters, and eventually sophisticated computers. State residents also wanted terminal services that could handle their personal needs, including modern baggage, dining, and parking facilities. Civic boosters, reminiscent of those during the railway age who had sought monuments to train travel, concurred. They demanded that their hometown airports be up-to-date showcases, thereby demonstrating to visitors that their communities were safe, convenient, and progressive, places of the future.[37]

Just as railroad depots evolved from simple structures to architectural marvels, airports in Ohio followed a similar pattern. The earliest airports were frequently sheds that adjoined grassy landing strips, not much different from the Wrights's complex at Huffman Prairie. A national guide to landing fields, prepared in 1923, listed ninety in Ohio, one of the largest numbers for any state. Most were designated "emergency" and contained directions and descriptions. Canton, for example, was noted as "Emergency; 800 ft. x 1500 ft.; west limits; good; lake 1 mi. N." The entry for Kenton read: "Emergency; inside track at fair grounds," and the one for Zanesville: "Emergency; 3 mi. NE; 900 ft. x 650 ft.; 'Zanesville' on building." The latter marking was not unique; there were many others. In the 1920s the Standard Ohio Company of Ohio, which sold such products as T-P Sohio Aero Oil, Red Crown Aviation Gasoline, and Sohio Ethyl Aviation Gasoline, as a navigational aid marked the roofs of its bulk plants and other buildings with the town's name and direction, noted by an arrow, to the nearest airport. With regular commercial aviation and an increasing volume of corporate and private traffic, better ground facilities became essential, but they cost more than civic groups, businesses, and others could be expected to finance. By 1930 municipal airports, built with public funds, were widespread. The U.S. Department of Commerce listed them in Akron, Belpre, Cincinnati, Cleveland, Gallipolis, Mansfield, Marietta, Middletown, Portsmouth, Springfield, Toledo, Van Wert, and Youngstown. Dayton, Defiance, and Fairfield claimed military installations.[38]

Development of Hopkins International Airport in Cleveland aptly represents the ongoing changes in aviation ground facilities in Ohio and shows once more how the state frequently led in transportation innovations. When Cleveland became the western terminus and soon thereafter a principal stop on the U.S. Army's transcontinental mail route, planes used Woodland Hills Park on the city's east side. This bothersome "snow belt" location was subsequently replaced by another eastside site, Glenn L. Martin Field, behind the Martin airplane manufacturing plant at 16800 St. Clair Avenue. But both landing strips lacked the lighting that the Army soon required for its proposed night flights and both needed major improvements.[39]

Cleveland civic leaders, worried that their community might lose its aviation prominence, wanted to build a state-of-the-art airport and preferably one removed from the worst snow squalls. Led by City Manager William Rolland Hopkins, the political establishment decided to

The modern art deco terminal at the "Port of Akron," located on the southeast side of the Rubber City, opened in the early 1930s. *(University of Akron Archives)*

make what would become Hopkins airport a publicly owned operation. Although by the mid-1920s Ohio had numerous examples of local "gas and water socialism," especially public electric light and water plants, municipalities lacked the legal right to construct airports. In early 1925 that roadblock disappeared when the general assembly empowered the city to use its bonding authority to build the facility. With this legislative green light, Cleveland named a blue-ribbon site-selection committee, which included Glenn Martin; Maj. Gen. Mason Patrick, head of the U.S. Air Service; and Capt. Eddie Rickenbacker, famous World War I flying ace from Columbus. With a recommendation in hand from these men, city council speedily approved a $1.25 million bond issue to purchase approximately one thousand acres of relatively flat land at Brookpark Road and Riverside Drive on the city's southwestern side and to erect the necessary improvements.[40]

The Cleveland airport rapidly took shape. Opening-day ceremonies occurred on July 1, 1925, highlighted by a "flying circus," with a crowd estimated at 250,000. The facility consisted of three small concrete block hangers, one of which later served as the airport's first administration building. In addition to these structures a graded one hundred acres of landing field, with appropriate lighting, handled a growing number of government, commercial, and private aircraft.[41]

As with other airports, changes repeatedly occurred. Most significantly, the runways, or "alleys," were replaced with a "landing mat," or "allway landing" field. "The entire field must be clear—no runways, no center lights, nothing that obstructs the free landing and departure of planes," explained a news release in 1929. "Runways have been found to be inpractible [sic]. With several planes arriving at or about the same time and all trying to land along the same runway that will keep them facing into the wind, you can see how congested the air would become. The pilots would have to wait for each other to land. That may be all right now, when there are not so many planes in the air, but it won't be in a few years from now." The allway landing mat, first grass and then asphalt with small sections of concrete, gave way during World War II to long (6,000 feet) reinforced concrete runways with set approaches. The nearby construction by the Fisher Aircraft Bomber Plant of heavy B-29s necessitated more substantially constructed takeoff paths.[42]

Although other airports employed the allway landing mat design, Cleveland was the first nationally to have a glass enclosed control tower with a 360-degree field of view. The structure was part of the art deco–style administration building that opened in 1929. Soon, too, the airport pioneered the use of two-way ground-to-air radio communications, which "established a model for air traffic control which was slowly accepted over the next 25 years."[43]

There were other improvements. A major addition to the terminal core took place in the late 1930s, responding to the giant increase in commercial air travel: 15,825 boardings in 1929 to 184,017 in 1936. Then greater usage prompted construction in the mid-1950s of a replacement facility; building the south concourse in 1970; and extensive renovations in 1978 and 1997, both of which involved expanded automobile parking.[44]

Related to betterments at the Cleveland airport (officially named the Hopkins Airport in 1961 and subsequently Cleveland Hopkins International Airport) was completion in 1968 by the Cleveland Transit Authority (CTA) of a high-speed rail line to the airport. This was one of the first modern rail links between a city center and an airport in the

This aerial view of Cleveland Hopkins International Airport dates from October 1974. *(Western Reserve Historical Society, Cleveland, Ohio)*

United States. Interestingly, the Cleveland & Southwestern Railway had tied Public Square with the airport (Riverside Drive) before the interurban's demise in 1931, and later the Cleveland Transit System operated a portion of the former trackage to accommodate visitors to the popular annual Cleveland Air Show. However, it was the success of the CTA line that prompted other cities, including Chicago, Philadelphia, St. Louis, and Washington, D.C., to follow suit.[45]

Part of the aviation history of Ohio has involved airports designed for private aircraft. Early flyers might have used a convenient "cow pasture" for their takeoffs and landings. With a dramatic increase in private planes after World War II, the federal government, through the Civil

Aeronautics Administration, began to provide funds on a matching basis for communities wanting to establish or to improve existing facilities. By 1950 a flurry of local airport construction was under way. Yet building failed to keep pace with need. In the fall of 1964 Gov. James A. Rhodes became distressed when he learned that fifty-eight of the state's eighty-eight counties lacked airports with paved runways and ten more could not accommodate business jets. Sensitive to the problem and convinced that "more industry is needed in Ohio," he included in the Capital Improvements Bond Issue financing for local airport projects. In the spring of 1965 voters approved this proposal.[46]

Although not every county received a new or improved facility, many did. Over a five-year span (1966–70) Ohio dedicated fifty airports, including the Neil Armstrong Airport, sponsored by the Auglaize County Airport Authority. Monies from the federal government also helped to provide Ohioans with these better facilities. By the 1990s the state had nearly two hundred public-use airports, usually with paved runways long enough to accommodate most business and pleasure craft. And Ohio boasted of being the foremost state in the nation in the ratio of paved, lighted runways to land area—one airport for every 207 square miles. This was fitting tribute to a state that claimed not only the Wright brothers but also John Glenn, the first American to orbit the earth, and Neil Armstrong, the first person to walk on the moon.[47]

Airways, along with high-speed roads, refurbished railroads, and well-maintained arteries, make Ohio as prepared for its transportation needs of the early twenty-first century as any American state. The tradition of Ohioans embracing better transport technology shows no sign of ending. The historic combinations of location, wealth, and leadership bode well for getting to and from and around "The Heart of It All."

NOTES

Chapter 1

1. Jay Abercrombie, *Ohio's Western Reserve: Discovering Nature and History in the Northeastern Corner* (Woodstock, Vt.: Backcountry Publications, 1996), 13–14; Henry E. Chambers, *Mississippi Valley Beginnings: An Outline of the Early History of the Earlier West* (New York: G. P. Putnam's Sons, 1922), 13–15; Archer Butler Hulbert, "The Indian Thoroughfares of Ohio," *Ohio Archaeological and Historical Publications* 8 (1900): 264–67.

2. Virgil T. Bogue, "The Girdled Road," *Ashtabula County Historical Society* 9 (June 1962): 1–2.

3. Ibid., 2–6; Lucy Hall Pancoast, "The Ohio Engineering Story: Girdled Road," *Ohio Engineer* 13 (June 1955): 19.

4. Charles L. Martzolff, "Zane's Trace," *Ohio Archaeological and Historical Publications* 12 (1904): 297–309.

5. See Hubert G. H. Wilhelm, *The Origin and Distribution of Settlement Groups: Ohio, 1850* (Athens, Ohio: Cutler Printing, 1982).

6. Norris F. Schneider, "The National Road: Main Street of America," *Ohio History* 83 (spring 1974): 123.

7. Richard T. Ferrell, "Internal-Improvement Projects in Southwestern Ohio, 1815–1834," *Ohio History* 80 (winter 1971): 12.

8. George W. Knepper, *Ohio and Its People* (Kent, Ohio: Kent State University Press, 1989), 111.

9. Farrell, "Internal-Improvement Projects in Southwestern Ohio, 1815–1834," 12; H. S. Perry, "A Story of the Ohio Highway," *Highway* 5 (February 1960): 47; William T. Utter, *The Frontier State, 1803–1825*, Vol. 2, *The History of Ohio* (Columbus: Ohio State Archaeological and Historical Society, 1942), 211–13.

10. Ethel Conrad, ed., "Touring Ohio in 1811: The Journal of Charity Rotch," *Ohio History* 99 (autumn 1990): 144; Emily Foster, ed., *The Ohio Frontier: An Anthology of Early Writings* (Lexington: University of Kentucky Press, 1996), 182.

11. George Rogers Taylor, *The Transportation Revolution, 1815–1860* (New York: Rinehart, 1951), 15–17; J. L. Ringwalt, *Development of Transportation Systems in the United States* (Philadelphia, Pa.: privately printed, 1888), 26–27.

12. Taylor, *The Transportation Revolution*, 16; Utter, *The Frontier State*, 206–7.

13. Knepper, *Ohio and Its People*, 145; Schneider, "The National Road," 118–19.

14. See Philip D. Jordan, *The National Road* (Indianapolis, Ind.: Bobbs-Merrill,

1948) and Karl Raitz, ed., *The National Road* (Baltimore, Md.: Johns Hopkins University Press, 1996). Thomas L. Harbin, "The National Road in Illinois," *Journal of the Illinois State Historical Society* 61 (1967): 16–17; Archer Butler Hulbert, "The Old National Road—The Historic Highways of America," *Ohio Archaeological and Historical Society Publications* 9 (1901): 436.

15. Schneider, "The National Road," 128–29.

16. Archer Butler Hulbert, *The Old National Road: A Chapter of American Expansion* (Columbus, Ohio: Press of F. J. Heer, 1901), 76–77; Schneider, "The National Road," 129, 135–36.

17. J. S. Buckingham, *The Eastern and Western States of America* (London: Fisher, Son & Co., 1842), 2:261, 291.

18. Schneider, "The National Road," 135. The basic idea of relays of mounted messages long predated the Ohio experiment, having been around at least since the Persian empire in the sixth century B.C.

19. Raitz, *The National Road*, 155.

20. *Wheeling (Virginia) Times and Advertiser*, June 10, 1845; *Mitchell's Traveler's Guide through the United States* (Philadelphia, Pa.: Mitchell & Hinman, 1837), 53–57.

21. Jordan, *The National Road*, 117–32.

22. See Paton Yoder, *Taverns and Travelers: Inns of the Early Midwest* (Bloomington: Indiana University Press, 1969), especially chap. 2.

23. Ibid., 85.

24. "William Renick and the Turnpike Road," *Pickaway County Historical Society* (winter 1965): 14–15.

25. N. B. Northrop, *Pioneer History of Medina County* (Medina, Ohio, 1861), 49.

26. *Weekly Chicago Democrat*, February 22, 1848; Remley J. Glass, "Early Transportation and the Plank Road," *Annals of Iowa* 21 (January 1939): 502–34; James H. Fairchild, *Oberlin: The Colony and the College, 1833–1883* (Oberlin, Ohio: E. J. Goodrich, 1883), 237.

27. *Altrurian (Denver, Colorado)*, January 1895.

28. *The Breeder's Gazette*, July 20, 1898; James J. Flink, *The Automobile Age* (Cambridge, Mass.: MIT Press, 1988), 3; *The Cincinnati Labor Exchange: A Brief Synopsis* (Cincinnati, Ohio: Cincinnati Labor Exchange, n.d.), 5, 7.

29. Schneider, "The National Road," 139; *The Cincinnati Labor Exchange*, 8–9.

30. David D. Van Tassel and John H. Grabowski, eds., *The Encyclopedia of Cleveland History* (Bloomington: Indiana University Press, 1987), 736.

31. Perry, "A Story of the Ohio Highway," 47; David A. Simmons, "Ohio Bridges from 1850 to 1950: Reflections of Society," *Old Northwest* 12 (spring 1986): 108–9. In 1909 U.S. Congressman Albert Douglas from Ohio captured, in part, why Ohioans liked the automobile: "It is this independence and feeling that you are not imposing upon a good horse as well as the lust for 'pushing on' that are elements in the pleasure of traveling by automobile." Albert Douglas, "Auto Trip over the Old National Road," *Ohio Archaeological and Historical Society Publications* 18 (1909): 506.

32. Wayne E. Fuller, "The Ohio Road Experiment, 1913–1916," *Ohio History* 74 (1965): 16–20, 26.

33. See *The Lincoln Highway: The Story of a Crusade That Made Transportation History* (New York: Dodd, Mead & Co., 1935) and Drake Hokanson, *The Lincoln Highway: Main Street across America* (Iowa City: University of Iowa Press, 1989).

34. Hokanson, *The Lincoln Highway,* 47.

35. James J. Flink, *The Car Culture* (Cambridge, Mass.: MIT Press, 1975), 187; John B. Rae, *The Road and the Car in American Life* (Cambridge, Mass.: MIT Press, 1971), 36–39, 74.

36. *The Complete Official Road Guide of the Lincoln Highway* (Detroit, Mich.: Lincoln Highway Association, 1924), 258–85; Frederick F. Van de Water, *The Family Flivvers to Frisco* (New York: D. Appleton & Co., 1927), 69–70.

37. Ruth Winters Odel, *Early Railroad Transportation in Jackson County, Ohio* (Barboursville, W.Va.: privately printed, 1986), 28.

38. Wayne G. Broehl, Jr., *Trucks, Trouble and Triumph: The Norwalk Truck Line Company* (New York: Prentice-Hall, 1954), 19–23; Merrill J. Roberts, "The Motor Transportation Revolution," *Business History Review* 30 (1965): 59–62; P. J. Russell, *The Motor Wagon: The Origin and History of Long-Distance Truck Transport* (Akron: Pioneer Motor Traffic Club of Akron, Ohio, 1971), 46. See also William R. Childs, *Trucking and the Public Interest: The Emergence of Federal Regulation, 1914–1940* (Knoxville: University of Tennessee Press, 1985).

39. Albert E. Meier and John P. Hoschek, *Over the Road: A History of Intercity Bus Transportation in the United States* (Upper Montclair, N.J.: Motor Bus Society, 1975), 1–9; Burton B. Crandall, *The Growth of the Intercity Bus Industry* (Syracuse, N.Y.: Sycracuse University, 1954), 6–13.

40. Green Line Bus Company public timetable, January 1, 1918.

41. Great Lakes Stages, Inc., public timetable, May 1, 1929; Great Lakes Stages, Inc., folder, "An Now—the Sleeping Coach," n.d.

42. Carlton Jackson, *Hounds of the Road: A History of the Greyhound Bus Company* (Bowling Green, Ohio: Bowling Green University Popular Press, 1984), 20–23, 39–58; *Ohio Official Motor Coach Schedules* (Columbus: Ohio Motor Bus Association, July 15, 1937), 23–32.

43. Jack Keenan, *Cincinnati & Lake Erie Railroad: Ohio's Great Interurban System* (San Marino, Calif.: Golden West Books, 1974), 205; George W. Hilton and John F. Due, *The Electric Interurban Railways in America* (Stanford, Calif.: Stanford University Press, 1960), 231–32.

44. See *America's Highways, 1776–1976: A History of the Federal-Aid Program* (Washington, D.C.: U.S. Department of Transportation, Federal Highway Administration, 1976).

45. Mark H. Rose, *Interstate: Express Highway Politics, 1941–1956* (Lawrence: Regents Press of Kansas, 1979), 30–31.

46. See *America's Highways, 1776–1876; Serving Ohio's Traffic* (Columbus, Ohio: Wilbur Smith and Associates, 1962), 2–18.

47. *Wheels in Motion* (Berea: Ohio Turnpike Commission, 1996), 3.

48. Ibid.; *Ohio Turnpike Commission Comprehensive Annual Financial Report 1986* (Berea: Ohio Turnpike Commission, 1987), 8–9; *Ohio Turnpike Commission Annual Report 1975* (Berea: Ohio Turnpike Commission, 1976), 4.

49. *Ohio Turnpike Commission Annual Report 1965* (Berea: Ohio Turnpike Commission, 1966), 8; *Ohio Turnpike Commission Comprehensive Annual Financial Report, 1996* (Berea: Ohio Turnpike Commission, 1997), 7–8, 16.

50. *Ohio Turnpike Commission Annual Report 1976* (Berea: Ohio Turnpike Commission, 1977), 5.

51. *Ohio Department of Highways: 4-Year Report of the Governor, 1959–1962* (Columbus: Ohio Department of Highways, 1963), 15.

52. Flink, *The Automobile Age*, 371–73.

53. Knepper, *Ohio and Its People*, 402–3.

54. Richard Wagner, *Golden Wheels: The Story of the Automobiles Made in Cleveland and Northeastern Ohio, 1892–1932* (Cleveland, Ohio: Western Reserve Historical Society and Cleveland Automobile Club, 1975), 3–24; Van Tassel and Grabowski, *The Encyclopedia of Cleveland History*, 1056–57.

55. Wager, *Golden Wheels*, 25–45, 53–69, 89–96, 256, 261–62, 265; Cornelius W. Hauk, "Cincinnati—Rival to Detroit? A History of the Automobile in Cincinnati," *Eleventh Midwest Concours d' Elegance for the Arthritis Foundation*, June 19, 1988; Van Tassell and Grabowski, *The Encyclopedia of Cleveland History*, 57–59.

56. Rosemary S. Hritsko, "The White Motor Story" (Ph.D. diss., University of Akron, 1988), 236–484.

Chapter 2

1. Richard C. Wade, *The Urban Frontier: Pioneer Life in Early Pittsburgh, Cincinnati, Lexington, Louisville, and St. Louis* (Chicago: University of Chicago Press, 1964), 66; Alice Wright, *The Ohio River* (Marietta, Ohio: Prettit-Seevers Printing, 1964), 3.

2. Charles Henry Ambler, *A History of Transportation in the Ohio Valley* (Glendale, Calif.: Arthur H. Clark, 1932), 21; Ethel Conrad, ed., "Touring Ohio in 1811: The Journal of Charity Rotch," *Ohio History* 99 (autumn 1990): 158; Henry S. Tanner, *A Description of the Canals and Rail Roads of the United States* (New York: T. R. Tanner & J. Disturnell, 1839), 207.

3. Wright, *The Ohio River*, 4–5; Ambler, *A History of Transportation in the Ohio Valley*, 25–26; H. E. Chambers, *Mississippi Valley Beginnings* (New York: G. P. Putnam's Sons, 1922), 22.

4. Leland D. Baldwin, *The Keelboat Age on Western Waters* (Pittsburgh, Pa.: University of Pittsburgh Press, 1941), 47–50, 52; Charles B. Duncan, *The Beautiful Ohio* (privately printed, 1971), 8; Timothy Flint, *Recollections of the Last Ten Years Passed in Occasional Residences and Journeyings in the Valley of the Mississippi*

(Boston: Cummins, Hilliard, 1826), 13; William J. Petersen, *Steamboating on the Upper Mississippi* (Iowa City: State Historical Society of Iowa, 1968), 48–56.

5. Duncan, *The Beautiful Ohio*, 8; John A. Jakle, *Images of the Ohio Valley: A Historical Geography of Travel, 1740 to 1860* (New York: Oxford University Press, 1977), 27; Wright, *The Ohio River*, 7.

6. Brian P. Birch, "Taking the Breaks and Working the Boats: An English Family's Impressions of Ohio in the 1830's," *Ohio History* 95 (winter–spring 1986): 107.

7. Jakle, *Images of the Ohio*, 28; Duncan, *The Beautiful Ohio*, 6.

8. Patricia Mooney Melvin, "Steamboats West: The Legacy of a Transportation Revolution," *Old Northwest* 7 (winter 1981–82): 342.

9. Ambler, *A History of Transportation in the Ohio Valley*, 120–21; *Liberty Hall (Cincinnati, Ohio)*, October 30, 1811.

10. Ambler, *A History of Transportation in the Ohio Valley*, 125–26; Louis C. Hunter, *Steamboats on the Western Rivers: An Economic and Technological History* (Cambridge, Mass.: Harvard University Press, 1949), 4, 19; Melvin, "Steamboats West," 342.

11. Ambler, *A History of Transportation in the Ohio Valley*, 127; Frederick C. Gamst, ed., *Early American Railroads: Franz Anton Ritter von Gerstner's Die innern Communication (1842–1843)* (Stanford, Calif.: Stanford University Press, 1997), 416.

12. Jay Mack Gamble, *Steamboats on the Muskingum* (Staten Island: Steamship Historical Society of America, 1971), 46; Wade, *The Urban Frontier*, 192, 329–30.

13. Melvin, "Steamboats West," 342.

14. Wright, *The Ohio River*, 26–27; Leslie S. Henshaw, "Early Steamboat Travel on the Ohio River," *Ohio Archaeological and Historical Publications* 20 (1911): 380; Jakle, *Images of the Ohio Valley*, 32–33.

15. Wright, *The Ohio River*, 18–20.

16. Duncan, *The Beautiful Ohio*, 25–27.

17. K. Austin Kerr, *American Railroad Politics, 1914–1914: Rates, Wages, and Efficiency* (Pittsburgh, Pa.: University of Pittsburgh Press, 1986), 13–16; John F. Stover, *The Life and Decline of the American Railroad* (New York: Oxford University Press, 1970), 161.

18. Ambler, *A History of Transportation in the Ohio Valley*, 423–48; Thomas F. Barton, "Twenty-five Years' Use of the 9-Foot Ohio River Channel," *Economic Geography* 33 (1957): 41–49.

19. John H. White and Robert J. White, *The Island Queen: Cincinnati's Excursion Steamer* (Akron, Ohio: University of Akron Press, 1995), 16–21, 76–94, 100–106.

20. See James Coomer, *Life on the Ohio* (Lexington: University of Kentucky Press, 1997); Knepper, *Ohio and Its People*, 461.

21. James Oliver Curwood, *The Great Lakes* (New York: G. P. Putnam's Sons, 1909), 159–74.

22. Grace Hunter, "Life on Lake Erie a Century Ago," *Inland Seas* 22 (fall 1966): 197.

23. H. Roger Grant, *Land, Air, Water: Transportation and Ohio* (Columbus: State Library of Ohio, 1979), 5.

24. "Conneaut Harbor," *Ashtabula County Historical Society Quarterly Bulletin* 10 (March 15, 1963): 57.

25. Grace Hunter, "Life on Lake Erie a Century Ago," *Inland Seas* 22 (spring 1966): 19, 23; Gamst, *Early American Railroads,* 415; Taylor, *The Transportation Revolution,* 61–62.

26. Hunter, "Life on Lake Erie a Century Ago," 24; Bernard E. Ericson, "The Evolution of Great Lakes Ships," *Inland Seas* 25 (fall 1969): 199.

27. Walter Havinghurst, *The Long Ships Passing: The Story of the Great Lakes* (New York: Macmillan, 1943), 121–44.

28. J. S. Buckingham, *The Eastern and Western States of America* (London, England: Fisher, Son & Co., 1843), 3:431.

29. Hunter, "Life on Lake Erie a Century Ago," 21; Gamst, *Early American Railroads,* 415–16.

30. Gamst, *Early American Railroads,* 417.

31. Hunter, "Life on Lake Erie a Century Ago," 25–26.

32. Ericson, "The Evolution of Great Lakes Ships," 200.

33. Ibid.; John N. Dickinson, *To Build a Canal: Sault Ste. Marie, 1853–1854 and After* (Oxford, Ohio: Miami University Press, 1981), 121.

34. Ericson, "The Evolution of Great Lakes Ships," 200–201.

35. Ibid., 202.

36. Ibid., 203–8; John and Alice Durant, *Pictorial History of American Ships* (New York: A. S. Barnes Co., 1953), 195–98.

37. Gary S. Dewar, "Changes in the Existing Bulk Fleet, 1945–1970," *Inland Seas* 45 (summer 1989): 95, 97–103; David D. Van Tassel and John J. Grabowski, eds., *The Encyclopedia of Cleveland History* (Bloomington: Indiana University Press, 1987), 658; T. A. Sykora, "1972—A New Era in Great Lakes Transportation," *Inland Seas* 28 (summer 1972): 131–33.

38. Dewar, "Changes in the Existing Bulk Fleet," 107–8; Richard J. Wright, *Freshwater Whales: A History of the American Ship Building Company and Its Predecessors* (Kent, Ohio: Kent State University Press, 1969), 245, 253.

39. *Wall Street Journal,* March 12, 1998.

40. B. D. Tallamy and T. M. Sedweck, *The St. Lawrence Seaway Project* (Buffalo, N.Y.: Niagara Frontier Planning Board, 1940), 3–6. See also William R. Willoughby, *The St. Lawrence Waterway: A Study in Politics and Diplomacy* (Madison: University of Wisconsin Press, 1961).

41. Tallamy and Sedweck, *The St. Lawrence Seaway Project,* 63.

42. Jay C. Ehle, *Cleveland's Harbor: The Cleveland-Cuyahoga County Port Authority* (Kent, Ohio: Kent State University Press, 1996), 39–47, 158–82.

43. *Wall Street Journal,* March 12, 1998.

44. J. R. Luoma, "Biography of a Lake," *Audubon* 98 (September–October

1996): 66–72; Glen Zorpette, "Mussel Mayhem, Continued," *Scientific American* 275 (August 1996): 22–23.

45. "Conneaut Harbor," 5–8.

46. Van Tassel and Grabowski, *The Encylopedia of Cleveland History,* 531; "Unloaded in 7 ½ Hours," *Erie Railroad Magazine* 43 (October 1947): 21; Frank E. Kirby and A. P. Rankin, "The Bulk Freighter of the Great Lakes," *Inland Seas* 34 (fall 1978): 221–22.

47. *The Proposed Lake Erie Ohio River Canal* (Pittsburgh, Pa.: U.S. Army Engineer District, 1962), 2–18.

48. Detroit and Buffalo Steamboat Company public timetable, March 26, 1908.

49. The Detroit & Cleveland Steam Navigation Company public timetable, April 1891; Van Tassel and Grabowski, *The Encyclopedia of Cleveland History,* 609; James A. Toman and Blaine S. Hays, *Horse Trails to Regional Rails: The Story of Public Transit in Greater Cleveland* (Kent, Ohio: Kent State University Press, 1996), 98.

50. Francis Duncan, "The Story of the D&C: The Modernization of the Corporation, 1898–1914," *Inland Seas* 2 (1954): 171–76.

51. Cleveland & Buffalo Transit Company public timetable, May 1, 1927.

52. Van Tassel and Grabowski, *The Encyclopedia of Cleveland History,* 609; *Sandusky (Ohio) Register-Star-News,* November 25, 1947; A. T. Zillmer, "The Lake Erie Excursion Company," *Inland Seas* 16 (winter 1960): 275–82; Toman and Hays, *Horse Trails to Regional Rails,* 258.

53. Van Tassel and Grabowski, *The Encyclopedia of Cleveland History,* 607.

Chapter 3

1. George Knepper, *Ohio and Its People* (Kent, Ohio: Kent State University Press, 1989), 6–7.

2. David H. Mould, *Dividing Lines: Canals, Railroads and Urban Rivalry in Ohio's Hocking Valley* (Dayton, Ohio: Wright State University Press, 1994), 13; "Ohio Canals," *Ohio Archaeological and Historical Society Publications* 34 (January 1928): 66–69.

3. Mould, *Dividing Lines,* 12–13; George White Dial, "The Construction of the Ohio Canals," *Ohio Archaeological and Historical Society Publications* 12 (1904): 462–63.

4. John S. Still, "Ethan Allen Brown and Ohio's Canal System," *Ohio History* 66 (January 1957): 22–56.

5. Jack Gieck, *A Photo Album of Ohio's Canal Era, 1825–1913* (Kent, Ohio: Kent State University Press, 1988), 1; Chester E. Finn, "The Ohio Canals: Public Enterprise on the Frontier," *Ohio State Archaeological and Historical Quarterly* 51 (1942): 5.

6. Ronald E. Shaw, *Canals for a Nation: The Canal Era in the United States, 1790–1860* (Lexington: University of Kentucky Press, 1990), 1–29; Ronald E. Shaw, "Canals in the Early Republic: A Review of Recent Literature," *Journal of the Early Republic* 4 (summer 1984): 123.

7. Ronald E. Shaw, *Erie Water West: A History of the Erie Canal, 1792–1854* (Lexington: University of Kentucky Press, 1996).

8. Harry N. Scheiber, "The Ohio Canal Movement, 1820–1825," *Ohio History* 69 (January 1960): 231–56.

9. Harry N. Scheiber, *Ohio Canal Era: A Case Study of Government and the Economy, 1820–1861* (Athens: Ohio University Press, 1969), 16–54.

10. Dial, "The Construction of the Ohio Canals," 465–66.

11. Harry N. Scheiber, "Public Canal Finance and State Banking in Ohio, 1827–1837," *Indiana Magazine of History* 65 (June 1969): 119–32; "Ohio Canals," 62–64.

12. Scheiber, *Ohio Canal Era,* 52–54; George W. Knepper, *Akron: City at the Summit* (Tulsa, Okla.: Continental Heritage Press, 1981), 24–26.

13. Shaw, *Canals for a Nation,* 127–29; *Cleveland Plain Dealer,* May 22, 1932.

14. John J. George Jr., "The Miami Canal," *Ohio Archaeological and Historical Society Publications* 36 (1927): 92–106.

15. Scheiber, *Ohio Canal Era,* 88–113.

16. Gieck, *A Photo Album of Ohio's Canal Era,* 125–26; C. P. McClelland and C. C. Huntington, *History of the Ohio Canals: Their Construction, Cost, Use and Partial Abandonment* (Columbus: Ohio State Archaeological and Historical Society, 1905), 34–38, 42.

17. Paul Fatout, *Indiana Canals* (West Lafayette, Ind.: Purdue University Studies, 1972), 42; Shaw, *Canals for a Nation,* 139–42.

18. *History of the Ohio Canals,* 31, 38.

19. Mould, *Dividing Lines,* 17–18.

20. McClelland and Huntington, *History of the Ohio Canals,* 40; Gieck, *A Photo Album of Ohio's Canal Era,* 210–12; Mould, *Dividing Lines,* 17–48.

21. Frank W. Trevorrow, *Ohio's Canals* (Oberlin, Ohio: privately printed, 1973), 23, 26, 28–29.

22. *History of the Ohio Canals,* 39; Scheiber, *Ohio Canal Era,* 127.

23. Gieck, *A Photo Album of Ohio's Canal Era,* 213–16; Trevorrow, *Ohio's Canals,* 21–22; McClelland and Huntington, *History of the Ohio Canals,* 40.

24. Harry N. Scheiber, "The Pennsylvania & Ohio Canal: Transport Innovation, Mixed Enterprise, and Urban Commercial Rivalry, 1825–1861," *The Old Northwest* (summer 1980): 107–9.

25. Ibid., 110–29; Harold E. Davis, "The Pennsylvania-Ohio Canal, 1823–1877," *Publications of the Hiram Historical Society* 1 (1929).

26. R. Max Gard and William H. Vodrey Jr., *The Sandy and Beaver Canal* (East Liverpool, Ohio: East Liverpool Historical Society, 1952), 11–25.

27. Ibid., 88–90, 120–24; W. H. Van Fossan, "Sandy and Beaver Canal," *Ohio State Archaeological and Historical Quarterly* 55 (1942): 165–77.

28. Gard and Vodrey, *The Sandy and Beaver Canal*, 141.

29. Trevorrow, *Ohio's Canals*, 37, 39–40; Fatout, *Indian Canals*, 149–55.

30. Charles E. Frohman, "The Milan Canal," *Ohio Archaeological and Historical Quarterly* 57 (July 1948): 237–46; Gieck, *A Photo Album of Ohio's Canal Era*, 203.

31. Scheiber, *Ohio Canal Era*, 79, 140–58.

32. Henry S. Tanner, *A Description of the Canals and Rail Roads of the United States* (New York: T. R. Tanner and J. Disturnell, 1840), 211.

33. Gard and Vodrey, *The Sandy and Beaver Canal*, 125–34, 152, 157–60, 172–75.

34. McClelland and Huntington, *History of the Ohio Canals*, 48–51; Gieck, *A Photo Album of Ohio's Canal Era*, 278–82.

35. McClelland and Huntington, *History of the Ohio Canals*, 47–48.

36. See, for example, Scheiber, "The Pennsylvania & Ohio Canal," 126–29, and Earl J. Heydinger, "The Pennsylvania and Ohio Canal, Part II," *Towpaths* 5 (July 1967): 29–31.

37. McClelland and Huntington, *History of the Ohio Canals*, 51, 55–56; Knepper, *Akron*, 97.

38. Scheiber, "The Pennsylvania & Ohio Canal," 119–21; Mould, *Dividing Lines*, 77–78.

39. George Perkins, "The Ohio Canal: An Account of Its Completion to Chillicothe," *Ohio Archaeological and Historical Quarterly* 34 (October 1925): 601–2.

40. Ernest M. Teagarden, "Builders of the Ohio Canal, 1825–1832," *Inland Seas* 19 (1963): 96; Knepper, *Akron*, 38.

41. See Gieck, *A Photo Album of Ohio's Canal Era*.

42. Ibid., 266.

43. Kenneth L. Nichols, "In Order of Appearance: Akron's Theaters, 1840–1940" (master's thesis, University of Akron, 1968), 17–22.

44. Shaw, *Canals for a Nation*, 153–54.

45. Gieck, *A Photo Album of Ohio's Canal Era*, 37.

46. Frederick C. Gamst, ed., *Early American Railroads: Franz Anton Ritter von Gerstner's Die innern Communication (1842–1843)* (Stanford, Calif.: Stanford University Press), 388; Fatout, *Indiana Canals*, 118.

Chapter 4

1. Ruth Winters Odel, *Early Railroad Transportation in Jackson County, Ohio* (Barboursville, W. Va.: privately printed, 1986), 131–32.

2. H. Roger Grant, *Ohio's Railway Age in Postcards* (Akron, Ohio: University of Akron Press, 1996), 7.

3. Paul F. Laning, "Frontier Railroads in Ohio's Great Lakes Region," *Inland Seas* 10 (1954): 182; Paul F. Laning, "Sandusky and Cleveland—Railroad Rivals in the 1850's," *Inland Seas* 28 (fall 1972): 190.

4. R. S. Kayler, "Ohio Railroads," *Ohio Archaeological and Historical Society Publications* 9 (1901): 189–92; John Prixton, *The Marietta and Cincinnati Railroad, 1843–1883: A Case Study in American Railroad Expansion* (University Park: Pennsylvania State University Studies, No. 17, 1966), 3; Harry N. Scheiber, "Urban Rivalry and Internal Improvements in the Old Northwest, 1820–1860," *Ohio History* 71 (October 1962): 236.

5. *Michigan (Monroe) Sentinel,* May 21, 1834; *Detroit Journal and Advertiser,* December 14, 1835; Alvin Harlow, *Road of the Century* (New York: Creative Age Press, 1947), 247.

6. Frederick C. Gamst, ed., *Early American Railroads: Franz Anton Ritter von Gerstner's Die innern Communication (1842–1843)* (Stanford, Calif.: Stanford University Press, 1997), 461–66; *Toledo Blade,* April 21, 1841.

7. John M. Killits, ed., *Toledo and Lucas County, Ohio, 1623–1923* (Chicago: S. J. Clarke, 1923), 542.

8. B. F. Prince, "General Mason and His Letter on Railroads," *Ohio Archaeological and Historical Publications* 17 (1908): 257.

9. Gamst, *Early American Railroads,* 398–408; John F. Stover, *Iron Road to the West: American Railroads in the 1850's* (New York: Columbia University Press, 1978), 114–58.

10. Walter Rumsey Marvin, "The Steubenville and Indiana Railroad: The Pennsylvania's Middle Route To the Middle West," *Ohio Historical Quarterly* 66 (January 1957): 11; Albro Martin, *Railroads Triumphant: The Growth, Rejection & Rebirth of a Vital American Force* (New York: Oxford University Press, 1992), 12–17. The desire to forge dependable, long-distance rail links explains why in 1854 the head of the Columbus & Xenia Rail Road urged the opening of the Central Ohio Rail Road for the latter's connections to the East: "Permit me to call your attention to the importance of an early completion of your road to Wheeling with reference to the 'through' freight business. Large quantities of pork, beef, lard, bacon, horses, mules, cattle, sheep, hogs, etc., etc., have been offered to us for transportation to an Eastern market, which we have been compelled to decline on account of the non-completion of your road." Daniel L. Frizzi Jr., *An American Railroad Portrait: People, Places and Pultney* (Bellaire, Ohio: privately printed, 1993), 61.

11. Gamst, *Early American Railroads,* 408–13; Laning, "Frontier Railroads in Ohio's Great Lakes Region," 184; C. P. Leland, "The Ohio Railroad: That Famous Structure Built on Stilts," *Western Reserve Historical Society Tracts,* Tract 81, 1892, 265–84.

12. H. Roger Grant, *Erie Lackawanna: Death of an American Railroad, 1938–1992* (Stanford, Calif.: Stanford University Press, 1994), 2–3; Leland, "The Ohio Railroad," 284.

13. Stover, *Iron Road to the West,* 129–30.

14. Ibid., 136–37; Grant, *Erie Lackawanna,* 2; Edward Harold Mott, *Between the Ocean and the Lakes: The Story of Erie* (New York: John S. Collins, 1899), 363–65.

15. H. Roger Grant, *Living in the Depot: The Two-Story Railroad Station* (Iowa City: University of Iowa Press, 1993), 7; Gamst, ed., *Early American Railroads,* 405.

16. H. Roger Grant, "The Combination Railroad Station in the Old Northwest," *Old Northwest* 4 (June 1978): 95–118.

17. Ibid.

18. Eugene O. Porter, "Financing Ohio's Pre-Civil War Railroads," *Ohio Archaeological and Historical Quarterly* 57 (July 1948): 215–26. For another example of system building, see Ivan M. Tribe, "Dream and Reality in Southern Ohio: The Development of the Columbus and Hocking Valley Railroad," *Old Northwest* 4 (December 1978): 337–51.

19. George H. Minor, *The Erie System: The Organization and Corporate History* (Cleveland, Ohio: Erie Railroad, 1938), 408–10; Edward Hungerford, *Men of Erie: A Story of Human Effort* (New York: Random House, 1946), 180–210; *History of Allen County, Ohio* (Chicago: Warner, Beer & Co., 1885), 399.

20. George W. Hilton, *American Narrow Gauge Railroads* (Stanford, Calif.: Stanford University Press, 1990), 75–117, 462–79.

21. John A. Rehor, *The Nickel Plate Story* (Milwaukee, Wis.: Kalmbach, 1965), 288–97, 312–14.

22. Hilton, *American Narrow Gauge Railroads,* 101–11.

23. Ibid., 110.

24. Ibid., 469; Norris F. Schneider, *Bent, Zigzag and Crooked: Ohio's Last Narrow Gauge Railroad* (Zanesville, Ohio: privately printed, 1960), 3–4, 6–9, 11–13, 15–16, 18–20.

25. Sherwood Anderson, *Sherwood Anderson's Memoirs* (New York: Brace & Co., 1942), 36.

26. *Suburban Homes* (Cincinnati: Baltimore & Ohio Southwestern Railroad Co., 1891), 7–25.

27. H. Roger Grant and Charles W. Bohi, *The Country Railroad Station in America* (Boulder, Colo.: Pruett, 1978), 3–10.

28. Ibid.; D. C. Saunders, *The Brasspounder* (New York: Hawthorn Books, 1978), 95.

29. Scott D. Trostel, *Bradford the Railroad Town: A Railroad Town History of Bradford, Ohio* (Fletcher, Ohio: Cam-Tech Publishing, 1987), 16–18.

30. John F. Moore, *The Story of the Railroad "Y"* (New York: Association Press, 1930).

31. Eugene H. Roseboom and Francis P. Weisenburger, *A History of Ohio* (Columbus: Ohio Historical Society, 1967), 257–58.

32. H. Roger Grant, "Depot: Economy and Style at Trackside," *Timeline* 1 (October 1984): 62.

33. Ibid.

34. Ibid.

35. Ibid., 63.

36. Ibid.

37. *Erie Railroad: Showing Changes from 1901 to 1914, Inclusive* (New York: Erie Railroad Co., n.d.), 3.

38. "History of the Akron, Canton & Youngstown Railroad Company," n.d., Akron, Canton & Youngstown Railroad papers, University of Akron Archives, Akron, Ohio (hereafter cited as AC&Y papers); *Poor's Manual of Railroads* (New York: Poor's, 1920), 1852.

39. Edward T. Heald, *The Stark County Story,* 4 vols. (Canton, Ohio: Stark County Historical Society, 1950), 2:596–99; Z. W. Davis to H. B. Stewart, memorandum, ca., 1908, in AC&Y papers; "Report on the Proposal to Extend the Akron, Canton & Youngstown Railway," 1913, 3–4, in AC&Y papers.

40. F. A. Seiberling memorandum, n.d., in AC&Y papers; A. W. Hochberg oral history, August 14, 1973, in AC&Y papers.

41. Ian S. Haberman, *The Van Sweringens of Cleveland: The Biography of an Empire* (Cleveland, Ohio: Western Reserve Historical Society, 1979), 50–64; James Toman, *The Shaker Heights Rapid Transit* (Glendale, Calif.: Interurban Press, 1990), 11–12; Herbert H. Harwood Jr., "Oris Paxton Van Sweringen [and] Mantis James Van Sweringen," in Keith L. Bryant Jr., ed., *Railroads in the Age of Regulation, 1900–1980* (New York: Facts-on-File Publications, 1988), 450–53.

42. Harwood, "Oris Paxton Van Sweringen [and] Mantis James Van Sweringen," 454–56; Richard Saunders, *The Railroad Mergers and the Coming of Conrail* (Westport, Conn.: Greenwood Press, 1978), 48–49.

43. "Memorandum on the Van Sweringen Railroads," n.d., 1–6, Barriger Collection, Mercantile Library, St. Louis, Missouri.

44. Ibid.

45. Harwood, "Oris Paxton Van Sweringen [and] Mantis James Van Sweringen," 456.

46. Ibid.; Haberman, *The Van Sweringens of Cleveland,* 105–20.

47. Harwood, "Oris Paxton Van Sweringen [and] Mantis James Van Sweringen," 457–58.

48. *Moody's Manual of Investments* (New York: Moody Investors Service, 1946), 855.

49. Edmund Keilty, *Doodlebug Country: The Rail Motor Car on the Class 1 Railroads of the United States* (Glendale, Calif.: Interurban Press, 1982), 29–33, 139–44.

50. *Yearbook of Railroad Information* (New York: Committee on Public Relations of the Eastern Railroad, 1936), 3; *Yearbook of Railroad Information* (New York: Eastern Railroad Presidents Conference, 1956), 7.

51. Interview with J. Gary Dillon, Akron, Ohio, December 8, 1995; Erie Railroad Company pamphlet, June 1943, 1.

52. John Grover, "Highballing Oil to the East," *Erie Railroad Magazine* 38 (October 1942): 8, 29.

53. Carroll L. V. Meeks, *The Railroad Station: An Architectural History* (New

Haven, Conn.: Yale University Press, 1956), 144, 160; Rehor, *The Nickel Plate Story*, 356–85.

54. H. Roger Grant, *Land, Air, Water: Transportation and Ohio* (Columbus: State Library of Ohio, 1979), 11–12.

55. *The Official Guide of the Railways* (New York: National Railway Publication Co., October 1951), 282–84, 342–45, 347–49, 351–52; *The Official Guide of the Railways* (New York: National Railway Publication Co., February 1962), 200–204; Amtrak public timetable, May 1, 1971; Grant, *Erie Lackawanna*, 166.

56. Interview with Gregory W. Maxwell, Moreland Hills, Ohio, June 12, 1989.

57. See Saunders, *The Railroad Mergers and the Coming of Conrail.*

58. Ibid., 95, 103–5, 120–21, 141–48, 178–80; Gus Welty, ed., *Era of the Giants: The New Railroad Merger Movement* (Omaha, Nebr.: Simmons-Boardman Publishing, 1982), 86–95.

59. Grant, *Erie Lackawanna*, 153, 161; interview with Jervis Langdon Jr., Akron, Ohio, April 26, 1990.

60. H. Roger Grant, "Erie Lackawanna: An Ohio Railroad," *Ohio History* 101 (winter–spring 1992): 16.

61. Ibid., 16–17.

62. Grant, *Erie Lackawanna*, 206–7, 212.

63. Welty, *Era of the Giants; RailOhio: The Ohio Rail Plan* (Columbus: Ohio Rail Transportation Authority, 1978), vi–vii, ix; Don L. Hofsommer, *Grand Trunk Corporation: Canadian National Railways in the United States, 1971–1992* (East Lansing: Michigan State University Press, 1995), 79–92.

64. See *American Shortline Railway Guide, 5th Edition* (Waukesha, Wis.: Kalmbach, 1996), 89, 233–35, 326, 346; interview with Jerry Jacobson, Akron, Ohio, December 2, 1994.

65. "Chronology of Ohio's High Speed Passenger System," Ohio High Speed Rail Authority, n.d; "History of the Ohio High Speed Rail Project," Ohio High Speed Rail Authority, n.d.

66. Ibid.

67. Greg Smith and Karen-Lee Ryan, *700 Great Rail-Trails* (Washington, D.C.: Rails-to-Trails Conservancy, 1995), 88–92.

68. See *Ohio Rail Development Commission: The Year in Review* (Columbus: Ohio Rail Development Commission, 1997). "Ohio Rail Map," Ohio Department of Transportation, 1996.

Chapter 5

1. Bessie Louise Pierce, *A History of Chicago*, Vol. 3, *The Rise of a Modern City, 1871–1893* (Chicago: University of Chicago Press, 1957), 506; Thomas R. Bullard, *The Columbian Intramural Railway: A Pioneer Elevated Line* (Oak Park, Ill.: pri-

vately printed, 1987), 3–7, 9, 12–13, 16, 18; Columbia Intramural Railway public timetable, 1893.

2. John R. Stevens, ed., *Pioneers of Electric Railroading* (New York: Electric Railroaders' Association, 1991), 1–8.

3. Ibid., xvii–xviii; George W. Hilton and John F. Due, *The Electric Interurban Railways in America* (Stanford, Calif.: Stanford University Press, 1960), 4–9.

4. Hilton and Due, *The Electric Interurban Railways in America*, 9, 21, 56, 71, 265; James M. Blower and Robert S. Korach, *The NOT&L Story* (Chicago: Central Electric Railfans' Association, 1966), 30; R. G. Morrison, *The Sandusky, Milan and Norwalk Electric Railway* (Cleveland, Ohio: privately printed, 1963).

5. Guy Morrison Walker, *The Why and How of Interurban Railways* (Chicago: Kenfield, 1904), 3–4; "The Farmer and the Interurban," *Street Railway Journal* 28 (October 6, 1906): 1497; Lake Shore Electric public timetable, September 7, 1909.

6. James Glen, "The Interurban Trolley Flyers," *World's Work* (January 1907): 8406–7; Samuel E. Moffett, "The War on the Locomotive: The Marvelous Development of the Trolley Car System," *McClure's Magazine* 20 (March 1903): 451–62.

7. H. Roger Grant, "Interurban!" *Timeline* 3(April–May 1986): 18, 29; William D. Middleton, "Electric Railway Freight," *Railroad History* 151(autumn 1980): 35.

8. George W. Hilton, "The Wrong Track," *Invention & Technology* 8 (spring 1993): 48; *Through the Heart of Ohio* (Columbus, Ohio: Columbus, Delaware & Marion Electric Railroad, n.d).

9. Hilton and Due, *The Electric Interurban Railways in America*, 10–11, 13; H. Roger Grant, "Electric Traction Promotion in Oklahoma," in Donovan L. Hofsommer, ed., *Railroads in Oklahoma* (Oklahoma City: Oklahoma Historical Society, 1977), 98; "Selling Energy Along Interurban Railways," *Electric Railway Journal* 48(October 28, 1916): 920–25.

10. David A. Strassman, "The Rise and Fall of the Interurban," *Trains* 9 (October 1949): 48–53; *Street Railway Journal* 21(April 13, 1907): 637–39.

11. David McNeil, *Railroads with 3 Gauges: The Cincinnati, Georgetown & Portsmouth RR and Felicity & Bethel RR* (Cincinnati, Ohio: privately printed, 1986), 191.

12. George H. Gibson, "High-Speed Electric Interurban Railways," *Annual Report of Regents of the Smithsonian Institution* (Washington, D.C.: Smithsonian Institution, 1904), 311.

13. Hilton and Due, *The Electric Interurban Railways in America*, 186, 255, 275; *Twelfth Census of the United States Taken in the Year 1900: Population*, Pt. 1 (Washington, D.C.: U.S. Census Office, 1901), 34; *Manufacturers, 1905*, Pt. 2, *States and Territories* (Washington, D.C.: Government Printing Office, 1907), 827–83; *Ohio: An Empire within an Empire* (Columbus: Ohio Development and Publicity Commission, 1950), 3; *Statistical Abstract of the United States 1915* (Washington, D.C.: Government Printing Office, 1916), 216, 829.

14. Hilton and Due, *The Electric Interurban Railways in America*, 25–41, 272–73.

15. *Work Done* (New York: Patteson Press, n.d.), 65, 67.

16. Hilton and Due, *The Electric Interurban Railways in America*, 255–75.

17. Ibid., 44, 273; Harry Christiansen, *Northern Ohio's Interurbans and Rapid Transit Railways* (Cleveland, Ohio: Transit Data, 1965), 99–100.

18. Oberlin broadside in the papers of the Bedford Historical Society, Bedford, Ohio; Stephen D. Hambley, "The Vanguard of a Regional Infrastructure: Electric Railways of Northeast Ohio, 1884–1932" (Ph.D. diss., University of Akron, 1993), 239.

19. U.S. Department of Commerce and Labor, Bureau of the Census, *Street and Electric Railways, 1902* (Washington, D.C.: Government Printing Office, 1905), 118.

20. Hilton and Due, *The Electric Interurban Railways in America*, 22–24.

21. Ibid., 23–24.

22. Ibid., 206; Bob Sell and Jim Findlay, *The Teeter & Wobble: Tales of the Toledo & Western Railway Co.* (Blissfield, Mich.: Blissfield Advance, 1993), 19.

23. Thomas R. Bullard, *Faster than the Limiteds: The Chicago-New York Electric Air Line Railroad and Its Subsidiaries* (Oak Park, Ill.: privately printed, 1991), 4–10; Mary Crane, "Chicago–New York Electric Air Line Railroad," *Trains* 6 (October 1946): 15–19, 26–29; Hilton and Due, *The Electric Interurban Railways in America*, 38–41, 48.

24. Grant, "Interurbans!" 18.

25. Max E. Wilcox, *The Cleveland Southwestern & Columbus Railway Story; The Sandusky, Norwalk & Mansfield Electric Railway* (Elyria, Ohio: privately printed, n.d.); Hambley, "The Vanguard of a Regional Infrastructure," 160, 308; Hilton and Due, *The Electric Interurban Railways in America*, 126–27; *Street Railway Journal* 28 (October 13, 1906): 681–82.

26. Hilton and Due, *The Electric Interurban Railways in America*, 109–12; Ohio Electric Railway public timetable, May 25, 1913.

27. *Along the Line* (Cincinnati, Ohio: Cincinnati, Lawrenceburg & Aurora Street Railroad Co., n.d.), 27; *Electric Railways of Northeastern Ohio* (Chicago: Central Electric Railfans' Association, 1965), 149.

28. Hilton and Due, *The Electric Interurban Railways in America*, 267, 270; Northern Ohio Traction & Light Company public timetable, May 15, 1915.

29. Harry Christiansen, *Lake Shore Electric, 1893–1938* (Cleveland, Ohio: privately printed, 1963), 5, 19; Cleveland, Painesville & Eastern Railroad public timetable, May 22, 1911.

30. Hambley, "The Vanguard of a Regional Infrastructure," 218.

31. *Report of the Railroad Commission of Ohio* (Springfield, Ohio: Springfield Publishing Co., 1910), 91–92.

32. Stephen D. Hambley, "The 'Green Line' Connection to the Green Lands of Ohio: The Cleveland, Southwestern and Columbus Railway," *Old Northwest* 14 (spring 1988): 6; Robert Lynd and Helen Lynd, *Middletown: A Study in American Culture* (New York: Harcourt, Brace, 1929), 255–56.

33. Hilton and Due, *The Electric Interurban Railways in America*, 130, 135;

James Greene and Stephen D. Maguire, "Lake Shore Electric," *Railroad Magazine* 56 (November 1951): 88–89; Grant, "Interurban!" 27.

34. Christiansen, *Lake Shore Electric*, 38–39; Greene and Maguire, "Lake Shore Electric," 76–90; William D. Middleton, *The Interurban Era* (Milwaukee, Wis.: Kalmbach, 1961), 392–93.

35. *A Deluxe Electric Line Chair Car Service* (Akron: Northern Ohio Power & Light Co., 1927).

36. Jack Keenan, *Cincinnati & Lake Erie Railroad: Ohio's Great Interurban System* (San Marino, Calif.: Golden West Books, 1974), 59–93; William D. Middleton, *Traction Classics: The Interurbans Extra Fast and Extra Fare*, vol. 2 (San Marino, Calif.: Golden West Books, 1985), 299–303; *Deshler (Ohio) Flag*, July 3, 1930.

37. Jeffrey R. Brashares, *The Southwestern Lines: The Story of the Cleveland, Southwestern & Columbus Railway between Cleveland, Elyria-Oberlin-Norwalk, Wellington-Lorain-Amherst, Berea-Medina-Wooster, Ashland-Mansfield-Crestline, Galion-Bucyrus* (Cleveland: Ohio Interurban Memories, 1982), 76.

38. Hilton and Due, *The Electric Interurban Railways in America*, 263; Toledo & Indiana Railroad public timetables, March 14, 1926; April 3, 1927; June 8, 1930.

39. Fort Wayne-Lima Railroad public timetable, July 15, 1929; Hilton and Due, *The Electric Interurban Railways in America*, 266, 268; Christiansen, *Lake Shore Electric*, 49, 74; Keenan, *Cincinnati & Lake Erie*, 205–6.

40. "Selling Energy Along Interurban Railways," *Electric Railway Journal* 48 (October 28, 1916): 920–25; *Highlights of Our First Century* (Canal Winchester: Ohio-Midland Light and Power Co., 1949); Northwestern Ohio Railway & Power Company public timetable, spring 1916.

41. Hilton and Due, *The Electric Interurban Railways in America*, 267, 270; George W. Hilton, *The Toledo, Port Clinton and Lakeside Railway* (Montevallo, Ala.: Montevallo Historical Press, 1997), 25, 29–32.

42. Hambley, "The 'Green Line' Connection to the Green Lands of Ohio," 21.

Chapter 6

1. James A. Toman and Blaine S. Hays, *Horse Trails to Regional Rails: The Story of Public Transit in Greater Cleveland* (Kent, Ohio: Kent State University Press, 1996), 15.

2. George Rogers Taylor, *The Transportation Revolution, 1815–1860* (New York: Rinehart & Co., 1951), 390–91; John H. White Jr., "Horse Power," *Invention & Technology* 7 (summer 1992): 41.

3. Larry J. Saylor, "Street Railroads in Columbus, Ohio, 1862–1920," *Old Northwest* 1 (September 1975): 294–95.

4. John M. Killits, ed., *Toledo and Lucas County, Ohio, 1623–1923* (Chicago: S. J. Clarke, 1923), 566–67. See also Richard Rhoda, "Urban Transport and the Ex-

pansion of Cincinnati, 1858–1920," *Cincinnati Historical Society Bulletin* 35 (summer 1977): 132.

5. William D. Middleton, *The Time of the Trolley: The Street Railway from Horsecar to Light Rail, Vol. 1* (San Marino, Calif.: Golden West Books, 1987), 12–24; Toman and Hays, *Horse Trails to Regional Rails,* 21–22; White, "Horse Power," 44.

6. Middleton, *The Time of the Trolley, Vol. 1,* 30–34; Richard M. Wagner and Roy J. Wright, *Cincinnati Streetcars, No. 1, Horsecars and Steam Dummies* (Wyoming, Ohio: Wagner Car Co., 1968), 22.

7. Wagner and Wright, *Cincinnati Streetcars, No. 1,* 22–23; Stephen D. Hambley, "The Vanguard of a Regional Infrastructure: Electric Railways of Northeast Ohio, 1884–1932" (Ph.D. diss., University of Akron, 1993), 88–97; Saylor, "Street Railroads in Columbus, Ohio, 1862–1920," 299; letter to author from Charles H. Stats, Oak Park, Ill., March 8, 1998.

8. Wagner and Wright, *Cincinnati Streetcars, No. 1,* 23.

9. George W. Hilton, *The Cable Car in America* (San Diego, Calif.: Howell-North, 1982), 11–147.

10. Middleton, *The Time of the Trolley, Vol. 1,* 45–51.

11. Hilton, *The Cable Car in America,* 289–98; "Cable Construction of the Mt. Adams and Eden Park Inclined Railway," *Street Railway Gazette* 1 (October 1886): 284–90; "The Mount Auburn Cable Railway," *Street Railway Gazette* 3 (February 1888): 22–23.

12. Hilton, *The Cable Car in America,* 454–56; "Cleveland City Cable Railway," *Street Railway Journal* 7 (June 1891): 277–81.

13. Hilton, *The Cable Car in America,* 293, 455.

14. George W. Hilton and John F. Due, *The Electric Interurban Railways in America* (Stanford, Calif.: Stanford University Press, 1960), 6–7; John R. Stevens, ed., *Pioneers of Electric Railroading: Their Story in Words and Pictures* (New York: Electric Railroaders' Association, 1991), 168–73.

15. Middleton, *The Time of the Trolley, Vol. 1,* 62; Toman and Hays, *Horse Trails to Regional Rails,* 33.

16. Karl H. Grismer, *Akron and Summit County* (Akron, Ohio: Summit County Historical Society, 1952), 246–48.

17. *McGraw Electric Railway List* (New York: McGraw-Hill, 1918), 135.

18. James M. Blower and Robert S. Korach, *The N.O.T. & L. Story* (Chicago: Central Electric Railfans' Association, 1966), 8–9.

19. *McGraw Electric Railway List,* 129; *Moody's Manual of Railroads and Corporate Securities* (New York: Moody Manual Co., 1908), 1165; letter to author from George Krambles, Oak Park, Ill., March 28, 1998.

20. Toman and Hays, *Horse Trails to Regional Rails,* 67.

21. Ibid., 48.

22. Tom L. Johnson, *My Story* (New York: B. W. Huebsch, 1913); Eugene C. Murdock, "Life of Tom L. Johnson" (Ph.D. diss., Columbia University, 1951).

23. Toman and Hays, *Horse Trails to Regional Rails,* 52; Saylor, "Street Railroads in Columbus, Ohio, 1862–1920," 306–7.

24. James A. Toman and Blaine S. Hays, *Cleveland's Transit Vehicles: Equipment and Technology* (Kent, Ohio: Kent State University Press, 1996); Middleton, *The Time of the Trolley, Vol. 1,* 118–21.

25. David D. Van Tassel and John J. Grabowski, eds., *The Encyclopedia of Cleveland History* (Bloomington: Indiana University Press, 1987), 1057; Toman and Hays, *Horse Trails to Regional Rails,* 85–87, 90.

26. Brian J. Cudahy, *Cash, Tokens and Transfers: A History of Urban Mass Transit in North America* (New York: Fordham University Press, 1990), 107–8.

27. Ibid., 164–66; Saylor, "Street Railroads in Columbus, Ohio, 1862–1920," 308–10; *Electric Railway Journal* 52 (November 1, 1918): 793.

28. Fred W. Schneider III and Stephen P. Carlson, *PCC from Coast to Coast* (Glendale, Calif.: Interurban Press, 1986); Winstan Bond, "A Streetcar Named Success: The PCC, a Product of American Research in the 1930's," in *Perspectives on Railway History, Working Papers in Railway Studies,* No.1 (York, England: Institute of Railway Studies, 1997); James Toman, *The Shaker Heights Rapid Transit* (Glendale, Calif.: Interurban Press, 1990), 99–100, 102–3.

29. Toman and Hays, *Horse Trails to Regional Rails,* 165–66, 242–43, 275; Glen Bottoms, "Dayton: One City's Approach," *Headlights* 35 (September 1973): 2–3, 6.

30. Van Tassel and Grabowski, eds., *The Encyclopedia of Cleveland History,* 1047; Cudahy, *Cash, Token, and Transfers,* 127–36; letter to author from Cornelius W. Hauck, April 18, 1998.

31. Cudahy, *Cash, Tokens, and Transfers,* 102–7, 190–92.

32. Grismer, *Akron and Summit County,* 592–93; telephone interview with J. Gary Dillon, Akron, Ohio, March 15, 1998.

33. Carl W. Condit, *The Railroad and the City: A Technological and Urbanistic History of Cincinnati* (Columbus: Ohio State University Press, 1977), 173–74; E. A. Munyan, "Cincinnati Subway Construction Presents Difficult Problems," *Gas Age-Record* 59 (June 25, 1927): 919, 934.

34. Toman and Hays, *Horse Trails to Regional Rails,* 253.

35. Ibid., 254–58, 262–63.

36. Ibid., 256.

37. Toman, *The Shaker Heights Rapid Transit,* 97–123; Toman and Hays, *Horse Trails to Regional Rails,* 324–31.

38. *Akron Beacon Journal,* October 23, 1997.

Chapter 7

1. Lois Walker and Shelby E. Wickam, *From Huffman Prairie to the Moon: The History of Wright-Patterson Air Force Base* (Washington, D.C.: Air Force Logistics Command, 1987), 1–5, 11–14, 25–30.

2. William M. Leary Jr., ed., *Pilots' Directions: The Transcontinental Airway and Its History* (Iowa City: University of Iowa Press, 1990), 1–3; *Cincinnati Enquirer*, July 14, 1911.

3. Roger E. Bilstein, "Putting Aircraft to Work: The First Air Freight," *Ohio History* 76 (autumn 1967): 249–55.

4. David McNeil, *Railroads with 3 Gauges: The Cincinnati, Georgetown & Portsmouth RR and Felicity & Bethel RR* (Cincinnati, Ohio: privately printed, 1986), 245.

5. Jeremiah Milbank Jr., *The First Century of Flight in America: An Introductory Survey* (Princeton, N.J.: Princeton University Press, 1943), 3–16; Tom D. Crouch, "Thomas Kirkby: Pioneer Aeronaut in Ohio," *Ohio History* 79 (winter 1970): 56–61.

6. Maurer Maurer, "Richard Clayton—Aeronaut," *Bulletin of the Historical and Philosophical Society of Ohio* 13 (1955): 143–50.

7. Milbank, *The First Century of Flight in America*, 120–22.

8. George W. Knepper, *Akron: City at the Summit* (Tulsa, Okla.: Continental Heritage Press, 1981), 204; Mansel G. Blackford and K. Austin Kerr, *BFGoodrich: Tradition and Transformation, 1870–1995* (Columbus: Ohio State University Press, 1996), 67–68; George W. Knepper, *Ohio and Its People* (Kent, Ohio: Kent State University Press, 1989), 362.

9. William M. Leary Jr., "At the Dawn of Commercial Aviation: Inglis M. Uppercu and Aeromarine Airways," *Business History Review* 53 (1979): 182–83.

10. Ibid., 183–86.

11. Ibid., 189.

12. Ibid., 189–92.

13. David B. Holmes, *Air Mail* (New York: Clarkson N. Potter, 1981).

14. Leary, *Pilots' Directions*, 55.

15. Carroll V. Glines, *The Saga of the Air Mail* (Princeton, N.J.: D. Van Nostrand Co., 1968), 82–84; Donald Dale Jackson, *Flying the Mail* (Alexandria, Va.: Time-Life Books, 1982), 84–87; Robert J. Serling, *Eagle: The Story of American Airlines* (New York: St. Martin's, 1985), 9–11.

16. R. E. G. Davies, *Airlines of the United States since 1914* (London, England: Putnam, 1972), 33; Henry Ladd Smith, *Airways: The History of Commercial Aviation in the United States* (New York: Alfred A. Knopf, 1942), 374–76.

17. *Now That Everyone Can Fly* (Dearborn, Mich.: Ford Motor Co., 1929).

18. Davies, *Airlines of the United States since 1914*, 39, 585.

19. Ibid., 28–40, 195; Stout Air Lines public timetable, April 1, 1929.

20. Stout Air Lines public timetable, April 1, 1929.

21. Davies, *Airlines of the United States since 1914*, 111.

22. Ibid., 112; Universal Air Lines public timetable, June 15, 1929.

23. H. Roger Grant, *The North Western: A History of the Chicago & North Western Railway System* (DeKalb: Northern Illinois University Press, 1996), 149; George H. Burges and Miles C. Kennedy, *Centennial History of the Pennsylvania Railroad*

Company, 1846–1946 (Philadelphia: Pennsylvania Railroad, 1949), 603–04; Transcontinental Air Transport public timetable, July 1, 1928; William F. Trimble, *High Frontier: A History of Aeronautics in Pennsylvania* (Pittsburgh, Pa.: University of Pittsburgh Press, 1982), 148–49.

24. Davies, *Airlines of the United States since 1914*, 85, 87.

25. Transamerican Airlines Corporation public timetable, April 1, 1932.

26. Ibid., 140–41; W. David Lewis and William F. Trimble, *The Airway to Everywhere: A History of All American Aviation* (Pittsburgh, Pa.: University of Pittsburgh Press, 1988), 16–20, 22–24, 26; Smith, *Airways*, 111.

27. Clifford Ball, Inc., public timetable, n.d.; Davies, *Airlines in the United States since 1914*, 602.

28. *The Official Aviation Guide of the Airways* (Chicago: Official Aviation Guide Co., October 1933), 10–13, 16–17, 20–25.

29. Davies, *Airlines in the United States since 1914*, 156, 191, 202–9.

30. Ibid., 388–420.

31. Ibid., 390, 402, 404, 410, 622; Lake Central Airlines public timetable, January 2, 1951, April 28, 1963.

32. Davies, *Airlines in the United States since 1914*, 482–83; TAG public timetable, May 1, 1961; interview with Thomas F. Patton, Cleveland, Ohio, June 1, 1989.

33. I. E. Quastler, *Air Midwest: The First Twenty Years* (San Diego, Calif.: Airline Press of California, 1985), 113–14; Lewis and Trimble, *The Airway to Everywhere*, 189–93.

34. David D. Van Tassel and John J. Grabowski, eds., *The Encyclopedia of Cleveland History* (Bloomington: Indiana University Press, 1987), 61, 1074; Liberty Airlines public timetable, 1982.

35. Comair public timetable, October 29, 1978, June 1, 1996.

36. Capital Airlines public timetable, April 27, 1958, June 1, 1961.

37. Edward J. Pershey and Christopher J. Dawson, "How Cleveland Invented the Modern Airport: Cleveland Municipal Airport, 1925–1955," paper presented at the Western Reserve Studies Symposium, Squire Valleevue Farm, Ohio, October 4, 1997.

38. *The Complete Camp Site Guide Including All Airplane Landings in the U.S.A.* (Washington, D.C.: National Aeronautic Association of U.S.A., 1923), 81–83; *ABC Book of Flying* (n.p., n.d.).

39. Van Tassel and Grabowski, *The Encyclopedia of Cleveland History*, 60, 241.

40. Ibid.; Pershey and Dawson, "How Cleveland Invented the Modern Airport."

41. Ibid.

42. Ibid.

43. Ibid.

44. Ibid.; *Cleveland Regional Airport Plan* (Cleveland, Ohio: City of Cleveland, 1946).

45. Van Tassel and Grabowski, *The Encyclopedia of Cleveland History,* 61; James A. Toman and Blaine S. Hays, *Horse Trails to Regional Rails* (Kent, Ohio: Kent State University Press, 1996), 155, 253, 278–79, 297, 323.

46. *The Ohio County Airport Story, 1964–1972* (Columbus, Ohio: Department of Commerce, 1972).

47. Ibid.; Damaine Vonada, ed., *The Ohio Almanac* (Wilmington, Ohio: Orange Frazer Press, 1992), 356–57.

SELECTED BIBLIOGRAPHY

Ambler, Charles Henry. *A History of Transportation in the Ohio Valley*. Glendale, Calif.: Arthur H. Clark Co., 1932.

Baldwin, Leland D. *The Keelboat Age on Western Waters*. Pittsburgh, Pa.: University of Pittsburgh Press, 1941.

Blower, James M., and Robert S. Korach. *The NOT&L Story*. Chicago: Central Electric Railfans' Association, 1966.

Brashares, Jeffery R. *The Southwestern Lines*. Cleveland: Ohio Interurban Memories, 1982.

Broehl, Wayne G., Jr. *Trucks, Trouble and Triumph: The Norwalk Truck Line Company*. New York: Prentice-Hall, 1954.

Bullard, Thomas R. *Faster than the Limiteds: The Chicago–New York Electric Air Line Railroad and Its Subsidiaries*. Oak Park, Ill.: privately printed, 1991.

Burges, George H., and Miles C. Kennedy. *Centennial History of the Pennsylvania Railroad Company, 1846–1946*. Philadelphia: Pennsylvania Railroad, 1949.

Cantelon, Philip, and Kenneth D. Durr. *The Roadway Story*. Rockville, Md.: Montrose Press, 1996.

Childs, William R. *Trucking and the Public Interest: The Emergence of Federal Regulation, 1914–1920*. Knoxville: University of Tennessee Press, 1985.

Christiansen, Harry. *Lake Shore Electric, 1893–1938*. Cleveland, Ohio: privately printed, 1963.

———. *Northern Ohio's Interurbans and Rapid Transit Railways*. Cleveland, Ohio: Transit Data, 1965.

Condit, Carl W. *The Railroad and the City: A Technological and Urbanistic History of Cincinnati*. Columbus: Ohio State University Press, 1977.

Coomer, James. *Life on the Ohio*. Lexington: University of Kentucky Press, 1997.

Crandall, Burton B. *The Growth of the Intercity Bus Industry*. Syracuse, N.Y.: Syracuse University, 1954.

Cudahy, Brian J. *Cash, Tokens and Transfers: A History of Urban Mass Transit in North America*. New York: Fordham University Press, 1990.

Curwood, James Oliver. *The Great Lakes*. New York: G. P. Putnam's Sons, 1909.

Davies, R. E. G. *Airways: The History of Commercial Aviation in the United States since 1914*. London: Putnam, 1972.

Ehle, Jay C. *Cleveland's Harbor: The Cleveland–Cuyahoga County Port Authority*. Kent, Ohio: Kent State University Press, 1996.

Electric Railways of Northeastern Ohio. Chicago: Central Electric Railfans' Association, 1965.

Electric Railways of Ohio. Chicago: Central Electric Railfans' Association, 1952.

Fatout, Paul. *Indiana Canals*. West LaFayette, Ind.: Purdue University Studies, 1972.

Flink, James J. *The Automobile Age*. Cambridge, Mass.: MIT Press, 1988.

———. *The Car Culture*. Cambridge, Mass.: MIT Press, 1975.

Foster, Emily, ed. *The Ohio Frontier: An Anthology of Early Writings*. Lexington: University of Kentucky Press, 1996.

Frizzi, Daniel L., Jr. *An American Railroad Portrait: People, Places and Pultney*. Bellaire, Ohio: privately printed, 1993.

Gamble, Jay Mack. *Steamboats on the Muskingum*. Staten Island: Steamship Historical Society of America, 1971.

Gamst, Frederick C., ed. *Early American Railroads: Franz Anton Ritter von Gerstner's Die innern Communication (1842–1843)*. Stanford, Calif.: Stanford University Press, 1997

Gard, R. Max, and William H. Vodrey, Jr. *The Sandy and Beaver Canal*. East Liverpool, Ohio: East Liverpool Historical Society, 1952.

Gieck, Jack. *A Photo Album of Ohio's Canal Era, 1825–1913*. Kent, Ohio: Kent State University Press, 1988.

Glines, Carroll V. *The Saga of the Air Mail*. Princeton, N.J.: Van Nostrand Co., 1968.

Grant, H. Roger. *Erie Lackawanna: Death of an American Railroad, 1938–1992*. Stanford, Calif.: Stanford University Press, 1994.

———. *Land, Air, Water: Transportation and Ohio*. Columbus: State Library of Ohio, 1979.

———. *Living in the Depot: The Two-Story Railroad Station*. Iowa City: University of Iowa Press, 1993.

———. *Ohio's Railway Age in Postcards*. Akron, Ohio: University of Akron Press, 1996.

Grant, H. Roger, and Charles W. Bohi. *The Country Railroad Station in America*. Boulder, Colo.: Pruett, 1978.

Grismer, Karl H. *Akron and Summit County*. Akron, Ohio: Summit County Historical Society, 1952.

Haberman, Ian S. *The Van Sweringens of Cleveland: The Biography of an Empire*. Cleveland, Ohio: Western Reserve Historical Society, 1979.

Harlow, Alvin. *Road of the Century*. New York: Creative Age Press, 1947.

Havinghurst, Walter. *The Long Ships Passing: The Story of the Great Lakes*. New York: Macmillan, 1943.

Hilton, George W. *American Narrow Gauge Railroads*. Stanford, Calif.: Stanford University Press, 1990.

———. *The Cable Car in America*. San Diego, Calif.: Howell-North, 1982.

———. *The Toledo, Port Clinton and Lakeside Railway*. Reprint, Montevallo, Ala.: Montevallo Historical Press, 1997.

Hilton, George W., and John F. Due. *The Electric Interurban Railways in America*. Stanford, Calif.: Stanford University Press, 1960.

Hokanson, Drake. *The Lincoln Highway: Main Street across America*. Iowa City: University of Iowa Press, 1989.

Holmes, David B. *Air Mail*. New York: Clarkson N. Potter, 1981.

Hulbert, Archer Butler. *The Old National Road: A Chapter of American Expansion*. Columbus, Ohio: Press of F. J. Heer, 1901.

Hungerford, Edward. *Men of Erie: A Story of Human Effort*. New York: Random House, 1946.

Hunter, Louis C. *Steamboats on the Western Rivers: An Economic and Technological History*. Cambridge, Mass.: Harvard University Press, 1949.

Jackson, Carlton. *Hounds of the Road: A History of the Greyhound Bus Company*. Bowling Green, Ohio: Bowling Green University Popular Press, 1984.

Jakle, John A. *Images of the Ohio Valley: A Historical Geography of Travel, 1740 to 1860*. New York: Oxford University Press, 1977.

Jordan, Philip D. *The National Road*. Indianapolis: Bobbs-Merrill Co., 1948.

Keenan, Jack. *Cincinnati & Lake Erie Railroad: Ohio's Great Interurban System*. San Marino, Calif.: Golden West Books, 1974.

Killits, John M., ed. *Toledo and Lucas County, Ohio, 1623–1923*. Chicago: S. J. Clarke, 1923.

Knepper, George W. *Akron: City at the Summit*. Tulsa, Okla.: Continental Heritage Press, 1981.

———. *Ohio and Its People*. Kent, Ohio: Kent State University Press, 1989.

Leary, William, Jr., ed. *Pilots' Directions: The Transcontinental Airway and Its History*. Iowa City: University of Iowa Press, 1990.

Lewis, W. David, and William F. Trimble. *The Airway to Everywhere: A History of All American Aviation*. Pittsburgh, Pa.: University of Pittsburgh Press, 1988.

Martin, Albro. *Railroads Triumphant: The Growth, Rejection and Rebirth of a Vital American Force*. New York: Oxford University Press, 1992.

McClelland, C. P., and C. C. Huntington. *History of the Ohio Canals: Their Construction, Cost and Partial Abandonment*. Columbus: Ohio State Archaeological and Historical Society, 1905.

McNeil, David. *Railroads with 3 Gauges: The Cincinnati, Georgetown & Portsmouth RR and Felicity & Bethel RR*. Cincinnati, Ohio: privately printed, 1986.

Meeks, Carroll L. V. *The Railroad Station: An Architectural History*. New Haven, Conn.: Yale University Press, 1956.

Meier, Albert E., and John P. Hoschek. *Over the Road: A History of Intercity Bus Transportation in the United States.* Upper Montclair, N.J.: Motor Bus Society, 1975.

Middleton, William D. *The Interurban Era.* Milwaukee, Wis.: Kalmbach, 1961.

———. *The Time of the Trolley: The Street Railway from Horsecars to Light Rail.* Vol. 1. San Marino, Calif.: Golden West Books, Rev. 2nd ed., 1987.

———. *Traction Classics: The Interurbans Extra Fast and Extra Fare.* Vol. 2. San Marino, Calif.: Golden West Books, 1985.

Milbank, Jeremiah, Jr. *The First Century of Flight in America: An Introductory Survey.* Princeton, N.J.: Princeton University Press, 1943.

Moore, John F. *The Story of the Railroad "Y."* New York: Association Press, 1930.

Morrison, R. G. *The Sandusky, Milan and Norwalk Electric Railway.* Cleveland, Ohio: privately printed, 1963.

Mott, Edward Harold. *Between the Ocean and the Lakes: The Story of Erie.* New York: John S. Collins, 1899.

Mould, David H. *Dividing Lines: Canals, Railroads and Urban Rivalry in Ohio's Hocking Valley.* Dayton, Ohio: Wright State University Press, 1994.

Odel, Ruth Winters. *Early Railroad Transportation in Jackson County, Ohio.* Barboursville, W.Va.: privately printed, 1986.

Prixton, John. *The Marietta and Cincinnati Railroad, 1843–1883: A Case Study in American Railroad Expansion.* University Park: Pennsylvania State University Studies, 1966.

Rae, John B. *The Road and the Car in American Life.* Cambridge, Mass.: MIT Press, 1971.

Raitz, Karl, ed. *The National Road.* Baltimore, Md.: Johns Hopkins University Press, 1996.

Rehor, John A. *The Nickel Plate Story.* Milwaukee, Wis.: Kalmbach, 1965.

Rose, Mark H. *Interstate: Express Highway Politics, 1941–1956.* Lawrence: Regents Press of Kansas, 1979.

Roseboom, Eugene H., and Francis P. Weisenburger. *A History of Ohio.* Columbus: Ohio Historical Society, 1967.

Russell, P. J. *The Motor Wagon: The Origins and History of Long-Distance Truck Transport.* Akron: Pioneer Motor Traffic Club of Akron, Ohio, 1971.

Sanders, D. C. *The Brasspounder.* New York: Hawthorn Books, 1978.

Saunders, Richard L., Jr. *The Railroad Mergers and the Coming of Conrail.* Westport, Conn.: Greenwood Press, 1978.

Scheiber, Harry N. *Ohio Canal Era: A Case Study of Government and the Economy, 1821–1861.* Athens: Ohio University Press, 1969.

Schneider, Fred W., III, and Stephen P. Carlson. *PCC from Coast to Coast.* Glendale, Calif.: Interurban Press, 1986.

Schneider, Norris F. *Bent, Zigzag and Crooked: Ohio's Last Narrow Gauge Railroad.* Zanesville, Ohio: privately printed, 1960.

Sell, Bob, and Jim Findlay. *The Teeter & Wobble: Tales of the Toledo & Western Railway Co.* Blissfield, Mich.: Blissfield Advance, 1993.

Serling, Robert J. *Eagle: The Story of American Airlines.* New York: St. Martin's, 1985.

Shaw, Ronald E. *Canals for a Nation: The Canal Era in the United States.* Lexington: University of Kentucky Press, 1990.

Smith, Greg, and Karen-Lee Ryan. *700 Great Rail-Trails.* Washington, D.C.: Rails-to-Trails Conservancy, 1995.

Smith, Henry Ladd. *Airways: The History of Commercial Aviation in the United States.* New York: Alfred A. Knopf, 1942.

Stevens, John R., ed. *Pioneers of Electric Railroading: Their Story in Words and Pictures.* New York: Electric Railroaders' Association, 1991.

Stover, John F. *Iron Road to the West: American Railroads in the 1850's.* New York: Columbia University Press, 1978.

———. *The Life and Decline of the American Railroad.* New York: Oxford University Press, 1970.

Taylor, George Rogers. *The Transportation Revolution, 1815–1860.* New York: Rinehart, 1951.

Toman, James A. *The Shaker Heights Rapid Transit.* Glendale, Calif.: Interurban Press, 1990.

Toman, James A., and Blaine S. Hays. *Cleveland's Transit Vehicles: Equipment and Technology.* Kent, Ohio: Kent State University Press, 1996.

———. *Horse Trails to Regional Rails: The Story of Public Transit in Greater Cleveland.* Kent, Ohio: Kent State University Press, 1996.

Trimble, William F. *High Frontier: A History of Aeronautics in Pennsylvania.* Pittsburgh, Pa.: University of Pittsburgh Press, 1982.

Trostel, Scott D. *Bradfrod the Railroad Town: A Railroad Town History of Bradford, Ohio.* Fletcher, Ohio: Cam-Tech, 1987.

Utter, William T. *The Frontier State, 1803–1825.* Vol. 2, *The History of Ohio.* Columbus: Ohio State Archaeological and Historical Society, 1942.

Van Tassel, David D., and John H. Grabowski, eds. *The Encyclopedia of Cleveland History.* Bloomington: Indiana University Press, 1987.

Wade, Richard C. *The Urban Frontier: Pioneer Life in Early Pittsburgh, Cincinnati, Lexington, Louisville, and St. Louis.* Chicago: University of Chicago Press, 1964.

Wagner, Richard. *Golden Wheels: The Story of the Automobiles Made in Cleveland and Northeastern Ohio, 1892–1932.* Cleveland, Ohio: Western Reserve Historical Society and Cleveland Automobile Club, 1975.

Wagner, Richard M., and Roy J. Wright. *Cincinnati Streetcars, No. 1, Horsecars and Steam Dummies.* Wyoming, Ohio: Wagner Car Co., 1968.

Walker, Lois, and Shelby E. Wickham. *From Huffman Prairie to the Moon: The History of Wright-Patterson Air Force Base.* Washington, D.C.: Air Force Logistics Command, 1987.

White, John H., and Robert J. White. *The Island Queen: Cincinnati's Excursion Steamer.* Akron, Ohio: University of Akron Press, 1995.

Wilcox, Max E. *The Cleveland Southwestern & Columbus Railway Story; The Sandusky, Norwalk & Mansfield Electric Railway.* Elyria, Ohio: privately printed, n.d.

Wright, Alice. *The Ohio River.* Marietta, Ohio: Prettit-Seevers, 1964.

Wright, Richard J. *Freshwater Whales: A History of the American Ship Building Company and Its Predecessors.* Kent, Ohio: Kent State University Press, 1969.

Yoder, Paton. *Taverns and Travelers: Inns of the Early Midwest.* Bloomington: Indiana University Press, 1969.

INDEX